DISCARDED

PILGRIMS OF THE SANTA FE

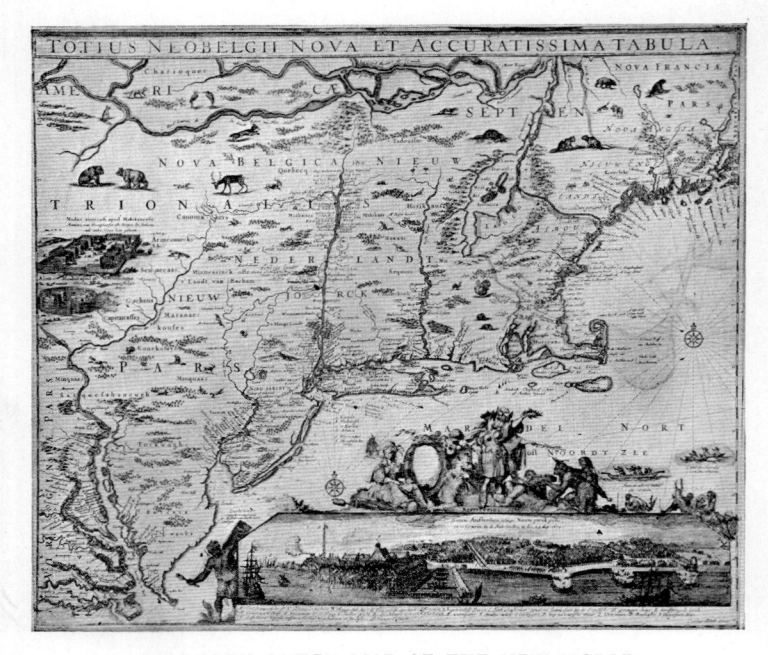

AN EARLY DUTCH MAP OF THE NEW WORLD

PILGRIMS OF THE SANTA FE

By AGNES C. LAUT

Author of "The Overland Trail," "Cadillac," "Conquest of the Great Northwest," etc.

WITH FORTY-FOUR ILLUSTRATIONS FROM PHOTOGRAPHS

LIBRARY OF
LAMAR STATE COLLEGE OF TECHNOLOGY

↑ 818472

FREDERICK A. STOKES COMPANY
NEW YORK   MCMXXXI

COPYRIGHT, 1931, BY AGNES C. LAUT

All rights reserved. No part of this work may be reproduced without the written permission of the publishers.

Printed in the United States of America

CONTENTS

PART I

THE SPANISH CONQUERORS

CHAPTER		PAGE
I.	PILGRIMS OF THE HOLY FAITH	3
II.	THE CONQUERORS AND THE SEARCH FOR THE SEVEN GOLDEN CITIES	15
III.	THE SEVEN CITIES ARE FOUND BY CORONADO AND HIS FRIARS, BUT THEY ARE NOT GOLD	27
IV.	CORONADO SETS OUT ON THE PILGRIMAGE OF THE HOLY FAITH. HE EXPLORES FROM SONORA TO THE BORDERS OF MODERN KANSAS AND NEBRASKA	41

PART II

THE FRENCH OPEN A CARAVAN ROUTE TO SANTA FE

V.	THE FRENCH OPEN A CARAVAN ROUTE TO SANTA FE	59
VI.	THE INDIANS OF THE SANTA FE TRAIL . .	73

PART III

A STORMY INTERLUDE

VII.	A STORMY INTERLUDE	99

PART IV

THE MORMONS ON THE PILGRIM TRAIL

CHAPTER		PAGE
VIII.	THE MORMONS ON THE PILGRIM TRAIL	123
IX.	THE MORMON SETTLEMENT	144

PART V

HERE COME THE CARAVANS

X.	THE CARAVANS COME RUMBLING AND TUMBLING OVER THE TRAIL	167
XI.	SANTA FE—PAST AND PRESENT	189

PART VI

THE AMERICAN ARMY ON THE SANTA FE TRAIL

XII.	THE AMERICAN ARMY ON THE SANTA FE TRAIL	207

PART VII

ARMY ANNALS OF THE SANTA FE

XIII.	WAR WITH MEXICO BRINGS THE ARMY ON THE OLD TRAIL	223
XIV.	OTHER ARMY PATROLS ON THE SANTA FE	246
XV.	SCIENTISTS' REPORT PARALLEL TO ARMY RECORDS	264
XVI.	GENERAL GEORGE ARMSTRONG CUSTER'S PATROLS IN THE SOUTHWEST	275

PART VIII

NEW MIGRATIONS FOCUS ON THE HOLY TRAIL

CHAPTER		PAGE
XVII.	FIVE MIGRATIONS NOW FOCUS ON THE HOLY TRAIL	291
XVIII.	HUMAN GHOULS AND VULTURES ON THE HOLY TRAIL	311
XIX.	BEFORE AND DURING THE GOLD RUSH	323

PART IX

WHEN RAILS CAME ON THE PILGRIM WAY OF THE HOLY FAITH

| XX. | WHEN RAILS CAME TO THE OLD SANTA FE TRAIL | 349 |
| | INDEX | 361 |

LIST OF ILLUSTRATIONS

An early Dutch map of the New World	*Frontispiece*

FACING PAGE

A relic of pioneer travel	4
Ox train fording a stream	4
Native houses in Tampico	5
A native home, tropical style	5
Old Palace of the Governors of New Mexico	36
Prehistoric pottery from Casa Grande	36
Taos	37
Open market, Mexico City	70
A Mexican boy peddling cakes	70
A Zuñi city	71
A wayside cross, Old Mexico	100
A rite of the kiva worship	101
Prison and custom house, Santa Fe	120
Overland wagon train with oxen	120
Freighting train known as "Bull of the woods"	120
The Black Mesa	121
Map of the mouth of the Chicago River, in 1830	132
The Enchanted Mesa	132
An early map of "New France"	133
March of a Santa Fe caravan	170
Kansas City, 1855	171
View of St. Louis	190

LIST OF ILLUSTRATIONS

	FACING PAGE
View of Omaha, 1868	191
Fort Dearborn in 1803	212
Fort Dearborn as rebuilt in 1816	213
Remains of wall of old Fort Leavenworth	213
Cartmen waiting for work	232
Mexican peons of today selling serapes	232
Rock trail, Frijole Canyon	233
A buffalo herd in the '70s	254
A Mexican cattle ranch	255
Freighting with an oxcart	292
Freighting with donkeys	292
A Mexican adobe hut	293
Dwelling of a native rancher	293
Kansas City, 1872	328
Fort Hall, near Pocatello	329
Fremont addressing the Indians at Fort Laramie	329
A windjammer	338
An excursion train at 1000 Mile Tree	339
Wagon train moving down Echo Canyon, bringing supplies to the builders of the Union Pacific	354
Grooves made by pioneer wagon wheels in solid rock, near Split Rock, Wyoming	354
Union Pacific and Central Pacific engineers at the driving of the golden spike	355

PART I

THE SPANISH CONQUERORS

CHAPTER I

PILGRIMS OF THE HOLY FAITH

WHY could a book on the famous Santa Fe Trail be appropriately named Pilgrims of the Holy Faith?

Because it was the faith which "removes mountains" that created the trail. It was not at first, as many other trails were, a game path to water and pasture, then a hunter's road, then a wheel highway for tented caravan wagon and rail. It was a Trail of Holy Faith in God ruling the future. That faith belonged quite as much to the first Spanish Conquerors with their priests as to the settlers in their covered wagons and the railroad with rickety cars to be superseded by motors and palace cars.

Who could foresee that in the brief period of a hundred years oil wells would be found, each exceeding in its yearly output all that the Washington Government paid for the entire area of Louisiana? What the settlers saw was a chance for free land, which "the thrifty husbandry of many years" could bring up in value to a good living in freedom; and they hied them to dangers and perils undreamed and in "the faith of little children" "laid them down and died" for that faith. Not far different was the faith of the first rail builders. What they foresaw was that a vast agricultural area under the toil of settlers would bring them great traffic both east and west bound; so they hied them out and laid them down in bankruptcy after bankruptcy for thirty years. Yet the assets of those roads to-day in many cases exceed a billion dollars. Faith has been justified in works and results.

The Wisest Teacher the world has ever known was not only a profound prophet when he quoted the proverb that "faith removes mountains," but he was an equally far-visioned economist. Hence the Santa Fe was really a "Trail of the Holy Faith."

The Santa Fe Trail crossed a far larger area than from the Mississippi to Santa Fe. It really began with the tramp of the Spanish conquerors from Pensacola, Florida, and from old Mexico City. This was in the middle fifteen-hundreds. Then the French came down and up the Mississippi from 1659 to 1700. Then, amazing to relate, followed in 1714 to 1716, the first caravan wagon procession from the Mississippi over the arid plains of the Southwest to Taos and Santa Fe and old Mexico City. It came to grief, of course, as many first ventures did; but it opened the way for the wheel. Still more amazing to relate, it was

A RELIC OF PIONEER TRAVEL

Courtesy of Union Pacific Historical Museum
OX TRAIN FORDING A STREAM

NATIVE HOUSES IN TAMPICO

A NATIVE HOME, TROPICAL STYLE

French, not Spanish, and it was not lured by the sordid hope of gain, but by a little god called Cupid. It is the only instance I know in North American history where the lure was neither furs nor gold but the pure chivalrous love of a young French knight-errant for his equally high-minded little dark-eyed Spanish señorita. Yet we are told the outworn lie that America lacks romance in her history.

From 1788 to 1888 there followed fast the procession of traders, rails, miners, cattle men, farm settlers. The least recorded but most heroic in all the long procession of trail finders were the army patrols. The army heroism has long been buried in oblivion. Perhaps that resulted from the fact that red tape of Washington could not endure the daylight of truth. If Custer had never suffered the awful sacrifice in the battle known as "the Massacre," his name would still be entitled to a place without a peer for his work in the Southwest.

As both Sherman and Sheridan wrote privately to friends, they did not agree with the policies of General Hancock and General Pope under whose direction the Southwest had come. Neither Hancock nor Pope understood the character of the Indian. They did not seem to know that the northern tribes of Cheyennes would raid so far South as the Desert area. Much less did they understand why settlers would pour to such an arid exposed region. Both were sticklers for red tape. Both had won great reputations in the Civil War; but under their régime such a hero as Custer was for a year deprived of his command in the Southwest for the two small offenses of causing the court martial and shooting of a desperado in the service and leaving his troops for a brief period to see that his wife was safe in a fort, where cholera was raging. Army men said frankly though unofficially that Hancock realized his policies had proved a failure in the West. He was jealous of Custer's popularity and used Custer as a scapegoat. It is unfair to ascribe motives to the dead, who cannot defend themselves. Hancock and Pope may have been hampered by Washington politics. Anyway, Grant, who understood the situation in the Southwest as Sherman and Sheridan and Grenville Dodge did, promptly reinstated Custer. Had the advice of Sherman, Sheridan and Dodge been accepted, it would have saved thousands of settlers from death and ruin.

But there was a shadow of darker hue than the Indian raider above the Santa Fe trail. It was the vulture moral pervert—the low-browed criminal, cunning and cruel as a wolf—slinking on his black midnight murders, an animal in human form running amuck in a no-man's-land where army patrols of fifteen hundred men had to scout and protect a circuit of three thousand miles. He was not the gay, carefree outlaw robber of mail coach and caravan—a picturesque though utterly lawless plunderer. One or two examples of such low criminal classes must be given as the story proceeds. The blackest were the Bloody Benders of Kansas. Their story was dug out by Mrs. Edith Connelley Ross for the Kansas State Report of 1926-28. It is a horror story unequaled in the annals of Borderlands and Outer Marches in any land; and Mrs. Ross has told it in a classic. More of this as the trail crosses Kansas.

When you come to the story of the settlers' wives and daughters, you do not know whether to close the book or weep. The rough rank and file of the army, who rescued them, wept. It is well for us in a softer civilization to remind ourselves of the heroines who won the West just as much as the rank and file of the army.

The poem General Miles quotes on the close of the Civil War, when Decoration Day became a national remembrance of heroes, applies to the graves of these pioneer women:

> "Cover them over with beautiful flowers,
> Deck them with garlands, those brothers of ours.
> . . . .
> Give them the meed they have won in the past;
> Give them the honors their future forecast;
> Give them the chaplets they won in the strife;
> Give them the laurels they lost with their life!
> . . . .

Cover the thousands who sleep far away,
Sleep where their friends cannot find them to-day;
They who in mountain and hillside and dell
Rest where they wearied, and lie where they fell.

Softly the grass-blades creep round their repose;
Sweetly above them the wild floweret blows;
Zephyrs of freedom fly gently o'erhead,
Whispering prayers for the patriot dead."

Leavenworth was the first radiating point for the army patrols. Fort Wallace soon supplanted it as the great jumping-off place to the unknown. If the fort had retained either its first name or its first location, it would be easy for any writer to tell the story of Fort Wallace; but it changed its name two or three times before becoming the famous Fort Wallace and it shifted its location half a dozen times from two to twenty miles before it shook down to the permanent walled adobe fort. Little remains of its ancient walls except crumbling adobe and a monument to mark the soldiers' cemetery; but it is a ghost city of the glorious sleeping dead who shall surely awaken to a reward which the world never accorded. Crooned by the summer wind, the prairie flowers bloom where once heroes' blood dropped and dyed the ground. They recall the old Grecian legends that the royal purple flowers would blossom and their hairy tresses toss to the breezes' rhythm. Boisterously blown by the wildest blizzards, one can fancy in the ghostly snow-chant the shout of raider and defender.

Down in old Santa Fe there comes a gentle summer mood to landscape and human dreams. There, too, was a hero era preceding the covered wagon. On my walls hangs a little old cross commemorating the victory of a Spanish general in the 1680's and '90's. It was given to me by the descendants of the very De Lunas and Oteros who first built Pensacola. In a cabinet lies the beaded tobacco pouch of that famous or infamous old Governor Armijo, who forced the American traders to pay him five hundred dollars a load in tax before he would permit a single pound to be unloaded.

Lapped amid the snowy peaks, little old Santa Fe is the one bit of the Old World set down in the New very much as built by the first white man. There you can dream pretty much any sort of dream; and it is true. Under the rain of blossoms from orchards planted by the padres of the Holy Faith, you can recall the tramp of iron heel from Mexico City to Santa Fe. Or within a short motor ride out to a famed canyon, you can look down on cave cities where prehistoric peoples once took refuge from an inundation of raiding tribes from the north. A people civilized, too, they were in their way. They wore woven garments when our ancestors of European forests used chiefly the skins of wild beasts as clothing. They had a pictograph language, which we are only beginning dimly to decipher. They had irrigation ditches for their corn. They had the Egyptian system of burial in walled tombs with the Egyptian secret of preserving mummies in fabric rolls of a flax linen for the dead. They had a secret, too, which the archæologists have only recently revealed. They could shrink their five- and six-foot dead to a length of three or four feet. This explains the little mummies of these caves in New Mexico and Arizona ruins, which for fifty years our learned men have inclined to ascribe to a diminutive race of dwarf men. More of all this anon.

Very, very old was this Pilgrim Path of the Santa Fe. It goes back certainly as far as the days of Jewish patriarchs. It has raised anew the controversy among scientists—was the cradle of the human race in Asia or America? Some day we may know. To-day we do not. That is the most any careful writer can say. It is easy to jump in the controversy. It is another matter to prove the case. When such careful scientists as Keith in England and Osborn in America hang back from decision, it is wise for the amateur to refrain from the fray.

How wide an area should we say the Santa Fe Trail embraced in its circuit? Certainly from Kansas City through Kansas and Colorado and

Oklahoma and parts of Western Texas through New Mexico and Arizona and on up through California, eastward through Nevada and Utah. There you meet another sort of pilgrimage—all west bound in a mad stampede. There were the Mormons to transform a desert to a garden. There were the gold-seekers of California and Colorado to win a fortune or bury their blasted hopes in a hole. The bones of these pilgrims bleached the path to a new Western Empire of which we are the heirs. It does not matter very much whether the faith that lured them was a will-o'-the-wisp or a true illumination. They opened the trail to a Divine Destiny. Tools they were in the hands of a Divine Sculptor; and we are the heirs to a new era for the human race. How long was the circuit? Certainly at least three thousand miles. Add up the length of the Santa Fe railroad. Add to that the length of the Union Pacific and its early brother, the Central Pacific—you get a circuit far exceeding three thousand miles.

How vast was the area in the circle? As General Miles wrote in 1898, you could lay all Great Britain and Ireland in New Mexico and not cover it. You could lay all New England, New York, New Jersey and Delaware in New Mexico and not cover it. You could stretch all Italy and Spain and Portugal up California to southern Oregon and not cover the Pacific area. As for the Central

Empire between the Coast Range of Sierras and Cascades to the main Rockies, you could lay in it all the empires of Central Europe and not cover the Central Inland Southern Empire.

Miles was one of the greatest of our modern army generals. It is only in recent years that people have begun to appreciate his services to his country. He was deeply appreciative of the Indians' best qualities and equally deeply versed by experience in their worst practises. He was the most unsparing critic of the white man's greed, treachery, perfidy in unfulfilled treaties; but even Miles, the friend of every Indian tribe from the Canadian Border to the Rio Grande, was unable to explain why the Indian was primarily a man-killer by vocation. To this were only two exceptions in the records of the Indian race in the Central Empire—the Mandans on the Missouri and the Aztec-Hopi tribes of the Southwest. Only self-defense compelled them to become killers and they are yet unexplained enigmas in American races.

When the Spanish white man came with horse and firearms, the raids can easily be explained. Every tribe had to have horses and firearms, or face extermination by hostile raiders. When the railroad followed the early traders, the Indians' fury turned on the white invader. The buffalo, his chief sustenance for clothing and food, began to go. As long as the buffalo had been hunted with only bow and arrow, it reproduced itself as fast as the Indian hunter depleted it, although there was never a more wasteful hunter of the buffalo herds than the Indian. He drove the great thundering, bellowing, stupid beasts over precipices, in quicksand rivers where their weight bogged them. He took only the best hides for tepees and clothes. He used only the hump, the nose, the spare ribs for food, and the intestines as sausage containers. He left the rest to the wolves.

With the railroad came the settler and cattle. Now cattle to the Indian were only a lesser buffalo to be raided and slaughtered as found. The Indian called the buffalo "cibola." In possession of long-range rifles, however bad, the Indian raider now became a peril that dyed the West in the Bloody Ground. With the settler came the fence and the bewildered Indian began to see his fenceless hunting ground cut up in checkerboard patches for the farm. Cheyennes and Crows from the north, Comanches, Apaches, Yaquis from the south, took to the war-path against all whites. In vain, wise old chiefs tried to restrain the raiding young bucks. The Indian chief could retain leadership only as he led. If he hung back, he was either ignored or defied. So the fifty dark years of the Santa Fe entered their tragedy. The Indian died by the weapons he had adopted—the sword and the bullet. It is a very sad page on both sides. The Civil

War shook Indian respect for white-man prestige and in this very era Hancock and Pope came to direct military affairs.

Before a Rob Roy or Robin Hood could be embodied in song and story, there was an old volume known as "Tales of the Scottish Borderlands." The various States have amassed the tales of their own borderlands. It is to be hoped the great poem, the great novel, will yet emerge from these human documents of early heroisms. For any one writer, or any one volume, to embrace all the heroism of the trail is quite as impossible and ridiculous as for one writer or one volume to embrace the heroism of all Europe.

Note
The casual traveler on the trail may perhaps skip this paragraph. It is for those who may wish to dig deep in annals. On early Southern Louisiana the best records are the French Archives of Quebec Province, whence directions were despatched from Louis XIV to the governors of Quebec. On the traders' era, Pike, Long, Gregg's "Commerce of the Prairies," Ralph E. Twitchell's "New Mexico" stand out preeminent. To these should be added such splendid records as exist in the historical museums of California, New Mexico, Colorado, Louisiana, Missouri, Kansas. The Kansas collection is unsurpassed, thanks to the late Mr. Connelley, who died in the heat wave of 1930, while these records were being written.

CHAPTER II

THE CONQUERORS AND THE SEARCH FOR THE SEVEN GOLDEN CITIES

FLORIDA seems a far call to the Trail of the Holy Faith—Santa Fe. Yet in Florida that trail began. "The Santa Fe Trail had more to do with the development of the territory" (Louisiana) "than any other trail that crossed the United States," says the Kansas State Historical Report of 1927-28; and the statement is true.

It began in the search for seven mythical cities of gold, such as Pizarro had found in Peru.

It is easy to-day for us to explain how such a myth grew and magnified in minds inflamed by the hoards of gold poured back to Spain from Peru. Younger sons of the nobility needed easy money—and needed it sorely. Some of the younger dons were good; some were bad; but all were knights-errant out with sword and bayonet and arquebus to mend lame fortunes. The newly discovered Americas seemed to offer such a chance. Thither such young officers flocked, eager to enlist under any banner that promised fortune.

Approaching from any direction the high mesas

and pueblo dwellings of New Mexico and Arizona, perched above yellow sands or precipitous rocks of ochre giving off glints of the sun in an almost cloudless land, one saw towns like those of Peru dyed in almost gold. The glassless windows of the three-tiered dwellings might be the portholes of strongholds. The ladders leaning against the steepest ascending rocks resembled defenders' devices against invading plunderers. The people of these mesas were known to all Indian tribes to be sedentary. That is, they dwelt in communal towns and cities. They cultivated corn and squashes and melons in the bottom lands. There irrigation and rivers afforded sufficient moisture. They were known to be great workers in metals and pottery such as the Spaniards had found in Peru. There seemed every lure to intrigue the imagination of an empire drunk in gold prosperity. It is a dangerous drink. It becomes an insanity of greed. That has been evident in every gold stampede. More is lost in human life and fortune than is found in the pot of gold at the rainbow end. The lucky few win in the lottery; so the myth grew.

Picture, then, the dark, almost unknown everglades of Florida in 1528. Hither came Panfilo Narvaez bent on fortune. He was tall, fair, wore a red beard and had lost an eye in some European war. With him was an officer, Cabeza de Vaca, he of the Cow's Head, who had been raised to the nobility by the Spanish king for guiding the royal army through a mountain pass by a cow's head. Narvaez landed in Florida near what is now Tampa Bay. There was also with Narvaez and Cabeza de Vaca a Negro slave of Morocco—Estevan. On Narvaez's five vessels were six hundred colonists and soldiers. On westward, he passed modern Florida. At San Domingo one hundred and forty of his men had deserted. He hurried southwestward with four ships, four hundred men and horses. The words with which he claimed all the unknown world for his royal master read farcical and grotesque to the point of laughter. The savages clustering in wondering groups round these newcomers with their fair skins, clad in chain mail and glittering helmets, were told that St. Peter and the King owned the whole world. Of course, they understood not a word of the loud harangue but they did admire those horses and those "sticks that thundered." Both were to transform the plains Indians in two centuries into conquering warriors on their own account.

Sailing along the Gulf of Mexico, the Spanish found cobs of corn and little bits of raw gold. Whence had come the gold? That was the question. Perhaps from another Peru; so the will-o'-the-wisp led on to tragedy. Little expeditions inland through the deep marshes of ocean-weed and bayous of swamp waters found no gold. The Negro Estevan, whose color seemed more akin to the Indians, kept picking up words of their language so he could make himself understood as interpreter. With his growing importance as intermediary between white and red chiefs grew his own appreciation of himself. He seemed to have no lack of wives wherever he went, and decked himself in bells down his calico trouser seams and feather head-dresses. The Spaniards plundered little wattle-roofed Indian camps of corn, beans and pumpkins, but found no gold in quantities beyond an occasional small bead. This plundering of corn angered the Indians, but "the thunder sticks" sent them scampering. News of the white warriors seemed to precede them. The Spaniards were received with bows and arrows. When the attacking soldiers entered a camp not a soul could be found in the abandoned Indian towns.

Narvaez's vessels became leaky, rickety, warped by the tropical heat on the Gulf of Mexico. The night fogs were so thick they rotted the sail-cloth. Narvaez called a conference of all his officers. Should he go on, or try to strike overland? To go on by sea, and try to reach Mexico City by the old Mexico route of Cortes, they would have to pause and rebuild new ships of lesser depth for coastal sailing. The vote was a compromise. They would rebuild ships, but keep an eye to a chance for a march inland to search for those Seven Cities of Gold.

Five light, shallow open boats were finished by September. Resin, which melts in heat, plugged the seams. Horses' tails were woven in fresh ropes. Shirts were used for sails. Old strong timbers from the wreck of their first vessels were hewn for oars. Horses were killed and carried along for meat. Skin bottles for fresh water were made from the tanned hide of the horses' legs. In the wide-open clumsy boat about fifty men crowded the deck. Forty men had died of disease.

Those horsehide bottles rotted. The Argonauts had to draw ashore for fresh drinking water. They were not so gay as when setting sail from Spain, but just as dauntless in hopes. The nights began to grow very cold and raw. Rounding a great swamp of yellow waters, Cabeza de Vaca—he of the Cow's Head—saw a great river. It was the Mississippi, discovered fourteen years before the coming of De Soto, over a century and a half before the discoveries of Marquette and La Salle, the French.

They had not done so badly, these young dons. Cabeza de Vaca had only five men strong enough to pull an oar. The others were weakened by disease and hunger. Then in November came a squall. The boat struck a reef of rock or sand. The crew waded ashore on an island off Matagorda Bay, Texas. Here, fortunately, the Indians were kind. They gave Cabeza's men fish and roots for food. They were clothed in fiber woven of Spanish moss. They conveyed the wrecked Spaniards to higher land. They sheltered them from the inclement weather—inclement, indeed, to men almost naked. Other boats wrecked in this storm reduced the wayfarers, hopeless, almost to cannibalism. Cabeza de Vaca, with some knowledge of healing from Salamanca medical schools, was regarded as a miracle man by the Indians, as a veritable miracle worker blessed of God by those friars who later wrote accounts of his adventures. Narvaez, as far as Cabeza could guess, had been drowned at sea.

Somewhere near what is now Galveston, Cabeza and Estevan the Negro and the rest of the followers determined that there was no course open but to try for the Seven Golden Cities overland. Others of the frail five boats were "never heard of more," as the friars later recorded. Though the desert of Texas seemed a terrible cactus land to wanderers now almost barefoot, the Indians were cheerful and merry and taught the Spaniards how to subsist on "the prickly pear" for both food and drink. They found buffalo, which the friars called "a cattle," and the Indians called "cibola." Old pictures of the period portray the Indians hunting "the cattle with bow and arrow." Birds were perched on the buffalo's hump, which is not so far amiss when we know the tricks of birds in arid lands picking both grubs and parasites from the fur of the hairy bovines. The Spaniards reckoned themselves now about four hundred leagues west of Florida. The reckoning was, of course, a guess.

Westward toward the Pacific, the survivors pressed their wandering way. As to the tribes met, scholars such as Bandelier and Hodge and Buckingham Smith differ. Estevan was ever the interpreter favored by the Indians. On discovering the smoke of a camp, he went ahead as scout; he entered their lodges fearlessly and got supplies of their dog meat, sometimes to be eaten raw, at other times cooked. It was very difficult to cook meat quickly. The Indians made fire with little sticks twirled in a stone. In the center hole of the stone were dry punk and resin. These Indians were great smokers. They used a tea of various barks. They conversed with one another in the sign language of the prairie. They made flour of beans. Again Cabeza traded his services as physician for shoes, clothing, food.

This section of the wanderings hither and thither could not be exaggerated in hardship by any subsequent annals written from memory. Cactus is cruel to naked feet as knife-points. Few stomachs unused to the acrid juice of the cactus can stand pulque to quench thirst. Add to that the fact that many of the pools around natural springs were caked with alkali. Mix pulque with alkali water and pour it in a stomach parched with thirst and meat diet. The effect was a violent dysentery with fever; and the men were marching under a torrid sky. The atmosphere was dry but the nights were cold from the altitude. Men dropped staggering to die. Survivors had no strength to bury the dead. Bodies were left for the wolves to pick and bones to bleach on the sands.

At last, the Spaniards came to Indians of fixed habitation. The whole face of the country had changed. The desert had rolled up to high rocky precipices on which were perched cities and towns. The people ate little soft nuts, of which they had abundant store. The nuts were thin—easily recognizable as the delicious piñones. There were many jack-rabbits, which the Indians cooked in earthen-like adobe ovens. Cabeza sewed up wounds, healed inflamed sore eyes, washed out infected skins, and bound up fractured bones. Where were they? Was it the mouth of the Pecos River, or far West amid the pueblo dwellers of New Mexico? Again scholars differ.

Anyway, they crossed another "Great River" at a shallow sand ford, some branch of the Colorado or Rio Grande. The ford was breast deep in shallow water. Cabeza felt he must now surely be near the Seven Golden Cities. He asked the Indians to conduct him to the Setting Sun. This the Indians declined to do. The Indians of the Rio Grande were at deadly enmity with the Hopi and Zuñi of the high mesas. Estevan, who could by then gabble in seven different languages, came back from a scouting reconnaissance with word that the people on the high mesas were civilized, sedentary, and lived on beans, corn, squashes, and pumpkins. When the plains Indians went almost naked, these people of the mesas wore fiber clothing that resembled flax, with blankets of cotton and used a soap root—the amole yucca—to keep their cotton shirts clean. Their necklaces were of turquoises and emeralds and garnets and rubies. It does not necessarily follow that the white wanderers were in the region of the Cerrillos turquoise mines. The turquoise might have come in trade; but the Spaniards were undoubtedly working toward old Santa Fe's first Indian site. These Indians worshiped a great god represented by the Sun, but not the sun. They held the serpent in great reverence as the finder of water and symbol of cunning wisdom.

Days and weeks had been lost in months and years. The lost crew of Cabeza was in a land not cold in winter, nor hot in summer, though far snowy peaks hung on the horizon and fed the valleys with bluest of blue pure water. Surely somewhere here were the apples of gold for the Argonauts. They had set out conquerors. They were now castaways. Hope rose phœnix-winged. It had to. There was no turning back. So the doors close behind every movement forward of the human race.

Winter floods filled the dry arroyo beds. They were delayed at one point two weeks and saw round the neck of an Indian the buckle of a sword belt and a horseshoe-nail. Where had they got such treasures for their necklaces of human fingers and bears' claws? From white men, who wore beards, had horses, lances, swords, and had gone south to the Sea of the Setting Sun, the Indians told Estevan. Again hope took a great bound upward; for Cabeza knew the Spaniards in possession of Mexico City were to send a ship up the Pacific; and these must have come from their ship. Was he near the Sea of the Setting Sun? If so, he might yet save the remnant of his followers; but he had not yet found the Seven Golden Cities, although he heard vague rumors through Estevan of seven such cities where the people were metal workers. On they wandered, seeing many signs of gold, also real pearls from the Gulf of California. Each night and morning, now, the Spaniards thanked God for hope. "At last," says Cabeza, "I came to four Christians on horseback, who seeing me in such strange attire were greatly startled. They could not find words to speak. I spoke first and told them to lead me to their captain, Don Diego de Alcazar." It was with horror Cabeza saw that these Spaniards on horseback raided the Indians, who had befriended him, and plundered and slew them ruthlessly. There, whether amid the Yaquis of Sonora, or Yumas of the California desert, we may leave Cabeza. "For two thousand leagues did we travel by land and by sea in barques, besides ten months more after our rescue from captivity, untiringly did we march across the land. Twenty horsemen ... accompanied us ... we reached Mexico City on Sunday, before the vespers of St. James."

Cabeza tried to obtain after his wanderings the reward of the governorship of Florida. This had been assigned to De Soto by royal edict. Cabeza was sent to Brazil. He was accused by enemies of "grave crimes," causing insurrection. He was called back to Spain and thrown in jail for six years; but his accusers were proven to be jealous liars and he died in Seville at a very great age. He was the first white to cross the North American continent from the Atlantic to within a few miles of the Pacific. He may have been north as far as Pecos (Ci-cuye), but he did not reach Santa Fe.

Note

There is such a host of authorities on Narvaez and Cabeza de Vaca that one hesitates to state which is right; but first place must be given Ralph E. Twitchell for exhaustive statement of facts; Hubert Howe Bancroft for bibliographical reference; Hodge and Bandelier and Prince and Buckingham Smith for scholarly research and knowledge of the topography; and undoubtedly for color and modern reference Leo Crane, the Indian agent in our own day. Could fireworks and a sense of bitterness have been left out of the more modern works, their evidence as to topography would leave one with a feeling of more reliability; but each writer is so deadly sure he is right and the other man wrong that it gives the reader a regret each did not state his case fairly, as Twitchell did, and let the evidence stand. For instance, how many survivors reached Mexico City? Some writers say ten, some four, some three. Was Narvaez ever again heard of? As far as known, he never was from the time the storm drove him out to sea. All that is known is Indian legend and no Indian legend tells of his survival. Was ever another such far-wandering recorded of American discovery? Only one in North American history—that of Vitus Bering the Dane, bound for Russia across Manchuria to Alaska, two hundred years after Cabeza's traverse.

CHAPTER III

THE SEVEN CITIES ARE FOUND BY CORONADO AND HIS FRIARS, BUT THEY ARE NOT GOLD

TO DE SOTO had been assigned the governorship of Florida. Florida was to the Spaniards of the fifteen hundreds what Louisiana became to the French a hundred and fifty years later. It was vaguely everything westward to the bounds of Old Mexico. As far as the Trail of the Holy Faith—Santa Fe—is concerned, De Soto's expedition may be set down in a few paragraphs. There was the same imposing panoply of adventure, romance, treasure-seeking, gay young dons, flying banners, as had characterized Narvaez's ill-fated Argonauts. Over six hundred officers and soldiers he enlisted under his flags at Tampa, Florida. Somewhere were those Seven Golden Cities in the far northwest. De Soto was going to find them or die in the attempt. He had been with Pizarro in Peru and knew that the loot of gold and silver there had enriched both rank and file. Small trouble had he enlisting both officers and soldiers to strive and fight for such a prize.

To the helmet and chain-armor mounted men, he added foot infantry with crossbows as well as the cumbersome old swords and arquebuses, which "thundered and lightened." He knew from Cabeza de Vaca's report that he was going to encounter fighting savages and, to the shame of white man, he took bloodhounds to track down all enemies. Indian runners by that mysterious wireless carrier of messages which traders later called the "Moccasin Telegram" carried news and warning of such advancing foes far ahead of De Soto's slow-moving marches through thickets of interlaced cypress, magnolias, gnarled low-set oaks, swales of freshwater bogs; and the precautions he took to ensure victory really created the hostility he met from the first.

Monks and friars were also in his cavalcade. A word as to these monks and friars of the Holy Faith. They have too often been set down as ruthless fanatical bigots, carrying the cross of the Prince of Peace in one hand, the sword of conquest and slaughter in the other. Of the friars and monks, this is not true. It is neither history nor fact. Of the friars and monks—chiefly, at this period, Franciscans—not one accepted salary or loot. Except in a cactus land, they went barefoot. In cactus and bramble marches they put on a solid sandal. They trusted to God for food and set out with neither treasure nor scrip as truly as ever apostles of old. They ate Indian fare, though in the hot lands it nearly killed them, and where the conquistadors fell back in defeat, mutiny, and desertion, the friars went on with no weapon but the cross and fell victims to disease and cruelest murder amid the red men whom they had come to save. When the infuriated white treasure-seekers, blasted of greedy hopes, sought to wreak vengeance on the Indians, the friars penned the truth about ruthless murder and seizure of food from defenseless camps and of victims seized for enslavement sold to work in the mines. These reports went direct to the King of Spain, who forbade any and all enslavement of Indians; but the King of Spain was far away; and the guilty viceroys of Mexico filed counter-reports that the friars were "the prize liars of the century." This, we know to-day, was not true. As Ralph Emerson Twitchell says, every document since extricated from Royal and Vatican records reestablishes the truth of the friars' reports, the shameless mendacity of the greedy treasure-seekers.

Briefly told, De Soto marched "hither and thither" "through the boundless wastes" of what we now know as Georgia, Alabama, Mississippi, compelling captives to carry baggage. When they refused, he slaughtered them. The unwilling, terrified Indians countered by scampering at night through thickets. Then the bloodhounds were set loose on their tracks; but the Indians knew a trick to throw bloodhounds off the trail. They waded up water courses, where the baffled hounds lost the scent; and the next Indian camp discovered was usually abandoned. The Spaniards plundered the palmetto-round wigwams of food—fish, corn, pumpkins, squashes, dried deer meats—and set the wigwams in flames. This was the smoke signal for the next nearest Indian camp to scamper and signal the approaching danger toward wigwams on the trail; so after two to three years of futile wandering the Spaniards, then a sorry cavalcade of wan and wasted men, reached the mighty river—Father of Waters—the Mississippi somewhere near the Arkansas. It was a turbulent roil of mud, sand, great rolling trees. They succeeded in crossing and pushed on westward. No cities of gold were found, but corn and "those horned cattle" and plains tribes hostile as hornets were seen.

There was nothing to do but turn back. No use trying to plunder tepee camps that could be torn down in a few moments and carried off by the prairie folk with nothing left but a dirty moccasin in derision. The Indian, in the slight sprinkling of snow as winter came on, would turn his moccasins backward and mislead pursuit. Even bloodhounds here were useless.

Back to the Mississippi, far south of the ford, tramped De Soto in silent despair. He did not know where he was and he did not care. He had not won a fortune in the march pursued by death. He uttered "few words"; for he knew he had lost all standing in Mexico and Spain. As the despairing company advanced south, De Soto fell deadly ill. It had grown hotter—hotter in fogs low-lying and thick as blankets. The low dank bayous were badly infested with the malarial mosquito, of whose poison in that age men knew nothing. De Soto grew weaker and weaker and died as he tried to march. Even then, his chivalrous dons were loyal to him in their way. To prevent his worn body being desecrated by Indians or torn to pieces by the wolves now skulking behind in ominous packs to pick the bones of the dead, the dons weighted the feet with stones and sank their dead commander in the yellow floods of the Great River.

Few if any horses had outlived the dreary march. Baggage and food had been lost or cast aside in the retreat. Armor had been discarded in the heat as useless weight. The remnant of the "gay array" of six hundred treasure-seekers had only one hope of escape—to build boats, to float down the turbulent Mississippi to the Gulf of Mexico and to try and find the way inland to Mexico City. Only three hundred ragged, emaciated, bearded, walking skeletons reached the Panuca in the vicinity of modern Tampico.

One may omit the next efforts to find the Seven Golden Cities; for the expeditions by the Pacific and by land never got past the River Colorado in the west and the Rio Grande in the east; but gold is an eternal lure. There were fewer than two thousand whites in Mexico City and they were needy adventurers. They could not finance their outfits with furs as France did; for the pelts in the land were only usable as leather, not in trade with Europe.

Mendoza, the new viceroy of Mexico, had bought that Negro, Estevan. Whether Estevan, who had been with Cabeza de Vaca, really believed his own lies, or, had been so flattered by Indian admiration that he longed Negro-fashion, for fresh admiration, is a guess.

Mendoza listened to his tales of marvels. Somewhere were Seven Golden Cities, where the people were sedentary, great workers in gold and silver and jewels. Mendoza was intrigued—to use that term in the sense of puzzled and lured and baffled. Among his subordinate officers was another man, who, like De Soto, had been in Peru. His name was Francisco Coronado. He was loved by the soldiers, a fearless fighter, friendly with the friars, and fair if not opposed by the Indians. He was regarded as a thoroughly dependable man. He had personal knowledge of the terrain as far north as the Colorado and Rio Grande. Twitchell describes him as deeply and sincerely religious, kind when kindness worked, stern when the sword was needed. His wife was a cousin of the King. He was rich through his wife and therefore had no incentive to become a plunderer. Coronado advised that any farther search for the Golden Cities avoid the desert toward the east by setting forth from some of the western provinces of Old Mexico. Then, if baffled, the expedition could retreat the way it had come and save itself the awful losses of Cabeza and De Soto by aid from these western Spanish presidios. So the search again began.

Coronado's march has two phases. On the first advance he went no farther than what is now the boundary of the United States; but thence, the fearless friar Fray Marcos de Niza went ahead as scout. On Fray Marcos' report, Coronado later accomplished his famous advance in what are now Arizona and New Mexico. Twitchell describes Marcos as "the worst slandered man in history." The Franciscans were not unacquainted with the Indians of the Pacific slope. Marcos, too, had been with Pizarro in Peru. Coronado himself knew Sonora and Sinaloa well. He had served as local governor in that Old Mexico territory. Estevan, the Negro, and certain very willing Indians who loved the friars, always went along with Marcos. Estevan still picked up enough Indian words to gabble as interpreter. Marcos, too, could converse in two or three Indian dialects—probably Yaqui, Apache, and Yuma. He, too, had heard of seven cities situated on high, rocky, inaccessible mesas, peopled by races who were civilized, workers in metals, wearing cotton and linen garments, fierce defenders of their invincible aerial forts, fighters with crossbow and with rocks in slings, whose houses were of two and three stories with wooden ladders outside, stone steps inside. More devices, too, they had for defenses—rocky arches under which assailants must pass, slippery steps in solid stone down which invaders could be pushed. Surely these precautions presaged great treasures defended. It was right on that point that military commander and friar were violently in conflict. The Spanish conquistadors considered they could plunder all pagans and be blessed of God. The friars condemned such policy. To go on with the story. The Negro, Estevan, was ordered to obey the friars. He doubtless tucked his tongue in his cheek.

Culiacan, the point of departure for Coronado, lay north and inland from the Pacific port of Mazatlan, or some five hundred miles south of the modern boundary. Many of the Indian slaves spoke a sort of babbling Spanish. They had been given their freedom in advance to go along. Fray Marcos saw to that—it would allay all apprehension of the tribes encountered. Marcos, going far ahead of troops, reached certainly the modern Yaqui and Yuma land. He sent the Negro about a hundred miles ahead with Indian scouts to be despatched back, and a cross was to be the signal whether to advance or wait. If nothing of importance were learned, the Indian scout was to fetch back a little white cross he could conceal in his hand. If it were safe to go ahead, the scout was to return with a cross the size of two hands. Authorities differ as to how far Estevan advanced, but the topographical army engineers say certainly as far as modern Tucson, Arizona. Blessed by the friar on Passion Sunday, with a full dinner under his belt and a chest swelling like a bullfrog with self-importance, Estevan set forth. Within four days back came a scout with a cross four times the good omen expected. He had heard of "the greatest find in the world"—the Seven Golden Cities were only thirty days ahead. Was he as usual lying? It is hard to say. An Indian runner could make the pace in a month to the inland mesas of New Mexico. A month was the usual period for sheepmen of New Mexico to go from Santa Fe to the Pacific; but it is doubtful if a modern motor car could cross this section at all in the rainy weather of spring, when adobe becomes glue. Much less could heavily armed marchers.

Fray Marcos hurried after the Negro and set up great crosses of possession for Christ and Spain. He was among the ancestors of the modern poverty-stricken Pimas. He was not far from that great house close to the boundary at Casa Grande. Tourists visit it to-day, for it is one of the splendid sights and types of an ancient civilization. There are the puzzling "cat holes" close to the floor, which we now know were for purposes of drainage in time of siege. There are narrow passageways from room to room that a person must sidle in sidewise. There are still narrower stone steps up and downstairs, where a flung rock, a push, a blow, would send an intruder to the bottom of the stairs with broken back or fractured skull; and the porthole windows and flat roof are lookouts far over sage-brush and sandy levels where an advancing foe could be seen for miles. A gong or drum was the signal for people to rally inside the Great House with pots of water and corn. Ascending to its flat roof, the friar could witness in imagination a most beautiful scene. The sand hills were dyed by the sunset in blood and fire and gold. He could easily visualize the clans rallying for protection to the Great House, the warriors stripping with crossbow ready and club and rock to welcome foe; but

OLD PALACE OF THE GOVERNORS OF NEW MEXICO
Now the State Museum

PREHISTORIC POTTERY FROM CASA GRANDE

TAOS

alas! Its people, whoever they were, no longer inhabited the Casa Grande.

Of course the Pimas told Estevan of the Moki and Zuñi cities far eastward, of Acoma, the beautiful, of the Black Mesa, and of Taos and other pueblo towns, which the Negro easily counted up to the Seven Cities of Gold. Poor Estevan! He advanced in a self-deluded glory like other folk to the grave of his own early death. Traditions come down about him among Indian legends as "the Black Mexican," who wanted their wives as slave pack-carriers. He heard of Oraibi and Hotoville the terrible—yes, terrible in hostility to whites right to this day.

The friar hurried forward following Estevan's trail. He heard the same story from the Indians—of Seven Cities. He saw strings of turquoise round the Indians' necks, and white shirts, and skin robes that must have been made from "the great cows"—buffalo. Estevan now sent back word that he had an escort of three hundred natives—Apaches eager to raid their ancient foes, the sedentary Aztecs, Zuñis, and Mokis. Fray Marcos had only thirty Indians as escort.

It was May. The forerunners had made amazing progress from Coronado's Pacific provinces in Old Mexico. Had Estevan's Negro vanity not mistaken the hostile motives of his Apaches, all might have gone well; but Estevan was now clad in belled trousers, in brilliant calico with feathered head-dress, which the poor fool did not know was the garb of a raiding medicine man. Partridges, deer, rabbit, turkeys, were now in abundance. Food was more than sufficient. What was there to apprehend? The crests of the mountains were covered with snow and the nights were cool.

Back came a scout to the friar with bad news. Estevan had reached a town and been plundered. The Indian scout was in tears. Back came two more Indians with worse news. Estevan, too sure of a welcome, had ascended a mesa, been kicked over a precipice and lay dead and bloody in one of the wide volcanic cracks.

Fray Marcos sought guidance in prayer. He was out to win the tribes for Christ. He persuaded two chiefs to go on with him to within at least sight of one of these fabled cities. What he saw afar was undoubtedly the modern Haw-ai-kuh with two hundred houses and one thousand people. It gladdened but saddened his good heart. He took possession of the country for Spain as a matter of course. He turned back, as he reports, with "more fright than food," hurried back to report to Coronado in Northern Mexico and to the viceroy in Mexico City.

If Estevan had only obeyed the friar, he could have proceeded safely enough; but he would clutter his train of followers with a baggage of wives;

and if there is one practise which the Zuñis, Hopis, Mokis, even to-day will hardly tolerate, it is mixing their blood with an alien; so they gave the vain fellow that fatal kick to the crack of a rock, which is their tribal burial for their own people. He was on the run in terror when kicked. The mesa Indians rightly guessed him a spy for some invasion; and they would not tolerate the degradation of a wife as pack-carrier—or slave.

They are as deeply suspicious to-day. I have ascended their rickety ladders and steep stone steps with clumsy boots, with no escort but a little child, who carried my purse, my kodak, my stick, to keep from sliding in the sand. I have ascended to their upper inner rooms and have the present of a corn-meal jar. The fact that I had no escort but a little child disarmed suspicion. My purse left with her at the foot of the entrance showed that I trusted them, and it was restored to me without so much as a dime missing. I could not have done that in any American or European city. The joyous laughter of the little Indian children, who escorted me back down through sand that touched the tops of my high mountain boots, rings in my ears to this day. Wherever the sliding sand threatened a scoot, little hands from the ragged rabble roped me erect. My only regret is that I had not a pot of dimes for reward at the foot of the slide. Take a pot of dimes with you when you go. You can reach it with a fast motor now. What a scene of beauty I recall! The sunset turning those yellow mesas to gold. The little folks, at the bottom, and the big folks at the top of the precipice waving arms and hands. Then the drive back through sagebrush in purple and blue bloom to our carriage hub.

CHAPTER IV

CORONADO SETS OUT ON THE PILGRIMAGE OF THE HOLY FAITH. HE EXPLORES FROM SONORA TO THE BORDERS OF MODERN KANSAS AND NEBRASKA

AS Coronado was enormously rich in his dower right and related by marriage with the royal court of Spain, he must have realized that any expedition searching treasure in the north was as much to extend Spanish empire as to expand his own private fortune.

Very seriously he and Mendoza down in Mexico City must have weighed evidence for and against those cities on the Seven High Mesas containing treasure. The expedition meant ruin or success to both. In Mexico City, as stated, was a white population of about two thousand. The majority, as the friars record, were like "corks on a bubble," looking for a chance of quick fortune. It was not unlike a modern mining town. Every one was on tiptoes, ears open to every whiff of rumor for a fresh stampede to a new find. Being shaved by his barber, Fray Marcos was asked were there really Seven Golden Cities in the north. Fray Marcos thought there were. The barber told his family. The whispered rumor ran riot, rolling bigger and bigger from mouth to mouth. Before Coronado was ready to move, there were from the rabble more than eight hundred applications to enlist at no pay but keep and equipment; but Coronado knew he must have more than a mob's support for the venture ahead; so over the riffraff scum of soldiers he placed three hundred young dons as commanders for the cavalry and light-foot infantry. Among them you will find the names of the best families in Old Mexico: the Tovars, after whom a great tourist hotel is named, and one of whose ancestors was said to have been with Christopher Columbus; the Lunas and Oteros and Alvarados and Armijos, whose names are commemorated from Pensacola, Florida, to Old Mexico. There was also a Diaz in the company, and a De Vargas, famous in the wars of New Mexico in the 1690's, undoubtedly an ancestor of the great general who reconquered Santa Fe from the revolting pueblo tribes. His feat is yearly celebrated by a beautiful procession.

Mendoza saw that the expedition was properly equipped as to armor, chain-mail, helmets, arquebuses, swords, horses, cattle and sheep to use for food to be driven on slowly by Indian herders. The families of the young officers loaded their pack-horses with supplies which had later to be tossed aside as useless baggage impeding swift advance. Coronado invested his entire private fortune in the enterprise. The families of the young dons mortgaged all they owned to outfit this chance of quick fortune. It was to be make or break for all Mexico. Who was it said, if hopes were false rainbows, fears might be liars? Poor Macbeth cogitating the witches' prophecies said the same. It is well to remember that Shakespeare's plays were not yet written. It gives an idea of the age of that Trail of the Holy Faith.

Mexico City was at this time torn by the intrigue of two cliques. Each clique was jealous of any other obtaining the royal permission to enter on a war of conquest. Cortes opposed Mendoza. He wanted Mendoza held back till he himself could send an explorer up the Pacific by sea. Mendoza and Coronado decided to take time by the forelock and to be on the ground first, as our miners say, "to get in on the ground floor." Cortes' spies knew this and were furious. The sea expedition which Cortes sent out was that under Ulloa, usually credited as the first attempt by the Spanish to explore the North Pacific.

There is a dispute as to whether Coronado set out from Culiacan, his western province, or from Compostella, some hundreds of miles distant.

Fray Marcos accompanied the party as far as Culiacan. He had been appointed head of the

Franciscans in Old Mexico; but he saw to it that friars brave and unselfish as himself were in the military company. One broke his leg in an upset from a fractious horse, and had to go back to Culiacan. The accident really saved his life from martyrdom. Of the friars going on, Juan de Padilla became a martyr in what is now known as Kansas.

There is also great dispute as to the exact date on which Coronado set out—was it Easter 1540, or Easter 1541? If we remember that it was only two centuries later that the yearly date changed from the old New Year's in Easter to our New Year's in January, that dispute settles itself.

The march made very slow progress. It was hampered by too much baggage. As supplies were thrown aside and cattle and sheep used for food, provisions became very scarce just when needed most—in the desert of eastern California, western Arizona, and central Mexico. Soldiers were sent ahead to hunt. One was shot in the eye by the arrow of a hostile warrior. When Coronado reached their brush and adobe camp, he promptly as a warning hanged half a dozen Indians to a tree. These Indians were either Yumas of California and the Mohave Desert, or Yaquis of the borderlands. This hanging had just the same reaction on tribes ahead as similar tactics by De Soto in Florida. It created furious hostility. It is fairly clear from Friar Padilla's account that they passed the Great House of Casa Grande in the full heat of midsummer and there paused to give their thin tired horses a chance to pasture. We can guess what the chain-armor and metal helmets meant in such blistering heat. After that arrow in the eye of an officer, who had raised his helmet, the dons kept their helmets down in danger. Coronado was deeply discouraged. At Casa Grande was that deserted Great House; deserted, as he could see, for centuries. Would the other Seven Cities of Gold turn out to be the same? Hardly; for Estevan had been kicked to death by living foes. With heat and thirst, the troopers were "almost dead." Some of the officers were so exhausted they "saddled their horses wrong-end foremost"— the friars said from fright. This is hardly fair; but by this time, Fray Marcos' report was being called a tissue of lies and the good Franciscan was being cursed aloud.

Which of the high mesas in Arizona did Coronado first see? There is hardly a doubt that it was the one sighted by Fray Marcos—the modern Haw-ai-kuh. Perhaps Marcos, after all, had not lied. Hopes again went up. There were the irrigated fields of stunted corn-stalks, pumpkins, squashes, beans. There were living people clad in white shirts. Coronado sent two friars, two officers and a small escort of cavalry to reconnoiter. They were welcomed with a rain of arrows. Coronado behind charged—charged up the rolling sands, up the slippery rocks, where a storm of great stones from overhead knocked him flat and might have brained him, "if I had not been protected by the very good head-piece I wore." "The city was taken with the help of our Lord." Tovar and Alvarado were badly bruised. The glittering armor was a perfect target for arrow and stone.

The mesa city was abandoned by the Indians scampering down ledges where the troops could not follow. The cool houses high above the heat and filled with food refreshed the exhausted Spaniards. Coronado now knew that while Fray Marcos' report as to the people was true enough, it was a blast of disappointment as to golden cities. He found a few trinkets of turquoise but no gold. The habits of the people he records much as Marcos had. The women ruled the house, the men the field. Some Indians of the other mesas came suing for peace. Coronado was both pleased and disappointed. He was glad to make peace with other mesa tribes, but disappointed on going ahead to find their pueblos abandoned. This was largely owing to the scum soldiers' treatment of Indian women. Mistreatment of their women, the mesa people would never tolerate, as the foolish Negro Estevan learned. She was absolute ruler of the house and neither her authority nor her person must be violated. Scum riffraff soldiers were always a curse to the army in these crimes. It was one of the constant topics of conflict between secular and sacred heads.

Moki land was visited by Pedro de Tovar. All the other high mesas were scouted or visited. Oraibi was reported to house over a thousand people. Diaz was sent back west to see what he could learn about Cortes' vessels' progress up the Pacific or of any rival march inland by Cortes' men. Whether he called the Colorado "Firebrand" because the Yumas carried firebrands to warm their naked bodies during winter, or from the fiery tints of the peaks lying in the great gashed canyon, we can only guess. He found the initials of a Cortes man on a tree. That was all. The Yumas were very sulky and hostile. One was put to torture and confessed to plans for attack on the white man. The Indian was forthwith ordered to be drowned. Diaz himself lost his life by throwing a lance at a bloodhound. It tripped his horse and penetrated his kidneys; and after great anguish he died and was buried in the "sandy wastes."

Pedro de Tovar reported another scouting sortie along the precipitous canyon of the Colorado; but from whatever point he approached the vast wild canyon of fire and sand, the banks were so steep that the soldiers could not descend, and the raging river below looked "a mere silver thread." The peaks below were described by all the scouts as "high as the Cathedral of Seville."

Meanwhile the Indians from the mesas were visiting Coronado from points as far distant as near Taos. One chief jocosely was dubbed "Whiskers." Whiskers told Coronado that north of Acoma he would find the "cow country." The friar Juan de Padilla went ahead right to Acoma. It is one of the most beautiful of all the old mesas now easily accessible to every tourist. It stands three hundred and fifty-seven feet above the sandy plains. The Acomas were very hostile. Coronado's men found the ascent difficult, as I did. Coronado's men must have seen the Enchanted Mesa, just northeast. This is one of the legendary heights of Indian lore. Here boys were sent up the precipitous walls to dream their vision of guardian spirits and pray to the gods and fast till the dream came. This custom persists to this day. See the Enchanted Mesa, when you go West. It is within easy driving distance from rail or motor route.

Near Taos, with its many-storied houses, Coronado met an Indian named the Turk, who seems to have lied more grandiosely than the Negro Estevan, either because he wanted to please the Spaniards or because he hoped to escape north to his own people. He misled Coronado into thinking perhaps, after all, the Seven Golden Cities

CORONADO SETS OUT ON PILGRIMAGE 49

were up in what we now know as Kansas and Nebraska. The poor fellow knew that crossing "the staked plains" of arid lava beds, the Spaniards would probably die of thirst and he might escape. He described big canals, golden eagles on the punt prow, golden bells in trees to lull great chiefs to sleep. Alvarado thought him a liar from the first; but Coronado was determined to settle forever the myth of the Seven Golden Cities. Coronado, his hopes of treasure blasted, had become very ruthless in his forays with all tribes; he seized and burned two hundred natives who had surrendered.

A slight pepper of snow blew down off the peaks and relieved the marchers of summer heat. The winter of 1541-42 was very severe, especially on the uplands crossed. The snow almost buried the floundering horses. The Indians fled. Those captured were reduced to slavery as pack-carriers. The Turk, now thoroughly terrified, often talked in his sleep. The superstitious soldiers said he talked to midnight devils. He doubtless thought he was among human devils and if he could, would have escaped; but the guide had to sleep between soldiers.

The Indians now became "more and more like Arabs." They dwelt in tents of tanned skins. They used the sign language of the plains. The herds of buffalo were simply in uncountable numbers. There was no doubt left in Coronado's mind; the Turk had been lying. Coronado called a council of his officers. The decision was to go on and if the Turk proved a liar, kill him. In a letter to the Spanish King, Coronado reported he was nine hundred and fifty leagues from Mexico City. He described the country as wonderfully productive—a second Spain. There is no doubt that he had crossed the Arkansas near Dodge City in Kansas. The Seven Golden Cities were then called by the treasure-seeking Spaniards Quivira. The trouble was—no gold had been found, and the young officers were furious at the Turk. The priest was more charitable. He knew the Spaniards had been as much lured by greedy hopes as the Turk was tempted to lie by hope of escape. Near the Great Bend of the Arkansas, in Kansas, the Turk's sentence was pronounced. "He was strangled when sleeping so that he never waked up." That report by the conquerors is written with as little concern as though they had wrung the neck of a chicken. Poor Turk! Juan de Padilla had had enough of the conquerors and their evil treatment of savages he had come to save. He decided to remain in Kansas as a soldier of the Cross.

Coronado had crossed sections of California, Arizona, New Mexico, Texas, Oklahoma, Kansas, and certainly an eastern belt of Nebraska; but he, too, had had enough of a will-o'-the-wisp which

CORONADO SETS OUT ON PILGRIMAGE

had used up all his personal fortune. How do we certainly know he was in all these great States, which are in area larger than European kingdoms? Because from Omaha to Texas, swords with his stamp, sword belts, buckles, have been dug out of the dry sands. Some are on exhibition in museums of these States. It was a page of heroic exploration and shameless bloody cruelty. There are hardly a half-dozen in the encircling pueblos —more than eighty in all—which Coronado did not pass or visit. In all he left a trail of bitter hostility to the whites for which they were to pay the price in their own blood down to the 1880's. Coronado out riding one day in Kansas suffered a bad fall from his horse. His rotten saddle-girth gave; he was pitched. The horse-hoof hit his head. He suffered so greatly that he decided then and there to return southwest as nearly as he could the way he had come; but this was no easy thing with no Indian guide, cattle all dead, supplies used, and hardly a horse left. Enough to say, the dreary retreat began in April, 1542. Friar Padilla, a lay brother and three Negro slaves remained. He heard some raiders were coming and on his knees awaited the glorious sacrifice of martyrdom for his Holy Faith. His slaves hastened after the retreating army and told what had happened. Padilla was killed while praying—the first martyr, so far as we know, in Kansas, the first hero of many in the army records of Kansas and the Southwest. Two other soldiers of the Cross remained behind the army. One perished near Taos, and another near the four great mesas of Arizona. Friar Padilla's death is given as November 30, 1544, but this is disputed by Franciscan records as a mistake for 1542.

From the day of beginning his retreat, Coronado's authority with his army declined. He was disobeyed and flouted. The moment the ragged band crossed south to New Galicia, the rank and file deserted. When the great commander reached Mexico City he was so depressed that he could hardly speak. Stragglers from his band came in ragged and heart-sick. Many of their families had mortgaged all they owned to outfit the glorious treasure-seekers. Sadness settled in the city. Deep gloom enveloped the viceroy circles. It is unknown what became of Coronado. He lost his position as governor of New Galicia. He probably did not want to go back to Spain in disgrace. All we know is he died a broken-hearted man. Cruel, yes; but he paid the penalty for cruelty in his own personal ruin and disgrace.

Juan de Padilla's life was not altogether wasted; for the Franciscans flocked to the mesas. There you can find the ruins of their first churches, and new churches that have risen on their ruins. In spite of evil practises in the Indian kivas, all the sacrifice was not waste. Hospitals were gradually built, schools established, blindness combated, the worst customs of torturing defeated foes stopped, the Holy Faith of Pilgrims extended in area, however deeply entrenched old habits of self-torture, of rotten morals as part of worship; and the old is still in process of giving place to the new.

When I visited Oraibi seventeen years ago, it was so indescribably filthy you had to hold your nose not to be nauseated. Smallpox and blindness were common. Wherever you looked were filth and the results in disease. The house builders were using the blood of animals and chickens to get the stains for tints on their abodes. To-day, there has been a universal clean-up. Smallpox is being eradicated. The blind are in government hospitals and many being cured. All this redemptive work began in the willing martyrdom of those early soldiers of the Holy Faith; but we cannot expect the habits of ten thousand years to be uprooted and changed in four hundred years. One thing, purely in the interests of scholarship, let us credit to the Franciscans. They did not, as the first French missionaries did, try to destroy the pictographs on the rocks of an ancient civilization as devices of the Devil. They did not try to force purely spiritual concepts on a physical race. They recognized, like St. Paul with the Athenians, that the tribes did worship a great Unseen God, and they tried to lead them gradually to that God. Pictographs were not portrayals of a devil. They were the picture language of a race without letters; so the Franciscans left such undefaced. Little images were not signs of idolatry. They were clan, family, tribal coats of arms—totems, as the Pacific tribes called them. The swastika was not the Christian cross, but it did point to the East . . . a symbol of the rising sun, which they seemed to worship both in the smokes and morning prayers; but it was not the sun they worshiped. It was the Maker of the sun. To be sure, the practises in kiva worship were dark and horrible, but no worse than the religion of the Greeks in the days of Christ. Their feasts were greedy gorgings, but had not the early apostles found the people of Crete and Athens and Corinth guilty of the same? "Gluttons," Holy Writ describes them.

There is a beautiful old legend of the Franciscan Padilla at Isleta, not far from Santa Fe and Albuquerque. It is worth treasuring, as the folklore of both races adoring the ancient friar. You will hear it when you go to Isleta, to see the Evergreen dance of September—the Indian Thanksgiving for the year. The church founded about 1629 has been rebuilt with thick adobe walls. "Bees drone among the cactus," says Leo Crane; "the magpies rasp blessing or curses." There the good fray martyr was buried beneath the loose

CORONADO SETS OUT ON PILGRIMAGE 55

plank floor. Once every twenty years or so, his body was supposed to rise in the coffin, push the planks up, and the ghost appear to bless his Indian children. Many Indians believe that miracle to this day. The coffin was of cottonwood, which legend says was packed down from Kansas, as Marquette's body a century later was brought by Indians from its first burial in the sands back up to Mackinac. The body of the friar wore a skull-cap. There was a wound in the left of the neck, where he had been stabbed. When laying a new floor to the church the spikes hit something hard coming up; but that was the last time Padilla's ghost came up. Perhaps the spikes held the floor down. Perhaps miracles had gone out of fashion by 1894. Anyway, Padilla's ghost is no longer seen.

The faithful friars alone seemed to remember the great empire discovered for Spain by the treasure-seekers of the Seven Golden Cities. They continued to go northward and establish missions; but for fifty years there were no other pilgrimages of the Holy Faith. Indeed, Santa Fe itself had not been founded. Blasts of disappointment do not usually continue for a half-century; but the fact is, the people of Mexico City were now becoming colonizers instead of treasure-seekers—becoming miners of precious metals, developers of vast haciendas; and as the friars yearly brought back word from the north to Mexico City of their own success in raising fruit, corn, or sheep, applications began to be made for concessions of land north of the Rio Grande. Juan de Onate of Zacatecas, who had married Cortes' granddaughter, was one such applicant. He offered to conquer and colonize New Mexico for Spain. In return he wanted the title governor and about ninety miles of land and profits from mines and ranches. His conquests and peace treaties with the pueblo Indians followed; but after changing the capital of the new province from its first site, he finally in 1605 to 1608—the date is in dispute—chose the site of Santa Fe.

There was everything to commend that site. It was the central hub of many pueblos but at the time unclaimed by any tribe. It had a pure supply of snow water from the encircling mountains. Its soil was fertile; its climate neither cold nor hot; and it commanded all great Indian trails north, south, east, west. It was ideal for a strong central fort. To it could come almost any missionary for protection. Around it schools, churches, fortifications would cluster in such a colony as already marked many a province of Old Mexico.

PART II

THE FRENCH OPEN A CARAVAN ROUTE TO SANTA FE

CHAPTER V

THE FRENCH OPEN A CARAVAN ROUTE TO SANTA FE

WHILE Spain was gradually extending her domain north of what we now call the boundary of the United States, another great European power had begun expansion north, west, south from the St. Lawrence. This was France. Radisson and Chouart Groseillers had discovered the upper Mississippi in 1659 to 1661. Marquette the Jesuit and Louis Joliet had discovered the middle sections of the Great Forked River fifteen years later; and in the 1680's, La Salle, who already knew the upper reaches of the river, came sailing over the Gulf of Mexico to ascend the current. The expedition circled much as Narvaez's had on the shores of the marshy seaweed and swale. He was assassinated by his own mutinous men. Then another third of a century was to elapse before the trail of the Pilgrims to Santa Fe could be resumed. This time the Pilgrims were lured by a higher god than gold.

Treasure the prize was, but the treasure was love of a little señorita, daughter of a Spanish don on the Rio Grande; and she had not the remotest notion that her fate was interwoven with the ambitious plans of two great European nations and a third American nation not yet born.

Louis XIV, Grand Monarch of France, was in friendly relations with Spain; but he knew Spain was slipping from her first place as a European power. He was preparing to snatch up what she let slip. Louisiana, named after himself, was regarded as pretty much anything between Spanish Florida, the English colonies along the Atlantic, and Spanish Mexico. Things had not been going well for France in Louisiana. La Mothe Cadillac, founder of Detroit, had been transferred to what is now New Orleans as Governor of Louisiana for France. Now La Mothe had been born and educated in the Pyrenees section of southern France. It is supposed he had some Spanish blood. While he knew that he must on no account embroil Louis with Spain over Mexican possessions, he always had his eye on trade with Mexico as a source of profit. The merchant trader of Louisiana had many goods—calicoes, grocers' supplies, broadcloths, silks,—which might be exchanged at great profit for the tooled leather, saddles, harness, gold and silver work of Old Mexico. Besides, Cadillac may have had secret instructions from the French

Court to block all Spanish advances from Santa Fe eastward toward Louisiana. Louis might have heard—indeed, through the Franciscan monks he would be sure to hear—of the terrible revolt among all the pueblo towns in New Mexico against Spain. Anyway, Governor Cadillac decided to send a scouting expedition westward from the Mississippi to learn all he could of Spanish trade and extension eastward toward Louisiana.

Among Governor Cadillac's junior officers in Louisiana in 1714 was a young member of the distinguished St. Denis family of soldiers. This youth spoke Spanish. He had been educated in the cadet schools of France in which many a Spanish lad of that period was trained. He was in his early twenties, graceful, handsome, fearless, offhand, generous, caring not for big treasure but caring very much to keep his honor stainless as his Damascus sword. He loved adventure. He could handle men. All men red and white trusted him. He was indeed a true knight-errant of the wilderness. He had been a subordinate officer at Natchez where the French treachery toward the Indians had provoked wide-spread antagonism among all western tribes. Yet in Natchez, Juchereau St. Denis was beloved and trusted by the Indians.

Cadillac sent for him and despatched him with instructions to take a wide circuit northwestward through what are now Arkansas, Oklahoma, New

Mexico and back down the Rio Grande to Presidio del Norte. Was he going as trader or spy? Undoubtedly as trader. His two trips could truthfully be described as the adventure of a knight-errant, who was no Don Quixote tilting at windmills. He was to go up the Red River from Natchez past the modern army fort of Alexandria. He was then to swing across from the upper Red or Canadian forks to the Rio Grande and so come on down the Rio Del Norte and across the hot plains of Texas (then New Spain) back to Louisiana. Recalling what had happened to Cabeza and Coronado in this semi-arid country, it was a pretty extensive commission for a young man in his early twenties; but St. Denis was keen for adventure and he found it. With an escort of twelve mounted soldiers and a drunken surgeon he set out. They were to depend for food on their guns. Up the Red in spring, the trip must have delighted St. Denis' heart. Here were adventure and beauty in plenty. The drunken surgeon's skill in healing wounds among whites and reds became a miracle that often protected their lives in Indian raids. When hunting deer, St. Denis permitted his men to toss off their hot metal shirts but when raided he and his men donned the metal breastplate, pulled down the helmet and spread a thick bullhide as protection against arrows across the horse's flank. Then he trusted their lives more to the fleetness of his black pony's feet than to the blood he might shed by the sword.

Alligators rolled and grunted in the swampy bayous of the Red. St. Denis struck north over higher ground. He must have risen at 2 A.M. to escape the midday heat and heard the mocking birds trill their divine song on the wing. Bed was on the ground with the rope of the horse's tether round one arm, a saddle for pillow and small thought of the scorpions, tarantulas, spiders and snakes which gave our modern army such trouble. St. Denis had more than likely learned how to forefend against these small poisonous pests by using a fur blanket below himself across which few earth parasites care to crawl.

He had made a circuit of one hundred and fifty leagues before he touched the upper Rio Grande. There at St. John the Baptist Fort, he found an old Spanish don in charge. These adobe forts were always at first disappointing to the French, accustomed to stockades and logs. The thick adobe walls looked like the inclosure of a barn yard round a ranch. The entrance gate was usually a rough tumble-down makeshift in small branch logs, or sparse timber, and the commandant's house a poor squat mud ranch house with face to gate and two wings at right angles leading back to cook-house and servants' quarters. A flag would be flying above the commandant's house to the whipping of a restless dusty wind that seemed never to quiet. Enter the door of the house! Instant transformation! The thick eighteen-inch wall excluded all heat. Deep well-worn rugs covered the rough timbered floors, the couches along the walls, the homemade chairs. Trophies of hunting trips decorated walls, with a picture of the good saint protecting the fort. Vegas, or light timber rafters, usually spanned the ceiling. Above this was a canvas. Like the inner walls it was often whitewashed with lime; or if not whitewashed, then more or less hidden by woven baskets suspended from the rafters. Indian pottery was used for water supplies. The drinking pots like the drinking canteens of the Far East had narrow necks with corks. Water for personal ablutions was held in open crocks. The commandants' houses were distinguished by silver service and pewters, which to-day are pretty nearly priceless as antiques of the Spanish period. The dress of wives and daughters was famed for lovely oriental shawls, mantillas, and delicate silks sent from Old Spain, which really came from oriental sources. These beautiful shawls are to-day almost priceless—one thousand five hundred dollars for many. The whole effect of such a dwelling on a newcomer was inexpressibly restful, cool, refreshing after a journey across a desert of dust and heat.

This fort was well named St. John. It was an

oasis in a desert wilderness such as that where St. John the Baptist had wandered. The commandant in charge of this fort we may call Don Pedro; for two great authorities differ as to whether his last name was Villescar or Raimond. There was an only daughter at this frontier back of beyond. The type of welcome by a generous Spaniard is elaborate.

"It is all yours, Seigneur," he bows his guest in.

St. Denis took the welcome literally; for he was gazing awestruck and almost dumb at the beautiful little señorita. He fell in love with all the passionate ardor of the Latin and his love from the first was reciprocated. From that moment, the Santa Fe trail took on roseate hues to St. Denis.

Don Pedro could make no trade treaties nor promises till he could gain permission from his superior officers in command at the pueblo of Taos. At Taos, unfortunately, was a rascal infamous for grafting in all trade permits. There is a legend that the rascal also had his eye on the señorita. His name is given Don Juan Gaspardo Anaya; and when St. Denis proceeded to Taos under guard of twenty-five men, he was forbidden to trade. St. Denis was too honorable to involve the girl of his love in an intrigue till he could obtain not only the fulfilment of his trade mission but the blessing of his commandant and her father on their union.

Vowing, under such low-hung stars and moon as

only the desert knows, to return from Louisiana next year, St. Denis with many a backward wave to the lonely little adobe fort put spurs to his fleet black pony and set out for Natchez on the Mississippi.

We can guess he "painted the lily red" and the prospects of trade with Santa Fe in roseate colors as he gave his verbal report to Governor Cadillac of Louisiana. He was eloquent of what the profits from trade must be; and later developments justified his prophecies. As for dangers, what did St. Denis care for danger? Could not he convert Indian foes to friends? He set out the very next year with many goods for trade—in rude caravan wagons with an army convoy. A wagon in those days was often transformed to serve either one of two functions: a home on wheels for the commander's wife and family, or a fort on wheels in case of attack, when feather beds against canvas siding and tin slope on the roof would bar out all raiders' arrows or chance bullets.

Bad luck hovered over St. Denis' second trip. The Comanches and other tribes of the Staked Plains were horribly hostile. Some of his escort were killed by the raiders and some goods plundered from the wagons. When he reached his former friend on the Rio Grande, he found that good don with orders from Mexico City to seize him and forward him to the dungeons of Mexico

City. St. Denis probably did not know those dungeons, or he would not have advanced so dauntlessly. Besides, later events in Mexico City seem to prove that his adored one and her uncle or father must have traveled with him. He certainly went ahead with no regret for his double chains of Cupid and an arrest. In the cool of morning the two lovers doubtless rode on horseback far ahead of the troopers' slow plodding beasts and slower wagons behind mules that seldom made more than twenty miles a day. As heat blazed from a flaming sun at midday, all the marchers would pause, the men to take a midday snooze under the shade of their wagons, the animals to sag and rest beside river or spring. It was easy to rig up a couch for the family in a wagon. Some old woman servant, cook or maid, usually accompanied the families to care for toilet and food.

Through cactus roof-high, sagebrush hub-deep, mesquite bloom yellow as gold, little cactus flowers like portulacas clinging close to the sands, St. Denis and his lady must have ridden for at least six weeks from the Rio Grande to Mexico City. Sunset is a filtered curtain of fire and purple in this land. Sunrise comes in a pale cool gold, not the copper red of a hot shield rising from torrid fogs in low lying tropic lands. Then the snowy summits of mountains swim in the far horizon and your path is dipping down gradually to Mexico City.

Little time had St. Denis then to admire the floating flowers of the lagoons and canals. He made up for the omission later. He was clapped in one of those terrible underground dungeons for which Mexico was notorious. The charge was interloper in trade, spy. This may have been to force blackmail for an escape; or it may have been that Spain knew very well what the Grand Monarch of France was about—a plot to pounce on Spanish possessions whenever chance permitted. The great viceroy Lenarez, to whom St. Denis might have applied as the loyal subject of a nation friendly to Spain, had died. Either a blundering or dishonest underling was in charge till the new Spanish viceroy could come out. Little light came through the slitted windows of the dungeons. Prisoners were chained to the stone walls so close to one another that their emaciated skeleton forms almost touched. The chains held both arms and feet. A pot of drinking water and corn bread were thrust in each day. One can imagine the condition of these pestilent stench holes, seldom cleaned of their accumulated cesspool filth.

Where was the little señorita all this while? Doing her best no doubt with her beautiful eyes to obtain the release of her lover, and crying her eyes out the rest of the time—a storm of Romeo and Juliet hope and despair.

St. Denis' long hair grew and matted to a tangle. His beard was "shaggy." He heard one morning "the trample of horses," then iron shod tread coming down the corridor to his own cell. The jailer came in followed by a file of soldiers. It was the firing squad. The officer in charge seemed to speak in an accent St. Denis recalled. "Who is this?" he demanded.

Before the corporal could answer, St. Denis had shouted:

"I, Juchereau de St. Denis, gentleman, gentleman from France, prisoner by oppression, and I demand justice from the Court of Spain for my men and myself."

This was the answer of no common felon.

"Bring him out to the light! Let me see him."

St. Denis emerged to the light "every inch a gentleman."

The Spanish officer drew aside the matted hair and uttered a loud exclamation.

"Jailer, we have made some horrible mistake! Off with those accursed chains! Set that man free! He is an old comrade of mine from the schools of France."

The two friends so young in years and old in experience could hardly speak for choking emotion. St. Denis was taken to the Spaniard's home.

He was clothed as a gentleman. The new governor had arrived from Spain. That very night, St. Denis dined in the halls of Montezuma and drank to their majesties, the kings of Spain and France. Amid the ladies sat the little señorita. St. Denis' cup of happiness seemed to fill to overflowing. He was lodged as guest in the viceroyal palace and detained for two months. It is said he saved the new governor from an attempted assassination. Every device that could be courteously applied was tried to detain St. Denis for service in Mexico. He was promised the señorita as an immediate bride.

Finally convinced that St. Denis was not to be detained from loyal services to the French King, the viceroy gave him his farewell blessing. "I shall hope the little señorita may persuade you to change your mind. You will meet her and her worthy father on the Rio del Norte. Give them my regards and bid them detain you with the gentler chains of love."

Did St. Denis and his men speed them back to that lonely little fort on the Rio Grande? Did the empty wagons sway and rattle dry and warped over the Pilgrim Trail? We can believe they did, the St. Denis horse far in advance. The old don on the Rio Grande was in a belt of perils. The Indians were about him in circles; but he had firearms, they had not; and St. Denis was welcomed

OPEN MARKET, MEXICO CITY

MEXICAN BOY SELLING CAKES

A ZUÑI CITY

back as lover, guest, defender. A good Franciscan united the lovers in life bonds of matrimony. The mission bell would ring. The old arquebuses would fire a volley. Whole oxen, whole sheep, with peppers, tamales and seasoning which the Spaniards might well add is as hot as their coffee would grace the wedding feast. The Spanish description of good coffee is the best I know. It is "sweet as love, dark as night, and hot as the inferno." I swear it is. It will keep you awake all night and is more stimulating than *aguardiente*. St. Denis and his bride returned to Mobile and New Orleans to find that Governor Cadillac had been recalled. The King of France was dead. St. Denis was appointed commandant at Natchez and within two years helped to capture Pensacola from the Spaniards.

For once the pilgrims of a new trail were led by Cupid instead of by beaver or coin.

As far as immediate trade was concerned, the first covered wagon venture was a complete loss.

Note

The best, in fact, only, authorities are Gayarré of Louisiana and Du Pratz, who was in Louisiana in the Cadillac régime. Gayarré drew his facts from the Marine Department of Louis XIV's reign, of which he was an indefatigable investigator. Many of these papers have been copied in the Archives of Quebec City as distinct from the Dominion Archives of Ottawa. These were comparatively recently issued. Reference will also be found to the earliest expedition in Du Harpe. Of Spanish records, Ralph E. Twitchell has the best; but Twitchell seems to have known nothing of St. Denis, which is not surprising considering that the documents bearing on Cadillac were issued by Quebec province as recently as in 1928-29. However Twitchell does give most fully the records of the various great governors in Mexico City, in Taos, in Santa Fe, and the guarded policy of New Spain toward all advance up the Rio Grande by the French of Louisiana. The great viceroys sent out as governors to Mexico City are given with their pictures. The rascals, for that is all one can call them, serving in Taos and Santa Fe, he also names. There is confusion of names both in St. John the Baptist Fort, in Taos, in Santa Fe. This is explained by the facts of the case. Few of these grafters in trade held office longer than two years. The posts were horribly dangerous after the great pueblo people's rebellion of the 1690's. Both sides of the picture can be gained by reading the French records, then the Spanish of the Cadillac period.

CHAPTER VI

THE INDIANS OF THE SANTA FE TRAIL

BEFORE the army heroisms of the Santa Fe can be realized, the character of the Indians in the Southwest must be known. These Indians differed as widely from the red men of the Northwest as an African from an Egyptian. They differed as much as a Frenchman from a German.

Lewis and Clark's classification of western Indians in the Southwest does not help. These explorers followed the northwest trail of the Missouri to the Columbia. Early travelers' descriptions of the Southwest in the main agree and are safer guide than purely ethnological groupings. Catlin was one of the first careful students of all Indians in the West and while his paintings seem crude, still they enable us to see what he saw. Then of the modern observers as purely laymen, General Miles, or such Indian agents as Crane are the surest guides. Arrayed against all layman conclusions are the findings and inferences from the spade-workers—archeologists and geologists. These two are again not in agreement. To these, add the old historians moving in a dense fog of ignorance as to whither and yon their lost armies of explorers and missionaries were wandering, and you have as nice a "boiling kettle of controversy" as exists in all America. The lay writer will look down in this "boiling kettle" and keep out of it.

Take a general rough outline first. One of the first questions that occurs is why were all these southwest nations so hostile to the whites. The immediate answer is because it was their own nature. There was not a tribe amid all these southwestern Indians that had not been long prior to the coming of white man fiercely antagonistic to the others. This will be taken up later. The bow was stretched to shoot, the poisoned arrow poised to wing its death, the skull cracker raised to brain, the scalping knife out to welcome all strangers to camp. Was that due to the haunting fear, the subconscious motive, which results in modern wars? Hardly. The Indian is a fatalist. He may fear disease and hunger, but death in battle he does not fear. Such a death he believes sends his "spirit walking to the Indian Happy Hunting Grounds." The body to the North American Indian as to the ancient Hermetics of Old India and Egypt was only "an old worn coat to be cast off," while the soul proceeded to Paradise whence Masters or Guides came back to guide the tribe. Then to the motive that his own nature urged him on to fight as a vocation, must be added a deep heritage of hatred and revenge from Spanish and French days. He would trade with both nations to obtain firearms, also liquor and such gew-gaws as bright calicoes, beads, looking glasses, tea, tobacco, condiments; but beneath the trade was masked antagonism to the white, masked hatred, masked seething revenge; also contempt for the lack of tranquillity among the whites. The Indian is essentially an oriental in his hidden mental processes.

The Spaniards had ever been cruel masters to the Indians. They had slain them by force of superior arms without mercy or reason. They had enslaved them for their mines. They had seized and traded them for blacks in the West Indies. The common Spanish soldier, often a riffraff blackguard or convict, was a menace to the families of the Indians wherever he went. Now the southwestern Indian was a monogamist—a one-wife man; and the woman ruled the house. A woman on marriage brought her husband to her clan. She increased the tribe; and any interference with women aroused a degree of hatred and vengeance comparable only to the southern white's defence of his daughters and wife. This attack on Indian women, the missionaries had fought, but in vain. The French were not cruel to the Indians. Their half-wild boatmen and horse brigade riders had usually married Indian wives on whose clans their own safety depended; but the French in trade did supply the Indians with an abundance of firearms and liquor pure and impure, doped and clear. Among the Americans advancing westward from 1802, the characters of the traders varied from "wildcatters" and "pirates" as some ruffians called themselves, boasting a nick in their gun for every dead Indian, to such saints as Jed Smith, whose Bible was his daily paper; or such a heroic gentleman in the army as General George Custer. There was certain trouble ahead for every advance of trader or pioneer.

One may roughly classify these Indians as plains tribes, mesa people, and desert dwellers. The difference between the plains tribes and the desert dwellers was that the plains man was a raider and rover, shifting camp with every season as the game shifted. The desert dweller was just as fierce a fighter as the prairie type; but he did not rove nor raid unless forced. He did not need to. His land was coveted by no rival. It was too arid. It was not a hunting land for game foods or furs. It was cut by rivers and arroyo beds of fine sand, where the waters evaporated at noon and seeped back to the surface in drinking pools at dawn and dusk. At these the desert dwellers could obtain water for home use, for herds of sheep, cattle, horses.

But these desert dwellers were themselves divided in two distinct groups: those who lived on the high mesa rocks resembling islands on a yellow sea of tumbling drifting sands; then the valley dwellers. The mesas were and are yet known as the Hopi, the Zuñi, the Aztec, the Moki or Moqui. It was their houses, going up two and three and four stories against the sky, which misled the Spaniards seeking for Seven Golden Cities. The desert dwellers were and are yet the Utes, the Navajos, the Comanches, the Yaquis, the Apaches. The Navajos are credited with being the most numerous pure blood Indians in the United States, almost forty thousand. The chances are they will absorb in the white race the slowest of all Indians. There is nothing to tempt any intermingling of blood. The traders are few. The wool clip comes only once a year. The woven blankets and jewel trinkets and tooled tents are carried to the nearest trader. Many of these trading posts you can visit in short drives, by buckboard or motor from main highways; but take a guide who knows where to find the water pools for noonday rest, and take, too, unless you are stomach proof against alkali waters a canteen of drinking water. Otherwise you will not be happy crossing these beautiful desert areas; and more varied majestic beauty I have never seen.

In the other desert dwellers, the Hopi, the Zuñi,

the Aztec, the Moki, you find one of the most puzzling, enigmatic race problems in the world. These Indians were as much community dwellers as the Mormons, or early Israelites. They were sedentary. They cultivated their outlying farms along the stream beds by day but came back to their eagle-nest adobe houses at night. They, too, were weavers, but their greatest craftsmanship was in pottery and baskets. Not all mesas had people of equally advanced standard. You will find that as you pass among them to-day. The people of Laguna and Acoma, yes! There are rooms in their houses as clean as any in your own. They wear shirts and skirts as clean as a white's; but when you go farther west in Arizona, you find mesa towns as hostile to decency and progress in sanitation as amid the most degraded races on earth. The three mesa towns towering above the sea of sand as you drive west are a good average—improving each year but pretty bad in spots yet, where the dead from such epidemics as smallpox are thrust down cracks in the rock. The blazing sun disinfects but the custom is odoriferous. But go on westward to Hotoville and Oraibi; and until the last ten years, you would have found just as much resentment amid these people, not only toward other mesa towns but toward white men's efforts to save children and aged from blindness by hospital treatment. It is said that this attitude of a chip on the shoulder arose from an ancient quarrel of centuries ago, when the caciques or governors of Oraibi and Hotoville quarreled with the other mesa chiefs and sulkily withdrew, and that the sultry strain of blood came down the centuries. I remember on my own first visit to them seventeen years ago, after I had parted friends with the Acomas, I could not evoke a smile, a gesture of friendliness from the Oraibi and Hotoville people. Only when we were coming back down the hill to our carriages with regrets that we had not had clothes-pins for our noses during the morning visit, did a little group of youngish women run after us and call, "We wish you well." Somehow it was too much like a kick to speed a parting guest. Long ago, as such ruins as Casa Grande show, these pueblo or community dwellings extended farther west, almost to the California bounds.

Where had these southwestern Indians come from? It is easy to believe that the pure plains tribes came from the same Mongolian origin as the Indians of northern areas. They had the small widely separated eyes, the high cheek bones, the strong, stern, sometimes cruel mouth and chin but seldom the squat flat nose. The nose was sharp and narrow with wide nostrils. Their faces were beardless. The figure till late in life was the rangy lank thin muscular type in men, perhaps stouter in women. The hair was lank and straight as a horse's mane. But the pueblo or town community Indian from the mesas had many Mongolian characteristics. He was short and stalky and thick-set. He wore his hair bobbed and bound back off the forehead, where the prairie man wore his in long braids. Though short, the pueblo Indian in a long even dog trot could out-pace and out-run a plains rider's cayuse; and he never showed the slightest sign of being wind-blown or exhausted in muscle. With an easy swing, he could reel off the miles day after day. I have passed them in my buckboard at noon, stopped for the night at some ranch house, and to my amazement descried the same two or three runners far to the fore the next day. But why had the pueblo Indians a community life where, till the white man came, the prairie rovers scorned fixed abode? This seems to point to an utterly different origin, when perhaps recession of glaciers and change of climate sent the plains men raiding the sedentary people, who took up their abode in the cave cities of the walled canyons or in the high mesas of the rocks that were islands in seas of sand. This would date their origins far back prior to Plato's account of a great change in the climate of the whole world about 10,000 to 20,000 B.C.

There was great resemblance, too, between the ancient civilizations of Egypt and the curious half-savage civilization of the pueblos. Take one example only. The Egyptians knew how to preserve their dead as mummies. So did the pueblo and cave people of New Mexico. You can see the Egyptian mummies in the Metropolitan Museum of New York. Go out to Frijole Canyon on the Santa Fe Trail. You will see the little body of a woman or girl preserved in one cave, wrapped in woven cerements of the dead. Near Casa Grande, much farther west, a little body was found several years ago to which the Forest Rangers gave the name, "Zack." It was barely four feet long but evidently the remains of a full grown man and mistaken for the remains of a dwarf race. We know now it was not a dwarf race. The cave people knew how to shrink their dead two or three feet, then how to harden the skin to almost flint. You will see examples of this in the great Huntington Museum of New York. The body was cleansed of all internal organs, then bones and skin were packed with some form of niter, which hardened to an almost flint.

Splendidly and heroically the old missions had begun with Padilla and continued down the centuries by holy padres from Mexico. You can see their churches, and remains of the walls of older churches lower down the mesas of the pueblo people. The word pueblo means simply a town of men, a community life, with farms lying round it. These churches the people still frequent on the visits of priests; but higher up, you find still the secret kivas, which an Indian agent can penetrate only in disguise and at risk of his life, as Crane tells. Side by side, the two forms of worship persist—the clean and the unclean, the merciful and the horribly cruel; and the curious phase of it is that the victims are willing sacrifices to the old devil gods who, all Indians thought, demanded sacrifices. Though half the Indian bureau is officered by employees of more or less Indian blood, the Government has no right to interfere with the religion of its wards, unless these practises cross the line of what is criminal; and that is a difficult thing to prove for a court of law as to secret ceremonials. Sacrifices—yes—the Indian always understands them as a part of worship; and there he mingles his old faith and his new in a fashion that has puzzled priest and laymen to eradicate. In one section of New Mexico on your way to Taos, you can witness a horrible example of this in a mestizo band, who mixed their old and new faiths, their open Christian worship and their secret lodges. There are the crucifixions and flagellantes. To atone for sin, it was customary for processions to be formed and the penitents to be scourged with cactus whips up to lone crosses on the summit of a hill. These whips were plied till the blood flowed in streams from naked backs and the willing victim staggered to his knees to crawl the rest of the way to the far cross. Not many years ago, the mock crucifixions so often ended in real death that such practises had to be stopped by the strong arm of law. Yet the victims were voluntary, just as voluntary as in the old Sun Dance lodges of prairie tribes who submitted their young men and boys to be tortured; and the youths who suffered the greatest tortures were accounted the greatest braves. Long since, the prairie people gave up their Sun Dance tortures. Not so the pueblo people. Their kiva worship is only another form of the Sun Dance sacrifices. In the Sun Dances, the women took no part except as spectators to applaud and healers to help the wounded. In the kiva worship, women and boys were too often the victims. In the crucifixion processions, men, women, girls, were eager contestants for the honor of martyrdom. Again let us not judge too harshly. We have only to read back in European history to the thirteenth and fourteenth centuries to find kings and emperors who from political or religious motives did publicly just such forms of penance. Let us say rather that the Indian and his half-blood descendant are still working up the painful pilgrimage to a higher faith from physical to mental, and from mental to spiritual concepts.

Yet with all the differences, the tribes of the Southwest had many similar features in customs, religions, beliefs, marriages, practise of a rude medicine and ruder surgery, knowledge of proper diets for certain seasons. In not one tribe were the people image worshipers. The little figures, which the first missionaries mistook for images, were either dolls or clan signs like our signet rings. All tribes worshiped the sun. The ignorant regarded the sun as a god, the moon as his wife, the stars as children or torch lights to the Indians' paradise. The deeper thinkers never regarded the sun as a god. They saw in the sun the symbol of a great Spirit, who clad himself in light, and to that spirit they offered at dawn their incense of a pipe smoke. The thunder-storm was an angry casting of forked lightnings to earth for some sin. The broadcaster of these fiery deaths was the Thunder God, to whom in great terror the Indians were apt to toss their slaves, their children, anything of value, to appease the god's anger. Weird chants, the tom-tom, the dance, the drama, were all vents for religious expression.

Wood, grass, stream, tree, beast, bird—all were animated by a spirit life; and these spirits the young Indians tried to enlist for familiar guides and companions all through life. Fasting till dreams of exhaustion came, the first vision of game, of bird, of tree, was to be the Indian's familiar spirit. Deep beneath all his white man's education and progress, that belief persists to this day; and the eagle is a favorite emblem for his far sight, and the serpent for his wily wisdom in finding water. Both, however, are symbols of the soul, of which more later.

Marriages were chiefly arranged by the parents but seldom forced against the wishes of bride or groom. The wife was often bought by a trader for five dollars' worth of goods. In the camp the wife's wishes were supreme; again the code was far superior to that of the north, where a husband could brain his wife, cudgel her, deface her, kill her, and go unpunished. The superior status of the wife in the Southwest arose from economic independence. At birth, it was customary to endow the child with a lamb, a heifer, a mare. The offspring of these became hers for life. On growth to womanhood, if she found herself married to an idler, a philanderer after other women, a worthless fellow, all she had to do was hang his saddle and bridle up on a pin at the door and the signal was, "Go off out of this: you are no longer wanted: you are divorced." The woman was not disgraced but the man was. He would not readily win a second thrifty wife on that mesa; and intermarriage among the mesa peoples was not common. To this day, it is not common with whites of the best character.

Their crude knowledge of medicinal plants and physics was probably built up as ours has been by age long experiments; but the results were kept secret, probably for similar motives, to prevent rash misuse by the ignorant and to preserve a sort of medical culture or standard or monopoly. The medical man had passed his knowledge on only to a successor chosen by himself. The medical woman did the same. We have lost, and it is to be regretted, many secrets of their medicinal plants. In the north, the sweat bath and purges were the cure for all rheumatism. In the south, plasters of plants applied did the same thing.

In the Southwest, the aged and blind were not abandoned as in the north. The community life always afforded a roof to the ill and helpless. From their crude rude surgery there is no possible conclusion to be drawn but that they had some knowledge of pain-deadening anesthetics. When a finger, an arm, a foot, had been shattered in accident, either the medicine man or the injured himself tied a twisted cord to prevent the spread of infected blood, applied a plant plaster, then with a notched shell or hunting knife amputated the injured part; and in a few days would be about the camp in perfect health, suffering no pain. Again and again many a trader gave examples of this; but though married to Indian wives, never learned the secret of such surgery.

Over the prairie tribes had come sinister changes since the first advent of Spanish and

French. They had firearms and they had them in abundance by 1802. They were turning the white man's weapons against himself. Up to the early 1800's, north and south tribes had little intercourse with one another except to kill. By the beginning of the new century, the tribes of the Platte had gained a new idea, which is not at all new to any white trader. It was to thrust themselves between North and South as middlemen taking toll of trade both ways north and south. Their chiefs could advise but they could not control the raiding young bucks. South lay a thousand miles of chartless plains. East and west lay more than a thousand miles. Over all blazed a tropical sun seven months of the year. Streams were few and rare, the North and South Platte, the Republican, the Smoky Hill, the Arkansas, the Cimarron, the Red, the Rio Grande. Dripping springs beneath cave shaped rocks were also rare and few, where the drop-drop-drop for centuries had worn out a natural basin. The narrowing canyon had carried subterranean tricklets of water to feed pools. Up between the narrow canyons to this day, you can see bands of wild horses led by a magnificent stallion sniffing air for danger come galloping at noon, or dawn, or nightfall, for water. The mourning doves frequent such oases in a desert in flocks of thousands, their purplish-gray plumage shadowy almost to the tints of the filtered air; and their sad threnody of a last call to daylight is one of the most pensive sounds in all desert life. It seems to question why all life should be so hard and cruel in the desert; and the brazen dome of the sky, whether filled by a blood-red hot moon or blazing with a sun that stabs the eye has no answer.

Now let us sketch briefly the records of the spade among "the master builders" of the ancient American world. Foremost of these great archeologists is Dr. Edgar Hewett of the Santa Fe School and Archæological Institute of America; and Dr. Hewett gives full credit to all his predecessors and contemporaries. It takes a very big man to do that—a very open minded and fair scholar. The little man tries to climb on the back of the man he has knocked down. Not so Hewett. He gives full credit to all. To Holmes, Cushing, Fewkes, Lummis, Hodge, Powell, Bandelier, Cummings, Morley,—whether he agrees or disagrees,—he gives credit for the sincerity of the purpose in each and keeps his mind open to all evidence because as he says "the spade keeps you guessing every minute."

Hewett like all workers in the Southwest and all visitors falls a victim to the charm of the desert land. It was formed by fire and water, volcano and prehistoric seas, antedating the great upheavals of which Herodotus and Plato tell, when

INDIANS OF THE SANTA FE TRAIL 89

some vast convulsive action in the Zodiac turned tropic to Arctic zones and Arctic to tropics, and heaved up deserts where once flowed seas, rivers, lakes. It threw down mountains two thousand feet sheer in such gashes below the level as the Grand Canyon of the Colorado. Whether man was a contemporary of the great sloths and giant marine life; or the sloth was a left-over from the ancient days, he wisely does not say, because he does not *yet* know. Emphasize "yet." It is the keynote to his liberal scholarship. To say that twenty years ago was as much as a scholar's life was worth.

"I know of no reason for thinking that America ever was discovered." "The cradle of the human race," he regards as one of "the follies of science," a "last myth" and false trail. "Let us find out," he says. Whence came the races here or whither and yon they were wandering, he does not say. Whether it was slow desiccation, the drying up of drinking water that wiped out every trace of some ancient people, he does not say. All he knows is that the disappearance of whole races began long before the coming of any white men. The spade has proved that. His dates would place "the building boom" from the Rio Grande to the Colorado as about contemporaneous with the same "building boom" that struck the Hebrews in King David's day—about 1000 B.C. The abandonment of vast community centers in the full tide of life he does not explain; but there lie the proofs in cities uncovered by the spade; and a racial chasm exists that cannot be bridged between people of those ancient days and ours.

You will not, in fact cannot, agree with all his gentle conclusions. For instance, he describes these sedentary people as peaceful. Yet he had to acknowledge also that long before the coming of the white man, the raids of Navajo, Comanche, Yaqui, and Apache were a terror to the mesa people. He has never witnessed in the kiva worship a ceremony "that was obscene," but he has to add the qualifying phrase, "from the Indian's point of view." One could say the same of the Greeks and Assyrians; but the point of view was too often that of the animal in human form. He gives the number of old pueblos very much as the friars gave them—eighty and the population of the Navajos as forty thousand; and "the Indian race is not decreasing in the United States." It is over a third of a million. Arousing self-pity he deprecates as the worst form of help by Indian lovers. Let them work out their salvation in their own way as we do ours and not try to engraft our ways of thinking on them. There was never any overpopulation and is not yet. Then why the raids? He cannot answer that. Of the town dwellers, there were seven in Zuñi land, seven in

Hopi, much shifted as to sites since the great rebellion of the 1680's. Two thousand people were in Laguna when the Spaniards came and are there yet. Acoma, he gives as fifteen miles from Laguna, three hundred and fifty feet high, with the best potters in the world. Zuñi Land—the scene of the fabled Seven Cities that did not exist, he says has two thousand people. Santa Fe was the site of a very ancient pueblo. There he is contradicted by some historians. Pecos was Coronado's Cicuye and it had two thousand five hundred people. It is a dwindling village of a few hundred to-day. He points out there were two distinct Casas Grandes, one just south of El Paso, the other in Arizona on the Gila. Both, he regards as great forts where rallied the tribe, called by a great hollow stone bell struck with a stone hammer, on approach of raiders. Taos was always prosperous and its four- to six-story houses exist much as they did in the Spanish era. It has become an art center to-day. Isleta has one thousand people yet and he gives it the island name because it once stood on an island, since bridged by sand or abandoned for a better site.

The Indian was profoundly religious and never separated his secular from his religious life. The drama, the dance, the song all sprang from religion. Their religious legends on the origin of life were not far different from the Christian and

Theosophist or those of the ancient masters of the Hermetics. Aquatic life came first, then the birds of the air, then the animals, then human existence created by the spiritual. The fall from heavenly spheres was a fall upwards, the result of disobedience but a blessing in disguise. The flood story too and the good omens from the birds were all embodied in pueblo religion. The plumed serpent resembled the oriental symbol of the Zodiac being a great serpent swallowing his own tail—a timepiece for all eternity guiding the universe, sometimes seen on the Milky Way, more humbly seen in the common snake, guide to all water; and the Southwest Indians had no fear of snakes, poisonous or harmless. Their weird Snake dances and dramas can be seen yearly in many of the pueblo towns and draw thousands of spectators, some few of whom understand the symbolism but many see only a hideously uncanny ceremony. Black was the sign of war and death. Of leprosy, cancer, goiter, numerous diseases, the Indians knew nothing. The great scourge was eye diseases from the dust storms and from lack of abundant clear water to clear out the eye. Infectious scourges came from the whites but help came also from the whites in preventions. There again, the white is giving generously of his services free of charge. Dr. Fox, the famous eye specialist of Philadelphia, yearly gives free treatment on some Indian reserve, and in the government hospital supervises such work and where necessary operates. I'll never forget, on one of my first visits to the Southwest years ago, seeing blind and half blind Indians tripping amid the cactus and stumbling pitifully hither and thither; then going out a few years later to another reserve and seeing young boys and girls in hospital wards spotless as any in costly Eastern clinic, lying with eyes bandaged but well on the road to recovery and with, what was better still, a smile of happiness and gratitude to the good Christian white physician who had worked on them what seemed to be a miracle. No wonder Indian agents like Crane grew hot under their collars when they went to rescue Indian children from blindness and found the chiefs of the village in possession of letters from foolish people in the East bidding them, "Resist—resist—resist," all efforts of the Indian Department to interfere with their rights. All who really wish to understand what is falsely called "the Indian Problem" should pause in their hurried scamper as tourists across the continent to see for themselves just what good work the Indian Department is doing among its wards. Infectious diseases, firearms, liquor and all its attendant evils, the white brought to the red man; but he also brought great blessings—the horse for travel, cattle for meat, and sheep for the wool that has resulted in new industries of weaving, which brings greater and surer revenue than the Indian ever knew.

Dr. Hewett calls the pueblo communities the "oldest republics" in the history of the world. They are. Their caciques or governors were elected and, differing from the northern tribes, elected not as war raiders but in councils of "elders" to advise and rule. There is no white government interference with that custom to-day. Wise heads guided the younger generation and whoever did not abide by their decision fell foul of an unwritten law and might be found outlawed by the community, pitched over a rock, secretly murdered. Wherever such murders are now discovered by the government agents, the murderers have to be punished; but the caciques' councils are held under oath of secrecy and, where detection may easily be traced, proof is hard to obtain.

The fable of Seven Golden Cities passed; but another myth took its place, which some future poet or novelist will yet embody. When the rebellion of the 1680's took place, the friars of the distant missions knew well enough trouble was coming; but they refused to abandon their missions. They gathered up what silver and gold they possessed and buried it in the earth. Many remnants of these old missions you can still see—walls two to three feet thick, twenty to thirty high, which have resisted the blasts of weather and war, and stand lonely, sad monuments to these pilgrims of a holy faith who perished. There the spade has not been plied by the archeologist but by the modern treasure hunter. If any treasures have been uncovered, the treasure hunter has not betrayed the fact; but from Indian legend and the facts of the case, there is not a doubt such treasures did lie buried near many an old mission.

Land of mystery, land of myth, land of romance, who has succeeded in resisting its elusive charm through all the long centuries?

Into this arena, a thousand miles long by a thousand broad, came tumbling and rumbling the traders' caravans, and after 1827 the army patrols with never more than one thousand five hundred men and often fewer than five hundred. These Pilgrims of the Santa Fe had the faith of little children chasing rainbow ends, though such hopes could hardly be described as very holy. It was all part of a great epic progress from stone-age man to civilization with its good and its evil.

PART III

A STORMY INTERLUDE

CHAPTER VII

A Stormy Interlude

THERE are interludes in human history when the whole world seems to rock. They are usually the earthquakes that throw down the old to rebuild a better. They are portentous.

Through such an interlude both America and Europe seemed to pass from the 1690-1715 period to the 1790-1815 era. Powers amid European nations rose to zenith and crashed. Old bounds faded in new. Nations were born. From 1817 to 1821, Spanish dominance waned. French monarchy shifted from absolutism to republic and back to monarchy. New Spain in America became in some cases republican, in others a dictatorship, none the less tyrannical because it first had itself elected. Except for a few small islands, France disappeared off the North American map. The United States was born from a little strip of Atlantic colonies so frail and disunited that it seemed impossible that such a nation could ever grow to inherit all that Spain and three-quarters of all France had conquered and more or less colonized;

but it was a terribly stormy interlude, with such changes as only a few prophets had foretold—"the extension of His Dominion from sea to sea"; the extension in that Holy Faith of a great epic pilgrimage.

Though Spain seemed to forget her northern provinces for a century after Coronado, not so the faithful friars. They tramped the desert with the Holy Cross their only weapon and fell martyr to the Holy Faith of the Pilgrim Trail. As already told, colonization had followed more slowly. Merchants of Old Mexico saw chances of trade in gems, tooled leather, saddles, bridles, silver, gold for horses, cattle, sheep, firearms, liquor, to the Indians. Powerful dons, with great flocks of sheep that could pasture on scant growth and move up the mountain slopes to watered alpine dells as heat waxed in midsummer, also saw chances to obtain vast grants of ranches along the acequia (irrigation channel) and arroyo stream beds. The acequias would irrigate on lower ground and the arroyos in times of flood could be dammed for reservoirs and drinking pools. Between the uplands and lowlands sheep moved in gray woolly bleating masses herded usually by little half-breed girls or boys, peons with faithful sheep dogs. Keep your eyes open and you will see the same to-day. These herders would work for a pittance wage, a few cents a day, wool for weaving, food, a few sheep

A WAYSIDE CROSS, OLD MEXICO

A RITE OF THE KIVA WORSHIP

with which to begin herds of their own. Still they were and are a happy lot. A chuck wagon was their summer home. An adobe hut near some strong ranch house made a cheap warm winter dwelling and their own branded herd multiplied so that at the age of fifty many could retire to little fruit and corn farms of their own. They wanted little and had all they wanted. They brewed their own light wines. They grew their own flax and spun their own linens. They cured and cobbled their own leather for boots. They wore their own blankets and if they sometimes forgot the marriage ceremony till they came in from the season's work, still they strummed their guitars, hummed all the old world ditties, fell in and out of love and lived a life of freedom from care. Though wages have advanced from cents to dollars, the peon herder is the same type to-day.

Then there were the mines of which the Indians knew. Turquoise, the Indian had mined from surface rocks by simply cracking a rock open with a stone hammer and taking out a beautiful green stone apt to fade to blue or darker green. Of opals, they did not know much and cared less; for the opal required polishing and was a very soft fragile gem. Silver surface mining, the Indians had always worked; but when the Spaniard began to go deeper for gold and silver and began moreover to enslave whole Indian tribes for such work, the tribes of all red men, both the sedentary pueblos and wandering desert rovers began to cherish a masked hatred for their cruel over-lords. This enslavement, enforced by whip and sword, the friars always opposed and the kings of Spain forbade; but the friars themselves needed protection by the scum convict soldiers and the kings of Spain were far away. The first friars on the ground were Franciscans, followed fast by Capuchins, Dominicans and finally by the Jesuit fathers. There was hardly a pueblo on the high rocky mesas amid the seas of sand from the Rio Grande to modern Colorado, which had not some form of mission by 1800. You will see their ruins from car windows and motors along every main highway.

The Apaches, the Yaquis, the Navajos—all desert rovers—were harder to conquer and almost impossible to Christianize. They were here to-day and off to-morrow, wild birds of passage and nearly all birds of prey, where white troopers could not follow. They waged ruthless war against the pueblo people. All tribes wanted firearms. Few wanted liquor. They could ferment their own sour intoxicating drink of pulque from cactus; and brewed strong it was a most exciting drink and a worse incentive to crimes of violence than any white man's liquor. Also it could be made on the spot and carried in dry skin canteens strung to saddle pommels.

How many people inhabited the pueblos, it was impossible for the missionaries to tell; for when one mesa was besieged by the desert rovers the people would clamber down the precipitous rocks on the other side by night and scamper to another mesa, where the two towns would mass to meet the raiders with great rocks hurled from above on all assailants. Desert rovers seldom fought at night. The odds were too dangerous in a warfare where close hand-to-hand fighting decided the victory. The missionaries put the population of over eighty pueblos and cave dwellings at seventy thousand fighting men; but this seems far too high. The most accurate mission observers numbered the fighting men at twenty-three thousand. If to this were added families of three to five, there were probably seventy thousand all told, which would average about ten thousand people for each of the seven mesas. Anyway, we know that by the time St. Denis the Frenchman came scouting out chances of trade between Louisiana and New Spain, there were twenty-four Franciscans north of the Rio Grande. There were not fewer than four hundred heads of families scattered from modern El Paso to Santa Fe. The Spanish families were much more prolific than the Indian.

Twelve was not an unusual number for one Spanish family.

St. Denis, it will be recalled, went on his scouting expedition for trade with the Spanish in the early years of the 1700's. He found the Spanish fort as far east as St. John The Baptist on the Rio Grande. He observed that the ranches were literally little forts walled in adobe, housing followers who could act as soldiers or servants, housing, too, European luxuries in the midst of savagery. How dared families, especially wives and daughters, follow their dons right into the midst of terrible perils? St. Denis' own experience with his beautiful little señorita explains that.

St. Denis, though young, must have known of the terrible outbreak of Indian rebellion against all Spanish dominance in the 1680's and the equally terrible suppression by De Vargas of the insurrection from 1690 to 1698. It preceded his own coming by only fifteen years. It explained the resemblance of any ranch to a fort.

In brief, the cause of the rebellion was simple. The Indians had seen the missionaries come first, followed by armies, succeeded by mining and ranching colonies, where their people were fed but enslaved. Therefore they hated the missionaries. They also hated the missionaries for interfering with their secret horrible kiva worship. They hated them yet more for calling on these criminal convict soldiers for protection. These convict soldiers were guilty of just as wicked crimes against women and children as the Indians practised in their secret underground lodges. Hatred, blazing resentment, fury, grew to the proportions of a rebellion, a resolution to slay ruthlessly every Spanish missionary and soldier north of the Rio Grande. That rebellion has never been told in story and never sung in poem. It will be some day. It resembled the rallying of the Scottish clans with a fiery cross carried by runners from highland to highland. The Holy Trail now became one of bloody defeat, fight, reconquest as well as of martyrdom.

This story alone would fill hundreds of pages. It must be compressed to a very few and is crisscrossed by confusion of motives, pious frauds, self-delusions and yet enough of truth to mislead every one of the eighty more or less pueblos. Other rebellions had ended in defeat, slaughter, enslavement. This one was to succeed by massing all the mesa people in one union against the Spaniards. Could the mesa Indians have trusted them, they would have welcomed the Yaquis, the Apaches, the Navajos, as helpers; but they could never trust these ancient foes, the desert rovers.

Popé was an Indian of uncertain origin. Whether he was a medicine man, or a self-deluded idiot, it is hard to say. He came from San Juan but had drifted to Taos as the best center from which to rouse rebellion and direct movements.

Its high houses were almost impossible to conquer. It had abundance of food and pasture and water. It could never be starved out. It could be approached only by narrow passes where a hundred Indians could defeat a horde of white soldiers. Popé used deer skins with crude drawings to rally the clans. These the Indians could read. The white man could not. He claimed to have had supernatural visions of three devils in the Taos kiva. These demons hated the Spaniards. They bade him, or he dreamed they did, make a rope, tie in it knots to the number of days to elapse before the universal uprising, then rise instantly and slay every white face on the spot. Secrecy was to be absolute as in all kiva worship. No woman was to be told a whisper of the great conspiracy. Popé suspected that his own son-in-law had babbled some inkling of the plan and with his own hands stabbed him to death.

Of course, the friars guessed something terrible was awry to bring about such a change of front from friendliness to sullen resentment. They sent back word to Governor Otermin to be on guard. Otermin himself had sensed a change in the good Indians of Tesuque, who frequented Santa Fe. You can see descendants of those Indians in Tesuque to-day, faithful workers with a curious mixed faith of pagan and Christian. Something was going on under cover among the Indians of every Spanish fort in New Mexico. It was a gathering storm. No one knew where it would burst. Taos, Pecos, El Paso, all felt the tense snapping atmosphere. Otermin sent word for all settlers to rally to Isleta, which he thought he could trust, or inside the walls of Santa Fe, which he could protect. Many settlers heeded the warning. The missionaries did not. The settlers abandoned everything they could not carry on their backs or bury in the ground in great rim-hooped trunks. In the trunks fortunately went gold and silver, solid table plate, rare silver heirlooms, and many of the beautiful household shawls and mantillas and jewels.

On August 14, 1680, the hurricane broke. Indians were in masses behind the sand hills of Santa Fe. Some say there were five hundred Indians, some said five thousand. They carried with them one red cross and one white, and bade the Spaniards choose. If the Spaniards desired peace, let them take the white cross and retreat at once south of the Rio Grande. If war, the Indians would slay every white, every saint, yes even the Holy Mary and the Spanish king and all his white chiefs in New Mexico. Otermin was not puzzled, nor did he regard the peremptory orders as ignorant bluff. It was backed by visible evidence that however misled the Indians were, they had overwhelming numbers, three thousand warriors against Otermin's paltry garrison of a few hundreds. The siege of Santa Fe lasted only a few days. Otermin ordered his men out to fight but he had to retreat swiftly to protect the settlers huddled inside the adobe walls. The Indians dammed and cut off the water supply. Every street was barricaded. Horses and people began to die of thirst. On the 21st of August, the Spaniards retreated, the majority on foot, the wounded on the few burros and horses still alive. The Indians watched day and night from behind the sand hills. Otermin and his dismal procession reached the friendly Isleta to find it deserted. Of course, exaggeration of what had happened in other pueblos ran riot among refugees crowding to the retreating Spanish rabble. One said a friar of Jemez had been tied to a hog and ridden to death. His body found later proved he had been slain by an arrow before being tied to the hog. Some refugees camped near Las Cruces for the winter, others fled west to the famous Casa Grande on the border of Old Mexico.

Victorious in Santa Fe, the Indians cast down and destroyed utterly every surface vestige of white occupation. Churches were burned. The friars' holy vestments were donned by the triumphant Indians and ridden on galloping wild ponies with riders boasting that they had killed the very Mother of the white man's God. They danced day and night. They forbade all Indians ever speaking the Spanish language. They tried in vain to involve the desert rovers in their rebellion promising in return to give for the first time in their history pueblo wives to Apaches and Navajos; but the desert rovers wanted more firearms and did not want any pueblo wives, who could order husbands to "go off there and get out."

Popé himself now lost his flighty head in triumph. He began to appropriate a lot of wives to himself and became the typical tyrant to 1688, when he died either naturally or by violence. How many Spaniards perished in the rebellion? Certainly all the friars outside Isleta and Santa Fe, and all settlers who did not succeed in reaching Isleta, El Paso, or Casa Grande. If radio waves could retain pictures of those eight terrible years, what a kaleidoscope the film would portray; for the Spaniards never died cowards. They died fighting in their boots.

Reconquest came just as ruthless as the rebellion and it lasted for almost ten years. It was not defeat on the field of action that drove the Spaniards from North America. It was misrule and the rotten diplomacy of European politics.

Again the story of reconquest must be compressed to a few pages and touch only on the high spotlights; and they are high in verity; high on the famous Black Mesa out from Santa Fe, high at Acoma and its neighbor the Enchanted Mesa, both of which you can see on a short run out from the main Santa Fe Trail. See both. There is nothing else just like them in North America; and thanks be, they can never be defaced by advertising sign board or tourist autographs on rocks black and hard as lava scoria. The desert wind will forefend against that. It wipes out desecration and tatters it to shreds. If you doubt that, try climbing the Black Mesa on a hot day.

It was well on in 1681 before the Governor was ready to prepare for a movement to reconquer Mexico. His old equipment of rusted armor was useless. He needed horses and saddles and bridles and more soldiers and sent to Mexico for these. They did not come. He could rally for the re-entry to New Mexico about one hundred Indians and one thousand horses. Suffice to say he was not welcomed back by the victorious pueblo people. As he began his march he could see the signal fires of the enemy from every sand hill; and the horrible desecration of churches and human bodies in abandoned forts and ranches was a bad omen. He did reach the friendly Isleta after a stiff fight and found the Mission church had been used as a stable, the holy images defiled and broken; and though the one thousand Indians then in possession declared loyalty to Spanish rule, Otermin soon enough learned the insincerity of such professions. Each night some Indians ran off behind the hills to join the encircling foes. There was no safe course for Otermin but again to retreat to El Paso. Otermin retired permanently to Old Mexico and let another governor take up the burden of reconquest.

So, for eight long years, the pueblos held what they had won. The foe had been expelled. If Popé, their leader, had not lost his head and become a tyrant, the chances are the reconquest could have been delayed much longer; but Popé had now lost the allegiance of his own people; and the ravages of the desert rovers, especially the Apaches, sent the mesa people scampering to defend their own home towns.

Finally came Don Diego de Vargas, one of the best soldiers Mexico had ever had. This was about 1692. He had few enough soldiers too, only three hundred armed men; but he was a commander of more determined fiber than Otermin. He was a dynamo of swift decision and almost terrible action. He marched up the sandy valley of the Rio Grande in September when the worst heat had passed and had surrounded the city of Santa Fe before the Indians off guard knew what he was about. There he did just what the Indians had done to the Spaniards, cut off their water and food supply—and waited. Then he sent spies inside to circulate reports of forgiveness and not a life to be taken if the Indians surrendered without one drop of blood being shed inside the walls. Taos, Tesuque, then Pecos, all surrendered within a month. The dispersed colonists flocked back over the Pilgrimage of the Holy Faith and with them the friars; but on the high mesas, De Vargas had real fighting to force surrender.

Acoma was the first of these, with its stone steps up solid rocks and overhanging arches and sands slippery as flour hills. De Vargas had cannon. Again he sent spies in and gave the Acomas their chance of surrender, or sword. Within a month of retaking Santa Fe, De Vargas was in Zuñi land. The Apaches had just raided the Zuñis. Deserted by their allies, the Zuñis like the Acomas made a graceful virtue of necessity and surrendered. Without the loss of a single drop of blood, De Vargas now held with a guard of about fifteen men in each mesa town all the strategic points of command.

Alas for the insincerity of the surrender.

De Vargas had hardly gone in 1693 to El Paso, where he expected reenforcements from Old Mexico, when the flames of revolt blazed anew. De Vargas was furious. Probably other generals, who had preceded him and failed, jealously raised the unfounded charge that of the almost forty-five thousand dollars allotted to De Vargas for the reconquest, he had spent only thirty thousand dollars and pocketed the difference; and the reenforcements had not come. Proceedings were actually in progress to have him arrested and imprisoned. It was the old trick of envy shooting at a shining target. De Vargas did not wait for arrest to defeat his plans. He marched for a second time in autumn up the sandy shores of the Rio Grande with eight hundred more colonists, and one hundred more soldiers. This time his sword was not to be sheathed nor bullets spared. When De Vargas made a promise, he kept it. When the pueblos made a promise, they must learn they must keep it, or stand for the consequences. Thirty people he lost from the border to Santa Fe; for his marchers were reduced to one pound of flour a day and had to eat horses for food and, in some cases, to sell horses to the Indians for firearms. He had to leave colonists to ride in their wagons floundering through sand and go ahead clearing the way of enemies. Of course, he had to fight futile raids all the way north. The Indians were all around Santa Fe but the Tesuque people were still loyal to Spain; and again on the 16th of December, 1693, on the eleventh hour of the day his old letter of the sixteenth says, "I made my entry into this town of Santa Fe . . . We arrived in the square where we found the said natives congregated, the women apart from the men, all unarmed and abstaining from hostile demonstration ... the fifteen monks ... of St. Francis chanting their divers psalms. I got down from my horse, my example being followed by corporals and officers, and the reverend fathers singing in processional order, a cross was raised where all present knelt down and saying psalms and prayers, I offered my vows to the praise of our Lord God and his Most Holy Mother."

It was on the occasion of De Vargas' reconquest that he swore that if successful, he would hold a yearly processional of thanks to God; and that yearly procession of thanks is held in Santa Fe today. It was the descendant from one of his leading officers, who gave me the cross made of wood from the Holy Land, which his family had used for two centuries.

His recapture of the old city had not been so easy as his brief report to the King of Spain might imply. Arrows and stones and boiling water were hurled at the Spaniards by the Indians on the walls. The gate had to be burned and battered down. The Indians had to surrender because of thirst and hunger and their leader hanged himself to escape punishment. Seventy of his assistant caciques were put to the sword on the spot and four hundred of their women captured and sold in slavery. De Vargas now knew that his former mercy had been regarded as fear and he determined to put fear in the heart of the foe. While the colonists began rebuilding the Holy City, De Vargas marched to the nearest places where Indians still held high points in defiance. The runners had forewarned Acoma, Zuñi, and Moki to prepare for siege. The Indians now realized they had to submit at once and take their punishment, or fight; and they had massed at the great Black Mesa. It seemed an impossible rock for any assailant to climb; but they mistook the character of De Vargas. In March of 1694, he had his troops encircling the Black Mesa. The Indians waited for the troops to begin to climb; De Vargas directed cannon to drive the defenders from the edge of the precipitous walls and then the soldiers began the climb. The climb lasted five hours. Eight soldiers despite protection of chain armor were badly smashed and hurt in the climb up the rugged hard rocks. The Indians then scrambled down the other side and tried to come on De Vargas to the rear. Ammunition ran out and De Vargas had to go back for rest and food and more soldiers. It was not a defeat. It was only a pause on both sides. He had captured all the corn the Indians had on the Black Mesa and one hundred of the horses. De Vargas was back by the 12th of April. This time he had troops enough to begin the climb on all sides. With a blast of trumpets, up the soldiers climbed. Showers of stones came down on them, followed by great clattering rocks. Up went bullets and cannon ball from behind the defense of large rocks. The Indians now began to scramble down by night. By the morning of the seventeenth, the fight was over in victory.

Again De Vargas had to rush back to defend Santa Fe. The Indians were around the Holy City sand hills like hornets; but the hornets scattered before this swift-marching white leader with guns and cannon.

How simple it all reads to us. Go out over the ground. The cannon must have been dragged across acequia irrigation ditches. The marchers must have floundered through heavy sands. There was not a point of defense the size of a carriage wheel till they reached the black rocks that concealed a foe.

Or consider the fight in August heat in 1696 at Acoma near the Enchanted Mesa. Of this, the records are scant but we can visualize the scene. His soldiers without too great sacrifices of men could not ascend to the summit; but he captured the cacique and sent him up to try to persuade the Acomas to surrender. The people refused. So De Vargas shot the four remaining captives in his hands and for the time withdrew to reenforce his troops and let that pueblo learn of what was happening in the other mesa towns.

It was at this period that the envious conspirators in Mexico City actually had De Vargas recalled, where he found his personal property confiscated; and the brave officer was imprisoned for almost three years. Thanks were coming to him from the King, but persecution from his petty envious foes in Mexico City. Of course, when the King got De Vargas' answer to his lying foes, he was restored as governor about 1703, and resumed the reconquest interrupted by fools and envious foes, who could not follow up his triumph; but his health and spirit had been broken. He died at Bernalillo and was buried under the altar of the parish church in Santa Fe.

Well are these years called the stormy interlude.

From 1702 better types of viceroys were sent from Spain to Mexico City, the Duke of Albuquerque, the Duke of Lenarez, whom St. Denis the Frenchman had encountered in his first memorable visit, that Duke of Arion, with whom St. Denis and his little Señorita had dined, when the French lover had so narrowly escaped the firing squad. So the years moved on till there were between eighteen hundred and two thousand white settlers back in settlements along the Trail of the Holy Faith.

Let us see what kind of a city Santa Fe was at this time. Twitchell, one of the most reliable of all authorities, gives the picture. You see it much the same to-day, except where American improvements have intervened in sanitation, in sewers and water supply; but happily for those who love old Santa Fe, there has been a determination by good taste to try and preserve the character of the Old Spanish city.

It lies in a sheltered lap of snowy peaks engirt by sand hills. "It is the oldest capital in the United States." The Palace, or residence of the old Governor has preserved its Spanish character. It is now a museum of art, achaeology, and history. San Miguel, the old church, stands over seventy feet long, thirty wide, thirty-five high. Vega rafters span the ceiling. Splendid paintings by old masters adorn its walls. The Cathedral of St. Francis is modern. It was built under supervision of Archbishop Lamy, one of the most saintly, beautiful characters, whose orchards you should visit in blossom time when the bloom seems to fall on your head like the benediction of the great bishop whose body lies in the church vaults. Again, as in San Miguel, fine art decorates the walls. From the first the Spaniards tried to combine beauty and happiness in worship. The Gareta, an old fortification of which American traders were to learn under General Armijo, the old rascal of 1837 to 1848, still stands. The Plaza as in all Spanish cities occupies the hub of Santa Fe and is also the center of a very informal civic and social life. Here the band plays. Here on certain festive nights, all classes parade and sing old Spanish ditties round piñon fires, the sad threnody of La Paloma, the mourning dove, or the peon songs with a whoop at the end of each verse, which will arouse the soundest sleeper not to condemn but to laugh over such an exuberant explosion of sheer happiness coming up to his window in hotel or apartment house. Famous points are only a stone's throw from the Plaza, where De Vargas made his entry, where General Kearny first floated the Stars and Stripes, where the American caravans for trade came tumbling and rumbling in to pay graft of five hundred dollars a wagon to old Armijo, before they could unload a pound, where Americanos came raw, dusty, rough to wonder at first how such a clutter of houses amid such filthy gutters could be so famous. Then, from scoffing they fell in with the happy carefree life like ducks first taking to water, and danced the fandango wild as the wildest Mexican peon, and fell victims to beautiful Spanish eyes as St. Denis the Frenchman had. A fine hotel now commemorates De Vargas' memory.

A bit sinister was the old prison at one corner off the Plaza. Bullet-spattered holes had embedded human hair, and the hair was not always the long straight black of an Indian. It was often blond and red. Many an Americano, who refused to pay graft to Armijo, knew that prison well. One taste of it was enough. They paid Armijo his graft and were set free. And over all there broods the peace of the majestic mighty opal mountain, the clear air of cloudless skies, and an ozone in the air that defies depression and creates in Santa Fe one of the greatest health resorts in the world for tubercular patients.

PRISON AND CUSTOMS HOUSE, SANTA FE

Courtesy of Union Pacific Historical Museum
OVERLAND WAGON TRAIN WITH OXEN

Courtesy of Union Pacific Historical Museum
FREIGHTING TRAIN KNOWN AS "BULL OF THE WOODS"
From a photograph taken on Main Street, Nebraska City

THE BLACK MESA

PART IV

THE MORMONS ON THE PILGRIM TRAIL

CHAPTER VIII

THE MORMONS ON THE PILGRIM TRAIL

IT matters not whether the world considers the Mormons Pilgrims on a Holy Trail. They considered it a Holy Trail in pursuit of a Holy Faith. We need only recall how the Spaniards and the French following a will-o'-the-wisp discovered and helped to found an empire. Perhaps as the Apostle Paul says each in his soul and each in his generation must follow the light according as his vision can absorb the light.

The furious dispute whether Joseph Smith, an ignorant farm boy, was inspired by a divine vision, which regenerated his whole being, or was deluded by a scholarly romance of early Hermetic teachings, cannot here be followed. That dispute tore the United States to tatters for a generation.

In the early 1830's and on to 1857, the United States was wallowing in hard times. Hard times leave people restless and discontented. The panaceas of all political parties are attacked. Conditions were much the same in Great Britain. Thrifty artisans and farmers were out of work.

Religious bodies were splitting up in countless sects more emphatic in their fanatic condemnation of rival systems than in proof of the right of their own faith. Every period of flux from old to new has been marked by just such features. Every mind was groping through a fog asking—which is right? On which can we rely?

Joseph Smith, the founder of the Mormons, thundered an answer—we are right. This is the new revelation to lead you to a new dispensation. He was attacked with a fury that we can hardly realize. His Latter Day Saint missionaries never seem to have attempted much work in such purely Catholic centers as Ireland. Proselytizing was not encouraged in purely Catholic centers but in the farming and manufacturing centers of Scotland, Wales, and England, the success of his disciples in recruiting members must have astounded Smith himself. The success is not hard to explain. His tithing system provided a perpetual emigration fund. For the ridiculously low initial cost of fifty dollars, emigrants were conveyed to New Palestine. They were urged to sell all they had, bring all their tools, looms, planes, carpenters' equipment, farmers' implements, family trinkets, and clothing of the strongest plainest best fabric; yet more. They were urged to bring all musical instruments, stringed and wind, instruments for orchestras and for bands. Many converts were orchestra and band masters of European fame. Neither is it surprising such types should have joined the Mormons. Music is the universal language. In hard times its leaders suffer want. Starved of emotional vent in their arid New England faiths, the first Mormon leaders—Smith and Young—determined that their followers should follow and always know the joy which had been denied them in their youth. Music, the dance, the play, every form of true art, was welcomed. "Eight hours' sleep, eight hours' work, eight hours' play"—that was to be the new régime; and there was to be no want by man, woman, or child in the new community life.

Ships were chartered and devoted exclusively to Mormon colonists. Such rigid cleanliness and wholesome diet were enforced in transit that not an emigrant died on his way to the new land. Man traps could not catch the people at Atlantic and Mexican Gulf ports. They were shepherded forward by keel boat, raft, barge, and what not to the new land of their hopes and dreams. No drunkards were ever taken, no idlers. All must be thrifty, God-fearing workers. No confiscation of all possessions was demanded; but the tithe of yearly earnings was. Every man, woman and child retained possession of each individual property. If any one would not work, he was cast out. If some one worked but did not make headway, an apostle, an elder, a teacher, was assigned to find why he did not, and he was taught where he had been making his mistake. Profit under this practical instruction began to show such astounding results that Smith, whose own mental vision and education from that of an ignorant farm boy, had expanded to that of a broad-gage strong man, began to be regarded as a second Moses. Over the strictest code of daily religious practises, Smith had the very great wisdom to maintain a glow of joy. The bands and orchestras were the features of all travel across the Atlantic and in the life of his first New Jerusalem—Nauvoo in Illinois on the Mississippi. Dancing was not forbidden. It was encouraged as a rhythmic expression of emotion. All innocent amusements were so encouraged.

For the first twenty-five years of Mormonism, polygamy was not practised. In fact, it was discouraged by Smith.

Up to 1850, there were going yearly from Scotland, Ireland, and Wales two thousand five hundred people, and their letters home proved that all Smith had promised was being realized to the full. The phenomenon was so astounding that the *Daily Chronicle* of London despatched a member of its staff to investigate for a number of years the secret of Smith's success. This reporter's own faith was that of a conservative hidebound churchman of the Church of England. He had little respect for Smith's alleged beliefs, which he regarded as "pious fraud," but he had to acknowledge the results surpassed expectations. His record is perhaps a better one to follow than the Mormon's own annals, which may be accused of suppression or exaggeration. It is a safer record to follow than the furious attacks of new evangelical bodies then in bitter feud among themselves— the Free Church, the Wee Frees, the Baptists, the Seventh Day Adventists, the Campbellites. But let us go back a lap in the story of these Pilgrims of the Santa Fe.

Joseph Smith was born in Vermont about 1805. Whether a visionary or "imposter," as the *Daily Chronicle* man calls him, he began in his twenties to ask himself which of all the religions was right. In 1830, he had exactly five followers. By 1851 he had three hundred thousand followers in all parts of the world. Let us ignore his visions. Many before his day had had them from the Hermetics of Egypt to Joan of Arc in France and Swedenborg the Norwegian while in London. The Catholic church had had its visionaries among its saints for centuries. All record practically the same experience, but all did not find golden or brass plates buried in the ground. The consensus of teaching by all these visionaries was that the so-called churches, creeds, politicians, bankers and scribes had lost contact with the true teachings of the Divine Master. They bound heavy burdens for the people to carry and the Devil laughed. That much for the birth of Mormonism. Smith after an infinite deal of trouble spiritual and material got his Book of Mormon or Golden Bible published. It seems almost irony to have to record that the man who helped him most and then fought him more bitterly had once been a Presbyterian and a Campbellite. Smith did not cast his precious "pearls before swine." His plates were not exhibited to any but the chosen few.

The chosen few multiplying so astoundingly from 1831 to 1851 were then organized in ruling elders, bishops, teachers and missionaries to every part of the world. The first declaration of faith did not differ far from the first declaration of faith by every reformed sect. God was regarded by all sects in that era as very much a personality and a material deity. Miracles were common especially among those suffering from nervous diseases and suppressed emotions.

Smith as the result of persecutions in the East, in Missouri, and in Ohio, where ruffians had tarred and feathered him, had moved his community up the Mississippi to Nauvoo in Illinois. The antagonism to Smith in Missouri really arose quite as much from Smith's policy toward colored people as from his teachings. Smith taught that all men are free. Missouri was the cockpit of the contest soon to break out in the Civil War; so he founded his New Jerusalem in Nauvoo, the Beautiful, and by 1851 had there fifteen thousand men, women and children. Its population exceeded Chicago's. Chicago was a backwater swamp of mud at this time. Nauvoo was the largest, most prosperous and best governed city west of the Great Lakes.

This little city seemed miracle enough in itself to excite admiration, wonder, envy, and slander. It seemed a true Utopia to his generation. Had Smith kept out of politics, the chances are he could have averted more trouble at least until the Civil War, when every section of the land was drawn into that struggle, free versus slave; but he most unwisely allowed his name to go before the public as a candidate for presidential nomination. He had expanded in his education, in his observation of public affairs, in his survey of other religions. He stood six feet in height, weighed two hundred and twelve pounds and was a magnificent orator both in hurling fearless defiance at all enemies and in setting forth his own views. He had no remotest hope of being elected. His object seems to have been to direct attention to the remedies offered for public ills in his own system. From that time, the Mormons became the targets of not only the envious but of religious and political foes. If you read his views on the policies of the United States in this period, you will find that they embodied many of our reforms in banking, in cooperative buying and selling, in freedom from bodily as from spiritual bonds, in tolerance to all religious faiths, and in giving to the state as representatives of the people implicit obedience but keeping secular and religious government absolutely and utterly separate.

In a few lines, from this time Smith could get military protection from neither state nor federal authorities. Smith was mobbed in Nauvoo and shot in Carthage near Nauvoo in June 1844. The martyrdom did what martyrdom always does. It hardened the faith of his followers to an adamant that could not be destroyed by the flames of persecution. It spread the tenets of that faith throughout the length and breadth of the land. When Smith's followers, now headed by Brigham Young, asked for the protection of state troops so that they could spy out another site for another Jerusalem and move thither, selling their belongings in Nauvoo, for what they could get, the governor of the state either could not or would not give that protection. This was from 1844 to 1848, when Oregon was becoming what Greeley described as "an insanity." In the midst of this universal persecution when the Mexican War broke out, the Mormons, who were undefended by the state, were requisitioned to supply a regiment for the war. To prove that they were loyal to the state always, they mustered at once a regiment for the war and reported at Leavenworth. Their heroism both in the California march and in Mexico will be given presently from army annals.

Leaving only a few Mormon leaders in Nauvoo to sell property for what they could get, the Mormons now gathered up their household belongings, their trinkets in gold and silver, their money possessions, their tools, implements, cattle, sheep, swine, poultry, and horses, and prepared for the great hegira to the far West beyond the Rockies along the Santa Fe, the Trail of a Holy Faith. But again, joy was not to be forgotten. Two pianos were packed across the Mississippi with all the band and orchestra instruments to cheer the marching hosts.

Let us finish with poor Nauvoo, the Beautiful, abandoned as the Children of Israel had fled from Egypt. Mobs began burning crops, barns, outlying houses. "Workshops, ropewalks, spinners' wheels, carpenters' benches, tanners' vats, houses, stood empty and desolate." All the beautiful statuary in the Temple had been smashed. Drunkards and sots wandered in the orchards and through the empty houses. Whether set on fire by incendiaries or struck by lightning, in November of 1848, flames were seen at dawn breaking through the spires of the Temple. In May of 1850, a tornado completed the utter destruction of the Utopia City.

Then began one of the most extraordinary hegiras known to modern history.

Says the London correspondent of the *Daily Chronicle,* "The first companies of the Mormons commenced crossing the Mississippi on the 3rd of February, 1846." There were sixteen hundred men, women, and children. They crossed the rivers on the ice. They continued to leave in detachments until July and August traveling by teams. The anti-Mormons asserted that the intention of the Saints was to excite the Indians against the commonwealth and that they would return at the head of a multitude of red skins to take revenge. Nothing appears to have been farther from the intentions of the Mormons. Their sole object was to plant the church in some fertile and hitherto undiscovered spot, where they might worship God in their own fashion unmolested by any other sect of Christians.

He then goes on to tell about the raising of the regiment to serve under General Stephen W. Kearny. He seems unaware of the fact that one of the first things the Mormons did on crossing the Mississippi was to sign a treaty with the raiding Pawnees for safe passage across the Indian lands and that the pact was faithfully observed by both

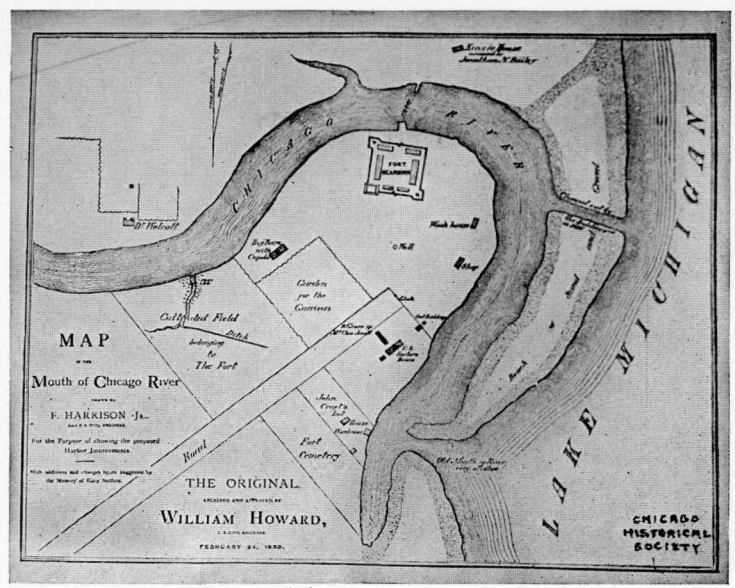

Courtesy of the Chicago Historical Society

MAP OF THE MOUTH OF THE CHICAGO RIVER IN 1830

THE ENCHANTED MESA

AN EARLY MAP OF "NEW FRANCE"

parties. The Mormons regarded all Indians as descendants of an older civilization, which had degenerated from the oracles of God. They welcomed Indians to their camps, fed them when that was possible but kept "powder dry" for defense. There is on record one case where a Mormon settler's home was entered by an Indian who demanded food. The woman gave it to him. Seeing her good man was absent, the Indian attempted liberties. She fled to an inner room and turned a huge mastiff dog loose with the words, "Seize him." The mastiff buried its teeth in the Indian's leg. By main strength she hauled it off. Then she medicated and bound up the wound. Never again was that woman's cabin molested.

The Great Salt Lake Basin was to be their future home. Colonel Kane accompanied the Mormons. In lectures to a Philadelphia audience he describes his visit to the Dead City of Nauvoo, the Beautiful, the hideous devastation, scenes where dying Mormons too ill from malaria to travel were left behind to face the grim shadow alone; mothers and babies and old people "bivouacked in tatters" across the river. The marching column of Mormons was seen disappearing over the horizon pursuing the phantom of a new home, "the cold was intense." There was little wood for good camp fires. Rheumatism crippled many marchers. Animals browsed on branches of cottonwood bark. Spring found the marchers only half way between the Mississippi and the Missouri. The plains became "a heavy mud." The most trifling streams were sloughs of spring thaw or raging water courses. Sickness increased. Burials were "terribly frequent." To cross sloughs and bogs, logs were cut and laid corduroy fashion. To make coffins for the dead, bark was stripped off; this was bound together round the corpses and the sad last services pronounced over lonely graves; but the march went steadily on. When provisions ran short with one band, that group cut daily rations to half and quarter. The strong young men gave their share to the weak and went off to hire out in Iowa and Missouri for wages, then to resume the march.

"It was not until the month of June that the advance of the emigrant companies arrived at the Missouri," says the London reporter for the *Daily Chronicle*. This party the London man joined at Fort Leavenworth, where he was the guest of Stephen W. Kearny. One would give a great deal to know what Kearny thought of these strange pilgrims but it is not given. The camp at Council Bluffs was covered with carts and wagons. It seemed alive with bright white canvas. Smoke rose from a thousand camp fires. Herd boys dozed. He counted four thousand cattle from where he stood. The women were washing their clothes in the river and laying them on the grass to bleach. Here he joined them on the Mormon road. However dark prospects to the Gentile onlookers seemed, no gloom darkened the light of their faith. Heavy anxiety as to the future must be thrown off as a proof of their faith. Each night old and young danced a cotillion to violins, horns, sleigh bells, or tambourine. They danced like a fox chase in full pursuit:—jigs and reels and gallops. As the sun dipped over Omaha Hills, the old choir of Nauvoo sang. Then an elder in a loud voice thanked God and blessed the day and all retired. It was from this point that the regiment for the war set off for Leavenworth. "The Battalion gone, the host moved on." The strict order of the march was like an army. Every ten wagons had a captain. The captain of ten wagons obeyed a captain of fifty, and he in turn a captain of a hundred. Each was responsible for every soul in his platoon. Sentries stood guard at night. Stock was tethered or herded in a corral.

One of the first camps for rest and refreshments was the Little Butterfly or Petit Papillon. It had a fine spring of cool good water. The wagons formed a square with a street down the center. Each guard had a repeating rifle invented by their own Mormon gunsmith. At night the cobbler mended worn shoes. Within two months of leaving Nauvoo, two thousand emigrant wagons were on the Mormon Road. Some wagons were heavy farm conveyances for families under the tented tops. Others were two-wheeled trundle carts pulled by a heifer or pushed like a baby cart. All —humans and animals—were given the rest of Sabbath to refresh. White horse-thieves on the frontier bothered them far more than Indian raids.

Nevertheless under the gaiety and faith lay many an anxious heart. One gay young fellow, whose fiddling was the delight of the dancers, fell very ill with a high fever. "Pah," he laughed, "I'm only homesick. Bundle me in a wagon and push on." The heat waxed to a blaze. He drank the bad alkali water. At the next night camp he died.

Bridge builders now went ahead. By stripping off all garments and plunging to their necks in water, the building brigade had piers erected, logs up and a bumpy crossing ready for the approaching teams. Where bridges could not be built across the shifting quicksand, flat-bottomed scows were used. Animals had to swim or flounder— thirty thousand of them that year. The rivers swollen with the snows of the far mountains frightened many herds, but across the herds were pelted and "I never heard an oath or exclamation of anger," says the London man.

Sometimes in the heat of the summer as many as thirty-seven per cent of a camp were "down with fever." The Mormons dubbed this section "Misery Bottom." The Englishman thought the illness the result of bad water, where frogs and dead grass had contaminated even the springs. In each "Misery Bottom," nurses and doctors went through the lanes of camps and waited on the helpless. August and September were the worst months. Good springs were low. Dead frogs and snakes cluttered the pools and alkali sediment on the banks aggravated the poison. The Englishman could not sleep for visions of "dismal processions" in his dreams. He would hear the cry for "Water—water"—then the deep sigh of the last sleep from which no morning trumpet call could waken the poor invalid; but the Mormons were following the phantom of their own faith.

It was quite apparent that the mountains could not be crossed before winter, so orders were given to halt and prepare for a string of safe winter camps. The first need was hay and fodder for the stock; and men with scythes dispersed to cut the prairie grass in those days almost waist high. Herders kept the cattle from straying. The hardest task here was to prevent horses and cattle mixing in with a stampede of buffalo drifting south for the winter. Red watch fires kept the buffalo off, but the howling of wolf packs made the night a hideous din. The wisdom of recruiting followers from tough-fibered farmers and artisans now became apparent. Winter camps like these, which might have saved the lives of many an Oregon pioneer, were no insecure makeshifts. Where a secure dwelling could not be made of branches and mud plaster, dugouts were built of sod with fireplaces inside and bake ovens outside. The women milked the cows, made the butter, baked the meal. On the march, butter had been churned by the swaying of the wagons. Now it was made in churns brought along or in kegs with a jigger made of a broken wagon spoke or axle. And always at night came the singing, the dancing, the prayers. The prayers at dawn are described as "a thousand-voiced murmur like babbling water."

Grand Island was a very sad camp. Thither came first news of the utter disaster back at Nauvoo. Some cripples from Nauvoo joined the procession here. "They came straggling on with faltering steps, without bag or baggage, beast or barrow," food or fodder. The Omahas and Pawnees kept faith with the Mormons, for the Mormons kept faith with them. The daughter of a La Framboise, a French half-breed, was an angel of help to the destitute Mormons. Peter Sarpy, the French trader from Omaha, had a log house and as Peter had an Indian wife, he, too, in his dirty log shack was kind to the Mormons, though a terror to any American frontiersman who called him a "squaw man." He would shoot a candle out in the ruffian's tepee, or plant a bullet neatly between the fellow's feet. No one challenged Sarpy to a shooting duel. "You are free," declaimed an Indian chief to the Mormons, "to cut and use all the wood you may wish. You can live on any part of these lands. Bon jour," by which he meant, "Bon voyage." In trade for hay and buffalo meat, the Mormons gave the Indians corn meal. It was a wise policy; for the Omahas and Pawnees protected the Mormons from the Sioux raids of the north.

The orthodox hard-boiled Englishman was getting some severe jolts to his orthodoxy. He was learning that there is a lot in the other fellow's heterodoxy; but it is doubtful if his London paper and publishers would have dared to publish all he thought. So slowly passed the hard winter of 1846-1847. "It was the severest of the Mormon trials." It was the turning point of Mormon fortunes. Yet the Englishman still thought it all a sort of "pious fraud." Yet here were a people doing what no other people had ever done.

The Mormons in spring sent ahead "a body of one hundred and forty-seven picked men with seventy wagons drawn by the best horses" to prepare their new Palestine for the main body of colonists. They carried with them tools and seed. They were to march swiftly and rely on rifles and game for food. South Pass did not bother them. Its ascent was gradual. There were good pasturage, good water, and game in plenty. So many writers have stated and reiterated that in no year did twelve thousand people ever traverse the Overland Trail that one is constrained to wonder if they have read the true record of how many passed that first year. Not fewer than fifteen thousand—the entire population of Nauvoo from Illinois.

After South Pass came the Utah Range and below the range lay the Great Salt Lake Basin. The advance guard lost not one man. Then five hundred and sixty-six wagons followed and the people from these had grain and vegetables in store before winter. Fortunately by 1848-'49 and '50, the battalions disbanded from the Mexican War joined the colonists of Utah and hastily built houses of adobe, fort walls, blockhouses, storage for crops and ammunition. The London observer did not see in Utah such a desert as the geographies of the period had pictured. He saw in it rather such a climate, soil, and scenery as in Switzerland, and many times vaster. The Salt sea puzzled him. In it poured fresh water streams. Yet the great lake was as salt as the Dead Sea of Palestine. It was beset by the goggle-eyed grasshopper with "legs of wire and a clock spring." The magpies and inland "gulls" took care of the pest, which the

Mormons ascribed to a miracle, the Englishman to the appetite of birds.

When the gold rush to California came in a stampede across Utah, the elders of the Mormons proved again their foresight. "Gold is for paving streets! Go not," they advised their flocks. "You will make more by building your houses, growing your crops and selling these to the Gentiles." As we know, this was true. The few amass great fortunes in a gold rush. The many lose all they possess in chasing phantoms.

The nutritious qualities of "bunch grass" for stock astonished all. Stock could winter out and come through the season fat. The Root Diggers were the Indians in possession. They were a brainless enough lot. The Utes were warriors and dangerous always. They rode like Cossacks on Spanish horses and had rifles and shotguns and abundant ammunition from traders. At first they did not molest the Mormons. They probably were ready to trade their horses and tooled leather for more firearms; and these amicable relations continued till the Mormons began to suspect traders east of the Rockies of plying the Utes with rum and with firearms to use against the Latter Day Saints, when bitter feuds broke out between the Mormons and such trade centers as old Jim Bridger's Fort. Perhaps there were faults on both sides in this bitter quarrel. Let us leave it aside. It ended in ruin for both sides. Each, suspecting the other, did ply the Utes with firearms and the firearms were used in raids by the Utes. The Mormons did not want outsiders to stir up trouble in their New Palestine. They wanted only to mind their own business and let the outside world mind its own business. Once when called on to umpire a dispute between two Mormons, Brigham Young responded tersely, "My advice is: mind your own business. Then tell the other brother to mind his." The dispute was settled on the spot. Each stopped interfering with the other.

I once asked a very aged Mormon how they subsisted in those early days when he was only a boy. "I'll tell you in few words," he said laughing, "but remember it is a bit exaggerated. We fed all we could raise to the stock. We sold the stock. What the hogs would not eat, we did; and we sold the hogs." The Mormons never favored a pork diet. It was too heating in a summer climate.

What then, was the secret of the amazing success of the Mormons' New Palestine? The London observer's conclusions are those which every disinterested observer must accept—a system of universal cooperation in buying and selling, the elimination of the middleman profiteer, and yet private ownership of real property—no one in want, rewards to all the thrifty, the casting out of all thriftless parasites by sheer economic pressure. People of the true faith refused to trade with an idler. He had to move out, or look out for himself.

CHAPTER IX

THE MORMON SETTLEMENT

THE Mormons like the early French and Puritans consecrated the ground of their New Jerusalem. They laid it out in wards with common store-houses, granaries, great public bath-houses. Hot springs warmed the bath-houses and prevented much disease. These also purged the systems of disease and cured rheumatism contracted on the march. The Mormons erected at once a yellow brick meeting-house one hundred feet long by sixty broad. They reserved a summit for the Great Temple. They had reached their Promised Land "flowing with milk and honey." Where other men had seen only a desert, their Faith saw a new empire.

They had not followed the Oregon Trail. They had struck south to the Overland Trail. Passing through a terribly narrow gate in the rocks, where the path had crossed the mountain stream forty times in five miles, they came abruptly to what lay below. "A ravishing panorama." Green and blue and gold and pearly the landscape seemed to float out endlessly west under a burnished sun. The Mormons lost all the repressed, depressed self-control of their wanderings. They cheered. They fell on their knees and prayed. They wept outright with sheer joy. Big men "completely dissolved in hysterics."

Before the Englishman departed, Salt Lake City numbered three thousand citizens not counting outlying farmers, and it had nineteen large merchant stores. There was a mail line. There was a music hall. There was a newspaper. There were no communists. They were classifying their mechanics for jobs. They were hunting for coal and iron ores. They raised fifty bushels of wheat to the acre and sold it at four dollars to the California gold-seekers. In four years, they had a settlement superior to Nauvoo.

Brigham Young in his address to all the Saints from Council Bluffs corroborates all the English observer recorded. "Their property in Illinois was confiscated. Their houses were burned by a mob. Those who sold any property sold it for almost a song." Their lieutenant, who had raised the battalion for the Mexican War died at Fort Leavenworth. The rest made their march on half rations almost to California. It was the scouts to the fore of the main movement of emigrants who found the Promised Land. The marchers had subsisted on the meat brought in by their hunters.

They had proceeded to the Rockies by Fort Bridger, South Pass. They had vacated the Omaha Lands in spring. Good firearms for hunting, Young demanded. Of false teachers let all Saints beware. Gold, trinkets, ivory, or ornaments, "to cast a fragrance" of beauty over the House of the Lord, Young also claimed as a part of all joyous service to God. "We are at peace with all nations, all kingdoms, all powers." "It matters not what a man's religious faith is, Presbyterian, Methodist, Baptist, Campbellite, Catholic, Episcopalian, Mohammedan, Pagan, if he will bow the knee, we hail him as brother." This was a broad welcome in that age.

The New Palestine formulated its own civil constitution for the simple reason there was no other law in this No Man's Land. In Utah rose the fountain head of the Missouri flowing southeast, the Colorado south, the Columbia west. A Cincinnati paper says that by the 1850's there were sixty thousand Saints in Utah, thirty thousand at least from Great Britain. It describes the classes from the British Isles as "farmers, mechanics, surgeons, miners, engineers, widows, shoemakers, tailors, stone-masons, bakers, potters, painters, carpenters, iron-moulders, dyers, glass-cutters, saddlers, gunsmiths." All worked at their trades wherever possible while crossing the ocean. Butter, cheese, and bread were taken by each family.

Canvas curtains were hung in the ship between each family and its neighbor, so that privacy could be preserved. Disputes were settled each day by elders. By eight in the evening, all water buckets and rubbish were gathered and thrown overboard. The cleanliness on board is described as "spotless."

The colonists from overseas came by New Orleans to St. Louis, thence to Council Bluffs, where all rested. From Council Bluffs to the Promised Land was figured as ten hundred and thirty miles. Each wagon had a bedroom and sitting-room. Meals were taken by the road side. The fifty dollars advanced for fare was expected to be returned to the General Emigrant Fund, as soon as it was earned by the colonist. There was small chance for the scamp "to jump his job" in Utah; for the way back or forward was too dangerous. By 1856 Young could say that "the banishment of the church had become a blessing of God in disguise"; but it was thrift had converted that tragedy to triumph.

One of the most remarkable instances of Young's foresight was that he foresaw the coming of rails across this very area. Only one railroad ran from Chicago westward. Poor Whitney dreaming of a great transcontinental in the east was regarded as a little cracked. It was only after the Civil War, that a Lincoln, a Dodge, a Sherman, a Sheridan, saw the necessity for "hoops of steel" to bind

East and West together; but Young foresaw that where land was fertile, mountain passes low, streams cutting a natural highway through canyons—rails must ultimately come. It is worth remembering that, when the Union Pacific came from the east and the Central Pacific from the west, it was in Utah the two lines met and completed that hoop of steel. The whole movement was so phenomenal in all colonization history that the eyes of the world were on Utah; and one could collect from many newspapers the same testimony as has been quoted from the Cincinnati daily.

A letter from a boy in Salt Lake to his father in England gives perhaps one of the best records. It is dated: Great Salt Lake, October, 1849. There were twenty-four in his group. "We were very merry" at first. "We traveled one thousand miles up the Mississippi. I am by no means partial" to such a type of river travel. "The accidents are innumerable. They arise from snags—pieces of timber sticking up in the muddy river—fire, collisions, and bursting of thin boilers under the saloons. In May, our mules were purchased and we were ready to start across the prairies. Our party had four wagons, each drawn by eight mules. We rode upon these combinations of all that is stupid, spiteful and obstinate." The boy did not know that the rough frontiersman called the saddle on a mule "the hurricane deck" of a ship in a tornado. "At daybreak we left our tents and were soon busy around the camp fire, preparing breakfast—coffee, bacon, hard biscuit. The weather became oppressively hot—one hundred to one hundred and ten degrees. This was very trying from the entire absence of shade on the ocean of land. These vast plains resemble the appearance of the dry bed of some mighty sea." (Not a bad guess for a boy in his teens.) The heat with the food produced bilious fever. "Half our number suffered from this. June 19, we had not been (in our tents) an hour before one of the dreadful storms swept over us. The horizon was the deepest purple, illuminated by flashes of forked lightning. Each clap of thunder resembled some immense cannon, shaking the earth. Our tent was blown over. I dropped my coverings under a wagon but found I was soon lying in a pool of water with saturated blankets, I then crawled in the wagon and was horribly bitten by mosquitoes."

The boy was ill for the rest of his journey to "the city." He found it built of logs and bricks from adobe, one or two rooms in each house. Round each house was an acre for a garden. The streets were wide and being planted with trees. A canal was being constructed for irrigation. The land that year produced eighty bushels of wheat to the acre. The price of a city lot was one dollar and fifty cents. "No men can be poor in this place," the boy says.

A *New York Tribune* man going to California gives almost the same testimony. He says his party on reaching the City, cheered, laughed, danced. All stores were crowded with buyers, but there was no drinking, no disorder, no idleness. He says the City was then only ten months of age. "The Mormon Empire may justly be considered the greatest prodigy of our time." The Mormons' worship, he describes as being solemn but very sweet and joyous with the music of the best quality. Brigham Young asked and gave no quarter in his sermons. He predicted that the love of gold would yet ruin and corrupt the United States. The constitution was being ignored and administration was being gradually undermined by corruption. The Mormon people were the most industrious he had ever seen. They had recovered from all illness of the trail and were in robust health. For gifts of food to passing gold-seekers destitute in Utah, the Mormons were reluctant to accept any payment. For provisions shipped on to California they charged the current market price and one estimate places the profit from gold spent by Californians at three hundred and seventy-six thousand, three hundred and twenty pounds (about eighteen hundred thousand dollars) in four years. The public sulphur-baths proved a boon to the gold-seekers and restored many a cripple to health.

The English reporter from the *Daily Chronicle,* of London, who had come to the Mormon people puzzled and prejudiced against a doctrine which he regarded as "a pious fraud," "a hoax," returned to London still more puzzled. It was an age when few men as yet regarded all religions as steps up a racial ladder to a higher sphere. We shall leave him with his puzzle and take scrutiny of the leader, who had succeeded Joseph Smith.

Brigham Young was a thick-set powerful man of middle age. His complexion was fair, blue eyes, brown beard, a very large but very firm mouth with lips clean shaved. He had begun as a carpenter when he stepped in the ranks of leadership in 1846. He believed intensely in his faith—that God would show the Pilgrims their way. His word was to be absolute law; but he always called in conference the twelve apostles. He never minced words to make his meaning clear. "Don't be so devilish hoggish," he used to say, "as to be afraid to do a day's work without getting pay for it. A man having such a spirit will be damned."

Brigham Young's life and record are worth giving in detail. They corroborate the evidence of Gentile observers. He was the first great empire builder in the region between the Rockies and the coastal region. He was born on June 1, 1801, in

Vermont, a Puritan of the Puritans. The stern discipline in that home "was a word and a blow but the blow came first." To quote his daughter, Mrs. Gates, "To listen to a fiddle, to laugh or shout on the Sabbath," was a crime. We can guess the reaction to this of a husky farm boy. He was sent to learn the trade of carpenter and painter. His schooling consisted in all of about eleven days. He joined the Methodist Church, but never in his heart subscribed to its severe condemnation of innocent amusements. His mother had taught him to read and the Bible was his only text-book. At twenty-three, he married. He was earning thirty-two cents a day. His wife was so fragile, in fact, then in the first stages of what we now call tuberculosis, that he always prepared his own breakfast and supper and took care of his children at night.

At this period he first heard of Joseph Smith's Revelations. He, like Smith, was confused by the welter of contradictory new sects. At thirty-one years of age, he joined Smith's Mormons. That very year, his wife had died and Young's night studies now became an almost furious search for truth. In winter, he then became a traveling missionary for the Saints. He married a Free Will Baptist and she, too, had become a Mormon. At a winter school he met a Hebrew scholar and from him began to study Hebrew. One of his trips took him to Illinois. He had now become one of

Smith's twelve Apostles. He, too, was often hounded by mob violence. He settled in Nauvoo, the Beautiful. He made a missionary journey to Great Britain for a year and observed, studied and came back to Nauvoo with an enormously expanded mental vision. When the prophet Smith was murdered, it was Young who thundered defiance to a hostile world and his election to succeed Smith came as a matter of course. From that time, his mind began to frame a national policy for the Saints. It was solidarity—unity in faiths, in works, in politics, in economic life.

Fremont's reports on the West, the Oregon craze, the fact of a great unclaimed No Man's Land—all these were known to Brigham Young. Ford, the Governor of Illinois, impotent to protect the Mormons, had advised Young, "Get off by yourselves where you can enjoy peace." So he became not only the Chief Apostle but the leader in the great migration. He led the first two thousand four hundred families westward. The band played not doleful airs but "The Girl I Left Behind Me," "Yankee Doodle," "Old Hundred," and many a rousing tuneful Psalm in which all marchers could join. He suffered; all his people suffered in the sleet storms of that first march, and Young it was who saw that hot drinks of ginger, pepper, cinnamon, were ready for the hosts, when they encamped. The bugle sounded at five A.M.

for all to rise. Two hours were permitted for breakfast. At eight P.M. all held prayers in wagons and at ten all were to be in bed; but there was no hurry. One of Young's great points was serenity, unruffled minds, quiet poise. Like David's army in Palestine, he had his overseers in every department of daily living. He provided sanitary inspectors, food distributors, musical leaders, women nurses for the sick, comfortable sleeping benches in the wagons for the women and children, preventers of waste, even of as much as one kernel of corn. It was he who arranged winter camps rather than winter marches, found ferryboats at Omaha, in which to cross streams, made pacts with the Indians for free passage across their hunting lands, laid corduroy roads across mud bogs, and secured rest wherever rest was necessary —always on the Sabbath Day. "If you work yourself or your animals on the Sabbath," he told his people, "you will find it does not pay. You will lose more than you gain. The Sabbath is made for man, not man for the Sabbath." It was he who advised the battalion for the Mexican War to show, "We are loyal patriots." "Not a man of the Saints shall lose his life in that war," he prophesied with an audacity that astounded; and while other troops did lose lives, Young's prediction came true. The secular captain from the regular Army died but no Mormon. His people ascribed

THE MORMON SETTLEMENT

this to miracle. The other troops wondered. Perhaps we moderns might explain this exemption from loss as due to care, to diet, to drill, to discipline, to serene confidence. Knowledge based on experience is easily called foreknowledge. It is but it is only practised by the wise.

At Omaha, there were winter quarters for three thousand two hundred people. As one company moved on, the next band of marchers took possession. Christmas Day, New Year's, July 4th, were always celebrated joyously, with booming of cannon, pies a foot deep, band music, night dances. Rations were apportioned as to any army, ample as long as they lasted. At first the north side of the Platte was followed. Old buffalo skulls left on the roadside were the mail boxes for group following group. When men grumbled at the strict rules, Young appointed a chief camp Grumbler and the fault finding was effaced in laughter. Once a Saint asked Young where they were really going if not to Oregon. Young answered gaily, "From somewhere to nowhere," but he had that band of scouts out ahead to find and prepare the New Palestine.

It was on the Little Sandy River that Young in June first met Jim Bridger, the famous Indian scout; and Bridger made the rash bet, "I would give a thousand dollars if I knew an ear of corn could be ripened in these mountains. I have tried it again and again and failed." Jim was speaking of the high lands east of the Rockies. Brigham had his eye on the warmer Inland Empire west.

Exactly what route did the Mormons follow? The Oregon Trail so far as they could; but from Laramie just what trail they could construct or ford amid floods, drought, sand drift; but it was chiefly the Overland Trail south rather than the Oregon Trail north.

Men from the disbanded California regiment met Young at Green River in Wyoming and urged him to go on to the genial clime of the coast. No, Young replied, there were other people of other faith there. He would find a No Man's Land for their New Palestine.

Through Echo Canyon with its towering precipices, that first group crashed their way leaving roads for the followers. From the next summit, they saw Great Salt Lake on July 19, 1847. It was heralded with shouts of joy. Down from the summit with wheels grinding on chain brakes, came Brigham Young in a light buckboard. The sight below him was like Moses' glimpse from Nebo and Pisgah. "This is the place," he said, "drive on." The next day was the Sabbath. The Lord's Supper was administered to all, not as a last doleful sacrament but as the sacrament of a new era.

The streets were laid out very much as they

run to-day with the site for a great central temple to equal Solomon's Temple in the Holy Land. Farm lands were checked off outside the main city in five, ten, twenty-acre fields, as each family could handle its area. Fort walls of adobe went up to protect the city from Indians. The walls were two feet thick, nine high. Roofs were brush covered with earth which baked to brick in the hot sun. Chimneys and fireplaces and bake ovens went up fast as masons could work and wheat and potatoes were planted at once. The first Temple was "a bowery of branches" for shade. Messengers went speeding back to cheer oncomers. Was Brigham Young's jaw hardening in these years? It was; but his eye was brighter, his sense of joy boundless, his repartee on the trigger, his thundering oratory a menace to foes, a clarion call to friends.

Cobblers made shoes from buckskin and ox hides. Weavers spun the wool yarns they had brought, women churned butter, cured meats and berries, knitted socks and mitts. Just once in those early years, all hearts sank. A pest of big crickets overspread the growing fields. They resembled the horrible grasshopper plagues. The Saints prayed. Came the inland gulls and not a cricket survived. To the Mormons, this was a miracle. I have seen similar flocks of ducks and geese on the vast lakes and sloughs north of the Saskatchewan and I can testify they darkened the morning and evening sky; for firearms had not come. Not a cricket or grasshopper could have survived as a pest amid such flocks of wild unmolested birds. This gull miracle is commemorated in one of the beautiful monuments in the Temple Block of the City to-day. The Saints now regarded themselves as an Army of the Lord. Sawmills, flour mills, factories, went up by magic; but it was the magic of hard work among thrifty people. For three years, every head of a family took stock of provisions needed for the winter and rations were apportioned for every soul in the colony. Irrigation dams were in use within a year.

There were no police, no courts, no drunks; in a word, no criminals, till the great Overland Stampede to California came tumbling through the city. Then courts had to be set up. Some of the Overlanders called themselves the Missouri Wildcats. They made trouble with the Indians, a story that belongs to army annals. Missionaries from other churches were welcomed and presented with lots for building, whether Catholic, Jewish, Protestant.

The New Palestine was called Deseret, "honey bee"; for all in the hive must work. Brigham Young was elected governor of the Provisional State of Deseret. The modern name Utah came from the Ute Indians, "good things to eat." When

THE MORMON SETTLEMENT 159

Washington officially despatched political appointees to fill offices in Utah, trouble followed. This also belongs to the army annals and it came the nearest to a terrific licking administered by pacifists' means that the army ever knew.

The sale of farm products to the gold-seekers without the intervention of any middlemen may have given Brigham Young his first idea of the great cooperation system, which has since become the corner stone of Mormon prosperity. Or he may have studied the communistic systems being tried out in England to relieve agricultural distress. There was a wide difference between the four dollars a bushel and twenty dollars a barrel the gold-seekers paid for wheat and the miserable prices of thirty to forty cents a bushel for wheat which was all the farmers of the Middle West could get till rails began to connect with outside markets; but Young recognized, too, with his New England farm shrewdness the causes of failure amid communistic experiments being tried out in England. Men will do their best only when assured of profits from their own thrift and labor. Therefore, each member of a cooperative community must share in proportion to what he produced. Cooperative stores can buy at lowest costs what the farmer needs. They can sell at highest market prices, what they deliver to the cooperative mercantile centers; so he began the organization of cooperative units in each farm center. The gold rush to California was followed by other gold stampedes to Colorado, to Montana, to Idaho; and to each of these mining centers farm supplies could be freighted at enormous profits.

"We see," said Young, "servants that labor early and late and have hardly enough clothing to go to meetings on the Sabbath. I have seen this in Europe." So began the cooperative movement. Shares were bought by the people at very low rates. Factories were built, tanneries, woolen and flour mills, which bought and manufactured what the farmers had to sell. Outside merchants were welcomed to Salt Lake City and could buy and sell unhampered by the Mormons; but the Saints' profits far exceeded such independent ventures. As far as I know this was the first entirely successful cooperative experiment tried out and found workable in the United States. It has had many successors—the raisin growers and citrus producers of California, the apple orchards of the Northwest, the wheat pools of Canada, varying in details from Young's plan but founded on the same principle. When the railroads came after the Civil War, such cooperative unions did exactly what Young had predicted as far back as 1846-48: prospered far more from farming than they ever could in mining. When great mines opened in Utah, again the producer prospered just as much as the big mining corporations. It is easy to see how Brigham Young's school of hard knocks back in Vermont had taught him much of the practical work of making ends meet and overlap in profit, much more than he could ever have learned from books. "Give people," he used to say, "iron and coal, good hard work, plenty to eat, good schools and good doctrines, and it will make them a healthy, wealthy, and happy people."

The Great Temple is seen by every tourist. It is world famous for its beauty, its music, its incomparable architecture. The work began in 1865 and 1871. It could seat ten thousand people. Again Brigham Young had studied in England the principles of architecture from St. Paul's, from Westminster and from all famed cathedrals. He aimed to combine beauty and durability. Gray granite from canyons twenty miles away was used. The cost when complete was four million dollars. Many features of Solomon's Temple were embodied, the brazen oxen, the sea of brass. The beautiful Grecian pillars and the Gothic spires were copied from later models. Music, which King David had insisted should be another essential feature of all worship, came also in Young's plans. The Temple choir is one of the best in the world. Here not only the Mormon hymns were chanted but the best oratorios of European masters rendered. Young never forgot how the hard narrow joy-killing atmosphere of much New England worship had nearly driven him to atheism. How could God, the Supreme Architect of beauty, prefer ugly hard forms of worship? Dancing came as a matter of course. Had not David danced in rhythmic chorus for very joy before the Lord? Let the Mormons do the same. The musical leaders were the best Europe could supply. Some were converts. Some were not; but the dancers and the music must be such as a God of love and purity would approve. The same rule applied to all theatricals given. Censors were not needed to exclude lewd plays. The audience with its box receipts settled that; and while Young could not control the character of Gentile tastes, with best of all forms of amusement presented in the most beautiful structures, the Gentiles gave little support to the worst of amusements amid ugliness and squalor. This was proved in the crowds scampering through the City to various mining centers.

On woman's rights Young was a pioneer. Obedience, yes, he counseled that; "but I never counsel a woman to follow her husband to the devil." Confession to the priesthood—no—Young was against that. "Don't proclaim your sins on the housetops. Ask forgiveness from those wronged; and if your sins are unknown, confess them to God, keep that to yourself"; sin no more and forget it.

Young died the husband of nineteen wives, and father of fifty-six children, in his seventy-ninth year. He had forbidden mourning in black because he regarded death as a rebirth in a higher sphere. His followers to-day number millions. The prophet of a lost cause led his people to a New Palestine and a New Jerusalem as far exceeding his dreams as the midday blaze of the sun exceeds the first faint beams of dawn. So has it been with almost every religion in the world. What is good has lasted. What is not has passed in a welter. The blind brain-bindings of yesterday burst asunder to wider freedom for each tomorrow on an epic Pilgrimage of Holy Faith.

PART V

HERE COME THE CARAVANS

CHAPTER X

THE CARAVANS COME RUMBLING AND TUMBLING OVER THE TRAIL

TO go back a little to our old French friend St. Denis of Louisiana in Cadillac's day of 1713 to 1717.

It was a natural sequence of events that the first traders should come rather from the French of the Mississippi than from the English Colonies of the Atlantic seaboard. The English, trading down the Ohio westward, had to fight both Indians and French. If successful, they acquired all the profitable trade they could handle; but that route became the Pioneers' Bloody Ground for more than half a century, whereas in Louisiana both the French and Spanish were eager for the interchange of goods at a profit, which left them rich in a few years. That is, it left them rich if they could keep their scalps and protect their caravans from raid by Comanches, Utes, Apaches, or Yaquis; but in this half century came such a topsy turvy upheaval of European and American bounds that it threw all traders' calculations in confusion. Louisiana governors first had sponsored trade with

New Spain in both Old and New Mexico, because Old Spain and Old France were in friendly alliance; so that many French traders under both Cadillac and Bienville had followed up St. Denis' first losing adventurous trip.

Friendship between France and Spain broke violently. Bienville, then an old man living in retirement just outside Paris, came from his retreat and on bended knee with tears streaming down his face besought the French ministry not to cede his beloved Louisiana to Spain; but the ministry was powerless. The treaty had been signed and Louisiana had to be ceded to Spain. Bienville retired to die of a broken heart. All the life work by himself and his famous brothers—the Le Moynes—seemed lost in a wicked shuffle of European politics. Little did he foresee that in another forty years all Spain's holdings in North America, all France's, would be deeded back to France in another shuffle and then sold by France for a song to a nation not yet born. The dates of these shuffles are parts of American history from Napoleon's sale, a sale made by the way while Napoleon was splashing in a bathtub raging about the victories of his arch enemy, England, over his own forces. The new American Republic bought Louisiana for a price less than the yearly output of forest or mine, oil well, or fruit farm, in a single county of a single state in that area to-day. Oils and mines may be regarded as freak outputs for a few years; but when one state in that area ships forty thousand carloads of fruit in a year and when six transcontinental rail lines depend for freight on what was once Louisiana, the statement that the United States made a bargain out-beggaring all Jefferson's predictions and hopes does not require proof. Faith again, boundless faith—and work.

Lewis and Clark completed their famous voyage of discovery and exploration by 1806. It was natural that Spanish traders from St. Louis should follow Lewis and Clark's voyage. Manuel Lisa was one of the first to send his traders both up the Missouri and across to Santa Fe. Of course he had been preceded by sporadic efforts of the English to try out that Spanish trade by the Ohio; but these usually ended in disaster. The English would hire a Frenchman to proceed to New and Old Mexico. The Frenchman took the caravan of goods and that was the last heard of him or of the goods entrusted to him. It was given out that he had fallen a victim to an Indian raid. Too often, he had not. He had succeeded in getting his caravans to Taos, to Santa Fe, to Chihuahua. There he sold the goods to native Mexican pedlers at enormous profits and thenceforward retired to a good or bad old age. He knew he could be neither followed nor traced, extradited nor brought to time. This type of rascal often perished in some tavern brawl.

Why was it cheaper for the Mexican pedlers to buy from the Louisiana traders than from their own Mexican merchants sending goods to Mexico City by way of Vera Cruz? From Vera Cruz goods had to be packed on mules. The single file trail was all up-hill, seven thousand feet. Loads had to be light, two to three hundred pounds. Every eight to ten mules had to have a separate Mozo with his yells—which you hear on the same trail to-day —"Mule ho! Mule-ah!", with curses and stones pitched ahead to force the laggard forward. The belled mules attracted raids by bandit and Indian. Camps were long and lazy in the heat of the day and equally long and lazy at night round camp fires. Compare this with the load of each wagon in a caravan. Many a wagon from St. Louis and later from Kansas City carried four thousand to six thousand pounds. The wages paid the muleteer from Vera Cruz and from the Mississippi were the same, five dollars a month, to ten dollars and forty dollars for the boss, with keep, which meant food, firearms, and not too strict audit if some good driver did a little trade with his own goods on his own account. All the driver and boss had to account for was every pound under the canvas of the wagon.

What were the enormous profits, which lured to such dangerous traffic? The prices paid from 1717 to 1846 answer that. Iron at one dollar a

MARCH OF A SANTA FE CARAVAN

Courtesy of Grace Raymond Hebard

Courtesy of Kansas City Chamber of Commerce

KANSAS CITY, 1855

pound, tobacco at four dollars a pound, flour all the way from twenty-five dollars to fifty dollars a barrel at certain dangerous mining centers; strouds and silks twenty-five dollars a yard, and calicoes four dollars a yard; teas and coffees at two dollars to four dollars a pound; what were described as hard sea biscuits, twenty cents a pound, dried meats one dollar and twenty-five cents to two dollars and fifty cents a pound, dried salt fish fifty cents a pound, cured smoked pork fifty cents up, brown sugar sixty cents, butter two dollars and fifty cents, molasses six dollars a gallon. If gold bullion were taken in trade, eight dollars would obtain twenty-four inches of irons ready for the blacksmith to hammer in horseshoes and wagon gear; but the most of the Mexican pedlers used unshod mules, or little two-wheeled carts with solid wheels and unrimmed tires of sections rawhided together till they warped and fell off. By then the local pedler had usually sold all his wares and was back to Taos and Santa Fe for the annual caravan fairs to exchange tooled leather, silver and gold bullion, for the next year's itinerary of a pedler's route. As nearly all the pedlers were mestizos of mixed blood, they could go where no trader in a caravan dared. Page after page could be given of these dizzy profits more alluring than the output of any gold mine. Wise was Brigham Young in the 1840's to bid his Mormon colonists stick to their farms and sell their output to the crazy gold-maddened overlanders at far higher profit than they could ever gain from a mine. Wise, too, were the pioneer Oregon settlers, who stuck to their farms rather than rush off to the mines; but few did. The California gold rush for a few years almost depopulated Champoeg near Portland.

Who were the first English and American caravan traders from the Mississippi? It is almost impossible to say, nor does it matter. They did small credit to their outfitters, whom they scandalously cheated. You can pick various names out from different records and then the man disappears. We know one Peyton a Virginian went as an independent trader in 1773 and was clapped in prison at Santa Fe and escaped barely with his life to St. Louis. We know a merchant of Kaskaskia sent a Frenchman, La Lande, in 1804 out on the Santa Fe Trail. Pike says he was a scoundrel and took the trade for himself. A Kentuckian, Purcell, joined a caravan early in the 1800's. As he had to work as a carpenter in Santa Fe, we may guess that his trading failed, where his carpentry left him well off. Purcell had met some Indians on the South Platte, who sent him to Santa Fe for permission to trade there. He was permitted to follow any trade except that of making powder and ball. Once he came almost to the hangman's noose for casting a little powder and shot for his own use.

Twelve other Americans led by Robert McKnight, James Baird, and Samuel Chambers crossed the plains to Santa Fe in 1812. They were arrested and sent prisoners to Chihuahua, where they were held till the revolution in Mexico overthrew all Spanish rule. One of the Chouteaus of St. Louis was far up the Arkansas in 1815 for the John Jacob Astor Company of New York. You will find the Chouteau name commemorated in Chouteau Island, just east of Bent's Fort. Two trips he made successfully from St. Louis to Santa Fe but on the third in 1817 he was arrested and his property confiscated. Spanish power was trembling and the viceroy exploded in such rages that he used to bang the table with shouts, "Gentlemen, we must have this man shot." It must have gone against Chouteau's pride to have to kneel down and kiss this rascal's hand. It was in those days that Kit Carson was a boy teamster on the Trail.

A Captain Bicknell of Missouri comes on the Santa Fe early in 1821. He had twenty-one drivers and three wagons filled with five thousand dollars' worth of goods. He did not want to follow the great bend in the Arkansas; so he risked the shorter route across the desert to the Cimarron. How terrible that desert was he did not know. He took very little extra water in canteens and kegs. His men were so desperate with thirst that they cut their dogs' and mules' ears to drink the blood; but that only made matters worse in the summer heat. They reached the Cimarron but it seemed dry. At night, water seeped up to the surface of the sands and all the caravan men and beasts were saved. This gives a very inadequate picture of the real struggle, when men staggered blindly in dust and heat, mules sank deeper and deeper, feebler with each plunge, in the sand, and the warped wagons groaned and pitched like a ship in a terrible sea. Nothing was more trying in the desert than the sudden dust storms. They beggar all realization to any one who had not been caught in them. The terrific heat generates such currents of air ascending upward that cooler currents rush in to fill the vacuum of "air pockets," and there is presently the tornado known as a dust storm. The mule and his little brother the burro sag heads, turn tail to the wind, close sleepy eyes and let the storm demon do its worst. Horses are apt to become nervous and halt and sink in the heat. Wise humans will imitate the mule, keeping mouths shut, and if sensitive to dust tie a handkerchief across mouth and nose. Such hurricanes seldom last more than a few hours and leave the air at sundown washed as if by a rain.

Whether Lieutenant Pike were a youthful tool in the hand of conspirators or just an innocent seeker of adventure, his annals give us the best early picture of Americans on the Santa Fe Trail. He followed the usual early route, through Kansas, Nebraska, past that great peak named after him but which he did not climb, through Colorado near Canyon City, so famous in battles among rail pioneers, often without food for days, with but nine ragged men. He was taken a prisoner to Santa Fe, where the Spaniards employed that Frenchman La Lande as a spy to find out Pike's mission. Pike was so angry that he kicked the spy out of the room. In Santa Fe, the Spanish Governor did not treat him badly. He gave him good clothing and entertained him at his own table. Pike needed a new outfit. He was down to rags for breeches, blanket coat badly torn, a cap of old red cloth mended with fox skins; but the Governor at Santa Fe had been ordered to send him on to Old Mexico. He and his followers were forwarded to Mexico by way of Albuquerque and down the Rio Grande. At all New Mexican forts on the route, they, now clothed as became army officers, were treated with regal hospitality. The trip was merry with fandango dances, songs and violins. In Old Mexico it was the same. They were set free and sent back to the United States. Pike came back to St. Denis' old headquarters, Natchez. He felt wherever he paused the coming revolution of all Spanish colonies in North America from Old

Spain. He sensed it in the very air. Perhaps it accounted for his gracious reception by all commandants. In a few years, the War of 1812 between the American Republic and the British had called Pike to Canada, where he perished in York, modern Toronto. Poor Pike! Had he been detained a few years in Mexico he might have escaped death in Toronto and become a valued agent of friendship between the new Mexican republic and the new American republic.

From the fall of Spanish power in Mexico, the lure of profit in trade from caravans became as enticing as the dreams of Seven Golden Cities in Coronado's day. First the mule was used as beast of burden because he was a tough desert traveler. He could make the night as hideous as did the yelps of prairie wolves, or the day sound like the honking of a motor procession; but the ox was more usable for the quicksands of a half dry river bed, or the dry sands of the desert. He could at a pinch be slain for food; but where fodder was scarce in the desert, the ox failed, too; so many a caravan set out with both. Hitched in one team, the mule and the ox did not agree. The mule kicked. The ox pitched and bolted; so according to the nature of the ground, one form of team would be hitched, the other driven along behind. They were long teams pulling tandem, eight to ten beasts in front of each canvas wagon. The driver rode or tramped abreast the procession with a long bull whip, which he could lash out with a yell, "Mule-ah! mule ho!" and hit any laggard with the expert aim of an arrow. Long pause was made in good pasture to cut hay, to let worn hoof regrow and have the local smith at the fort reshoe. Often, too, at such forts near the base of the mountains as Bent's, worn beasts could be traded for fresh mules and oxen. Pike, Gregg, and Twitchell describe these forts as "ports of call in a sea of mountains and desert"; and the ports took on many of the phases of sea ports on a long ocean voyage. The drivers danced and gambled and drank in an orgy wild but short. There were señoritas good and bad. There were Indian squaw partners, which the drivers like sailors left behind them, a bride in every port. Forts like Bent's could not possibly house the drivers of the caravans; but the caravans usually formed a corral four square of wagons outside the adobe walls, where they left sentries on guard night and day, and then hied them to make merry and trade away all their wages inside the fort. These forts were private not official structures on a No Man's Land beyond reach of law; but such forceful characters as the Bent brothers and Bridger saw to it that lawlessness was not tolerated inside the walls, nor so far as they could prevent it outside among the Indians. The safety of these private forts depended too much on the good will of the Indian tribes to permit ruffianism among the tribes. The Bent brothers always preserved an attitude of great dignity and distance toward all underlings and traders; but all did barter to the drivers liquor for the hilarious frolics and took wages in return for fresh bizarre clothing, colored Indian sashes, beaded moccasins, trousers of buckskin, and coats worked in porcupine quills the shades of Joseph's coat of many colors, which excited such envy among his Hebrew brothers. It has been only in very late days that artists like Remington and Russell saw as much that was picturesque in these rough pilgrims of a new trail to empire as older artists saw in the mailed helmet and chain armor of a Coronado.

Nor was the missionary absent in these wild pilgrimages. Any missionary of any faith was welcomed to the mess table and given a room to hold services and another room in which to refresh himself inside the fort. There was no hunger. There was no want. There were no rumblings of discontent however loudly the axles of the caravan wagons screeched to high heavens the need of fresh grease. Tortillas of corn in paste and husk wrappings, frijole beans cooked with such hot condiments that they would take pain out of any stomach poisoned by alkali water, tamales yet hotter, fresh fruit and fresh water, sent "Los Americanos" out on the trail southwestward gay as birds of passage, singing, eternally singing, and strumming guitars and banjo and playing the mouth organ or squeaking concertina. It may have been the Latin temperament. It may have been the carefree life. It may have been the chant of an eternal youth eager for a fresh adventure each day; but at wages of five dollars to forty dollars a month they were a much happier lot of men than their outfitters, who might make a fortune in a year, or wind up the season down to a last dime.

Of all the early caravan traders on the Santa Fe Trail, Jedediah Smith stands without a peer. He was an ardent Methodist New York boy, and came west to St. Louis before he was twenty-one, probably with aspirations to make a quick fortune, then retire to a literary life. He had first joined Ashley's fur traders from St. Louis. By 1826, he and two other partners bought out Ashley and resold to the Rocky Mountain Fur Company. As fur trader before he was thirty-five, Smith had been down Snake River and across country south to San Diego, where he doubtless gained his first inkling of how much greater the profits from the Santa Fe barter were than the profits from the fur trade in the north. His expedition was one of the strongest that ever left the Missouri. He had twenty wagons and eighty frontiersmen. He had followed the Arkansas westward but on coming to the great circle near the mountains decided to risk trying to cross the desert by a quick rush. But it was in the heat of mid-summer; the tornado dust winds had drifted over human trails and left only the buffalo's deep-rutted single-file wanderings hither and thither as guides. Smith was aiming to strike the Cimarron in a couple of days. That was too brief for his heavy wagons. The third day without water or food his oxen began to lag and stagger and lie down. Smith came on a buffalo trail. He knew it must lead to water. Bidding his teams pause, till he found water he followed the path southwestward and came on the dry bed of the Cimarron. Smith knew that up through these dry sands would seep water at night and he had stooped to scoop up a drink for himself before going back with the good news for his caravan to come on by evening which would be cooler travel, when he was struck by two Comanche arrows. He staggered to his feet and had fired two shots when he fell dead. The Comanches and Apaches had at this period become the worst raiders on the Trail. They had learned there was just as much loot to be taken from the returning caravans in silver and gold and bridles and saddles and firearms as from the westbound pilgrims with their oxen and mules so easily raided and stampeded. Independence and Westport, and Kansas City, were now the jumping-off spots to the wilderness westward rather than St. Louis. Leavenworth just north of Kansas City was now the headquarters of the army patrols to the south.

In the New Mexican official forts, where annual fairs were held for the meeting of pedlers and caravans, the church and the commandant's house were the center of activity. Taos and Santa Fe were the chief centers of activity in these official centers. There the sinners confessed their sins and it is to be hoped were forgiven; and there the wicked old local governors of whom Armijo of 1838 to 1848 was one of the very worst, demanded graft of five hundred dollars before a pound could be unloaded for trade. The "loose language" was awful; the gamblers like our glorified gangsters were decked in diamonds that stabbed the eye, their "ladies" were worse examples of bad taste and of worse morals; but though there was cock-fighting on Sunday afternoons after most sacred services at churches in the morning, there was no bull-fighting in New Mexico.

Jewels were a passion almost as great as gambling, with high classes and low classes. There was very little outright drunkenness; for the Latin is not a drinker of rums and whiskies. He drinks light wines, partly because he himself brews them, partly because strong liquors are fatal in a hot climate at high altitudes. Horseback racing and vanity parades were also another passion. Spurs were silver, bridles silver and tooled leather, saddles of tooled leather embossed with silver fit for a king's mount. When the poor could not afford an expensive mantilla, they wore serape blankets with a hole for the head to come through in the center, and the brightly dyed border made as beautiful a picture or color as ever the most expensive silk shawl or pearl-embroidered lace veil. It was not hard for the rough caravan drivers to fall in love with their ladies of the fandango as St. Denis had fallen in love with his señorita a century prior. The narrow alleys, called by courtesy streets, named after this saint and that, might stink with filth, but behind the shuttered windows were whitewashed adobe houses and piazzas with fountains of water and fireplaces to warm the chill of nights.

What was the exact route followed by the caravans? There was never any exact route. You will find this out when you study the army maps issued for the guidance of the patrols. In rail days after the Civil War, the route cut the great circle of the winding streams to the mountains and followed the diameter from Topeka down southwestward through Raton Pass and Las Vegas and so on through Santa Fe and Albuquerque and westward through New Mexico and Arizona and across the

Grand Canyon of the Colorado, through the Mohave Desert to Los Angeles—the Mission of the Angels. Whether you go west by motor or train you can to-day see along this route all the Indian land of Zuñi and Hopi and Navajo and Mohave. You can indeed see many of the Indians' pueblos differing little from the days of the caravan. Pause if you can. If you can not, use your eyes day and night and get off your train or motor to meet the modern descendants of these ancient peoples, who change so slowly.

You can see their best handicraft spread for sale, rugs, pottery, baskets, where they squat awaiting the passing of trains. Books endless have been written on all these crafts. You can buy exactly the value for which you pay. Just remember two to three points. Baskets woven so tightly that they hold water are the most expensive. They have hardly a mark of white man's influence. Loose-woven baskets of rushes are cheap but do not last. Pottery in soft gray glaze chips and breaks easily and does not last. Pottery in black with corked necks for water is usable in a dry climate but chips and cracks and disintegrates in damper zones. Jars and jugs in a shining almost iridescent hard brown are the best and most expensive, but the glaze lasts. If you are wise and want samples true to Indian life, buy only what has, stamped or drawn in, the symbols of desert life amid the pueblos. The animals may be crude drawings, the rope work in clay be jagged, the pictures of sun or clan, very imperfect circles; but they are true Indian symbols. When you come to buy blankets and rugs, beware of too bright colors. They are usually aniline modern dyes and while the rug will last as long as you live and defy wear and tear, it is not pure Indian. The best rugs are close woven. The nap has usually been combed off. There are no bright colors. The ground work is gray or dull white, the borders black or brown native wools. These rugs are everlasting in wear and cost the most. They are worth it. The yearly demand for southwestern rugs has sent prices up to dizzy zones. What I bought seventeen years ago at fifteen dollars to thirty dollars, I could not buy to-day for one hundred dollars to one hundred and fifty dollars; but I bought direct from the Indians on the reserves.

Preceding the rail and motor days, the caravans followed either the Arkansas to Bent's Fort, then traveled down past Las Vegas to the Rio Grande, or cut the distance south from Fort Dodge to the Cimarron and on to Santa Fe. The route followed from 1821 to 1831 was from the Missouri to Bent's Fort, then over the Raton Pass and so to Taos and Santa Fe. The ports of call from Kansas City along the river route were Council Grove a hundred and fifty miles from Kansas City (not the

Council near Omaha), Pawnee Rock, Fort Larned, Cimarron Crossing, Chouteau's Island, Bent's Fort. The terribly dangerous sections were Raton Pass, which required five days to cross, and the Jornada (journey) across to the dry Cimarron section, not far as it looks on the map, from sixty to one hundred miles, but terrifying to the caravans in hot dry weather, when slow moving oxen might make only fifteen miles a day and the wagons could not carry enough water in kegs and skins to quench the thirst of man and beast. The jockeying to gain first place in the long line of wagons was to avoid the dust. Trumpets and horns sound the "up-up" at dawn. "Catch-up, catch-up" was the cry to get in line. The teamsters yelled at their "mulas." The bells of the leaders jangled. The wagon chains clanged. The frying pans pitched in wagons added to the clatter and the burros raised their long donkey necks and brayed in a key between a dog's howl at the moon and a trumpet snort. Then the drivers yelled, "Stretch out," and the long line was in motion. Bent's Fort was an island haven in a torrid sea. It was five hundred and thirty miles from the Missouri. The walls were eighteen feet high and six thick. There were bastions with a powder store at each corner. There were sixty men trained to fight. Kit Carson, the famous scout, was the hunter to bring in game. The Bent brothers lived in what was really a baronial castle of the middle ages, rude, crude, rough with Indian and halfbreed retainers but with food and furnishings far exceeding in comfort and luxury, the regal fort of many a highland chief in Scotland. There were few hours in the day when the odors of prime ribs of roasting beef, deer or fowl did not assail and tempt appetites ravenous from labor and outdoor life. Round the fort, the grass grew waist high.

When caravan travel was at its height, trains often had twenty-six wagons, twenty-five filled with freight, one a chuck or mess table for all hands. Each wagon had five yokes of oxen, and there were six to ten teams for extra use or emergency. Worn beasts were left by the way. Such heavily loaded caravans were very slow; eighteen miles was the high speed for a day.

How many wagons were on the Trail to Santa Fe in a year? Just preceding the advent of the rail as many as six thousand.

Coming from the desert, travel-stained, dust-encrusted, scorched by sun and wind, the caravan would mount a rolling sand hill, or pass between two and lo!—beneath lay a squatty collection of what seemed mud houses round a drain that seemed dry. They looked, says Gregg, like a little hovel at the foot of a cliff; but after the desert, Santa Fe seemed a New Jerusalem. Natives ran out shouting "Los Americanos—Los Carros—La Caravana." Men and beggars flocked out. The muleteers had spruced up with clean-shaven faces, sleeked hair, bright big red, blue, green handkerchiefs round the neck, and the caravan rumbled and tumbled down, as proud as a modern flying express to the plaza of Santa Fe. The import duties were not heavy; but the graft was according to the whim of the governor. In the year 1846, there were three hundred and seventy-five wagons on the Trail with almost two thousand mules, two thousand oxen and five hundred men. This had increased to six thousand wagons by 1866. When stage coaches began about Civil War days, the fare from the Missouri to Santa Fe was two hundred and fifty dollars, forty pounds of baggage. For all over forty pounds, there was a charge of from one dollar to fifty cents for each excess pound. Though much faster than the caravan, with relays of horses and mules every one hundred miles, coach travel was terribly dangerous. The coaches coming out eastbound were so often carriers of gold and silver, that they were a temptation to white bandits, who could hide in the caves, or Indian raiders "sicked" on by the white brigands. You will find many an old cave along the Santa Fe famous as a rendezvous for the stage robbers. At some dripping pools in the desert, you will find the well known marks of certain gangs, not always in red, not always in black, but in signs telling comrades which way to follow or where to meet for the next pounce on mail-bag and bullion.

I have ceased to wonder why Americans say their own land lacks the past of a romance era.

CHAPTER XI

SANTA FE—PAST AND PRESENT

R. L. DUFFUS, who has captured the charm of the Old Trail as few have says that the complete final story of the Trail can no more be written than of the trail from India and Egypt, and that the caravan route was a living flexible thing never to be mapped.

It can no more be mapped than the paths of a wriggling snake. Not that the snake is a sinister comparison. Far from it. The snake was the sign where water could be found—always a good augury to the Indians of the Southwest. In winter, snake signs did not matter much. Snow fall could be scooped up to allay thirst of man and beast. But snow fall banked and barred the narrow high mountain passes to Taos and Santa Fe, the places of the fairs, when goods brought in were exchanged for goods brought out. Thus, expeditions had to set out in spring. This brought the caravans across the hot desert zones in the full blaze of midsummer. A week, two weeks were allowed for barter and rest. Forty-six days in and forty-six days out were considered fast time. The Spaniards might be leisurely laughing philosophers. Apart from their wild outbursts of fun and rough horse-play at the fairs and just as wild outbursts of hilarity on return to the Missouri, the caravan men were work demons.

Let us again go over this living snake trail on its various and vagrant wanderings. It had begun with St. Denis in the 1714-17 era, then moved up to St. Louis and Franklin in a century. Franklin, undermined by earthquake and treacherous river, tumbled off the bank and drowned in wild waters its hopes of becoming a great city. Then the jumping-off place to the wilderness of a lawless No-Man's-Land became Fort Leavenworth. Leavenworth was an army post from 1829. You will hear much of it anon. From 1827 to 1833 steamers began wriggling up the Missouri. Against the flood tides of spring with only cord-wood fuel and nightly stops to avoid sand-bars and log snags, the steamers could seldom reach Leavenworth before late spring; so Independence, now a suburb of Kansas City, became the jumping-off place. From Kansas City to Santa Fe was about 780 miles according to the cut-offs risked. Cut-offs became a pioneers' phrase for avoiding long bends by river routes and risking rushes across the desert between such bends. The shortest cut-off was across from the Arkansas to the Cimarron.

A VIEW OF ST. LOUIS

Courtesy Union Pacific Historical Museum

VIEW OF OMAHA, 1868

This was known as the Jornada. Jornada simply means journey; again, this Jornada had three trails. From Santa Fe to Old Mexico were another nine hundred miles; so the Trail of the Holy Faith became a very long one. It was assaulted by danger every mile of the way. When lone horsemen had to make it, they slept by day and rode by night, to escape the heat. It also brought the riders to pools for drinking water at night, when water seeped up through sands or down through rocks. When Brown, an army officer, was sent out in 1825 to make a survey for the Washington government, though thirty thousand dollars was provided to put up trail marks for the army patrols, the marks were never set up. He had probably exhausted his appropriation in his survey.

A treaty was made with the Osage Indians and others, to permit passage across their lands, eight hundred dollars to each tribe. Alas, the Pawnees were not a party to this treaty. Neither were the Navajos. Nor were the Apaches and Comanches. It was this treaty of August, 1825, which gave Council Bluffs its name. The Bluffs were a lovely park-like center of trees—really not bluffs at all but the shadow of trees in an almost treeless plain, stood up like "a great rock in a weary land." Pawnee Rock was named either from a Pawnee spy camping there, or from the Pawnee scouts lying in wait to observe the strength or weakness of the caravans. Brown's route was an excellent one.

Heat and Indians were not the only perils on the long journey. The beds of rivers with sinkholes of quicksands were just as dangerous. There the only recourse was to use the slow ox with broad hoof, or chain the mules so that if one floundered down bogged, the others in the team pulled him out, with such a jingling of bells and cracking of merciless whips and yells as outdid the whoops of Comanche raiders. Chouteau's Island far up the Arkansas was the jumping-off place to cross the Jornada to the Cimarron. The mountain route for reasons given became avoided in favor of that by the Bent brothers' Fort southward. Then came the Raton Pass over to New Mexico. It was a horror to the caravans and often required five days in a traverse. If you want to experience thrills, drive a motor over the beautiful highway to-day; but use a good car and take a skilled driver. You can see part of it to-day by the rail route; but you get the real thrills in a car, where you lose count of the sharp corkscrew twists. I have heard skilled drivers say on reaching the highest point, "Well, gracias a Dios (thanks to God) that is over." In olden days, the coyotes' howls on the Raton Pass were described as the howls of "souls lost in the inferno of the abyss" below. Yet few lives were lost on the Pass. It was so dangerous that precaution against disaster had to be taken; but it gave the boss driver bad dreams and the aching wagon men worse nightmares. Las Vegas and Pecos came next. After such perils the road to Taos and Santa Fe seemed easy.

When you compare Brown's distances with Gregg's years later, there is very little difference.

By 1827, old Spanish power had been cast off, but it is very doubtful if all New Mexico's pure blood white population exceeded five thousand people. I set this figure down very tentatively. The best census is a guess. How then could the old Trail carry such vast concourse of caravans? Because the goods bartered at Taos and Santa Fe went on down by pedlers to Old Mexico.

In later days, Fort Wallace, not a great distance from modern Dodge City, became the hub of the wheel for army patrols.

Now let us try to picture Santa Fe as it lay spread out a squatty adobe town to the vision of the caravans from 1827 to 1857. Keep in mind that the New Mexican was an ardent Catholic, so ardent and sure he was right that he did not much mind nor know alien faiths. He was sincere, too, in his religion. Though many Missourians were Catholics, many were Protestants of a rough frontier brand with less tact than a mule's hind kick. This accounts for the amazingly different first impressions. The rough frontier Protestants came with their prejudices. Enough to say their prejudices fell before the subtle charm of a city older than Manhattan, older than Plymouth Rock of the Pilgrims, older than any city of the James or Chesapeake. It was a sort of American Cairo. Human nature as far as youth is concerned is, as George Eliot says, "pretty much of a muchness." Before coming over the sand hills, the wild drovers had paused to shave, spruce up, don clean shirts, clean high boots, dust off hats and tie big colored bandanas round necks. Having been exposed to blistering heat and high winds, they were still a pretty wild-looking lot.

When the welcome shouts to the Americanos from the Mexicans and the answering yell from the drovers had subsided and the dark eyes lining the sandy trail had exchanged glances, the caravans tumbled, creaked, grumbled their tipsy way on tipsier wheels round the plaza toward the Gareta, or custom house to which was annexed a prison with walls six feet deep. Then the head man was summoned across the plaza to the Governor's Palace to show his bill of lading, pay the import tax—which was not heavy—and then an extra tax which was according to His Excellency's whim. His Excellency's whim being to extort as much graft as possible, this extra tax was in Armijo's day five hundred dollars a wagon—quite a nice little total when you figure that many a caravan numbered from twenty to forty wagons.

Armijo—if you can regard a scoundrel as picturesque—belonged to the land pirate picturesque type. He was very pompous, stout, wore a tremendously stern expression as well as profusion of gold and silver buttons, and used to emphasize his brief demand with one smashing blow of his fist on the table. Armijo was well born, though he seems, like many another descendant of good old Spanish blood, to have developed a system of morals at variance with his ancestral strain. It is said that having wasted his patrimony gambling, he rebuilt his fortunes by sheep stealing. That is, he would mix his herds with other ranchers' flocks and when the two herds were separated somehow or other a few extra good ewes and their bleating lambs would attach themselves to Don Armijo's lot. Be that as it may, he often resold the good ewe back to its original owner.

While Armijo was figuring up totals of taxes to be paid by the head caravan man, the drovers were standing by their wagons before the old Fonda or Exchange Hotel, quenching a long thirst in Mexican wines, or wandering more or less aimlessly round the plaza. They saw the little burro or donkey come trotting in loaded with sticks called fire-wood, also often with a lazy peon sitting on its rump, feet dangling almost to the ground. The milk vendors went calling from house to house with milk in cans and canteens strapped to saddle sides. The burros honked or brayed their notes through upturned nose or blinked lazily in the sunshine. One can guess the dumb amazement of many a rough Missouri boy at one spectacle hung in festoons between the portals of the Governor's Palace. The Missouri boys were not above pretty rough border warfare themselves; but this went one beyond their limit. At first they had mistaken these strings for ears of red corn drying in the sunlight. Closer inspection revealed the strings as festoons of Indians' ears, hung in grim warning to the natives stalking about the plaza. In other words as plains tribes took scalps as proof of victory, these ears represented dead foes and rewards were paid for human ears taken from tribes raiding Spanish settlements.

When taxes had been paid, the drovers were free to go their way and play, while the pedlers assembled to barter for imported goods. Their play did not run to drunkenness. High proof liquors were not the drink in Santa Fe; but high play in gambling was the vogue; and it is to be inferred that wages for three to four months went often in a night over the card table or at the roulette wheel, in wild betting over horse races, or in smaller betting on the poor sport of cock-fighting. Here again, the Missourian got a shock. Gambling wages away in a night was no new experience to him; but it was a new thrill for him to stand beside women of high rank, who wore no masks but hid faces under beautiful scarfs, and chanced jewelry, necklaces, rings, coins, on dice, cards, or wheels. He gasped at first but ended by taking customs as he found them. American girls, who had accompanied any caravan in a coach, were shocked beyond measure to see the Spanish señoritas with skirts so short they were above the ankles. Whether they acknowledged that skirts above ankles were sensible in a dusty land, the annals do not say.

All comers were admirers of the picturesque dress of men and women. The sombrero had gold or silver cord about the brim and crown. Jackets were cheerful in color and bright with metal decorations. Trousers might be so tight that one wondered whether the wearer had been dropped into them, or hauled; but one had to admire the graceful fit. Even the Americano leaders had to acknowledge that the señorita's scarfs of lace were better than little hats perched on heads, where a wrench of wind sent the hat off and brought the hair down. Courtesy was the rule of all the Spanish life. Hospitality came next and it was abused most outrageously.

The vesper chimes from the towers of the numerous churches were a charm, even to the most prejudiced Missourian. The bells were not rung. They were struck in unison by hammers. The first clang was a rude almost harsh crash. Heads bowed, hats came off in a moment's prayer. Then the next strokes were a joyous chime, fast and harmonious, symbol of sins forgiven, new life, joy. Then followed the evening parade of all classes round the plaza. There was mingling of classes but little intermixture of good and bad. Each found and kept his own level. The night often ended in the singing of the peons below tavern windows and the shower of small coin by visitors on the singers' heads. The airs often began plaintively and slowly like the dances but ended like the vesper bells in quick joyousness. The most prejudiced Missourian did not go back quite so prejudiced. To his own amazement, he often returned with a Spanish bride.

In the next era after the caravans, lumbering, swaying, grumbling, over sandy jornada and Kansas prairie like the creaking caravel of early Spanish ships, came the armed battalions of the 1848 Mexican War. Soldiers are soldiers world over; and in these visitants, the sleepy old Santa Fe town encountered a type perhaps more spick and span as to dress but less chivalrous in heart than the rough drovers of ox and mule. "Gringo" and "greaser" now became terms of exchange not so polite as the old names of señorita and don and Los Americanos.

How much truth there is in the tradition, I do not know; but some ascribe the term "Gringos" to the army song "Green Grow the Rushes, O," and the soldiers repaid the epithet by calling the Mexicans "Greasers." Legend also has a story of Mexican peons welcoming the rough Missourian with "Gracias a Dios—not an Americano."

Two of the darkest tragedies in the caravan and coach days occurred to the Chavez and White families. The Chavez family was and is yet one of the oldest in New Mexico. Don Antonio was going out to Independence, Kansas City, in February, 1843. He had as usual servants for his family, mules for his wagons and much raw bullion in silver and gold. He had been three months on the way and was proceeding down from the Arkansas. There was very bad feeling between New Mexico and Texas at this time. Texas desperadoes, ruffians of the type who provoke the bad feeling in border camps, encountered Chavez. They plundered his caravan and shot Chavez on the spot. Ten of the white bandits were captured, one hanged, and the others fined and imprisoned.

The White family tragedy occurred to a coach coming back to Santa Fe from Leavenworth. The Apaches were on the rampage in 1849. Dr. White was riding ahead in a coach with his family and servants. Indians surrounded Dr. White's coach. He refused to buy them off with presents. The

Apaches shot every soul except Mrs. White and a baby whom they carried off captives. When news reached Santa Fe, Kit Carson the scout and a company of American soldiers rode in hot pursuit. Carson advised the soldiers to charge at once. Foolishly, they paused to parley. The raiders shot Mrs. White and rode off with the child. The Apache chief wore a necklace of Dr. White's teeth. The child was never again heard of. The name White seemed ill-starred on the Santa Fe Trail. There was another family of Whites, who suffered worse in the army era, whose story shall be told later.

When the rail period came, rails had to follow the easiest grade and the shortest line. Santa Fe had to be left aside off the main line. The short line up to Santa Fe diverged from Lamy, named after the great bishop. The little rail station there is one of the gems on the desert. In furnishings and architecture, it reproduces the old Spanish type and one can do worse than pause there for a night or a day, and study both the building and its beautiful old furnishings. Santa Fe thought its ruin sealed for all time, when the railroad passed it by. Quite otherwise think visitors to-day. Its age has become its charm. The Palace stands much as it stood when Americans first saw it. The shutters lie back, opening from the inside against the deep wall casements, just as in Mexico City.

Fireplaces have been uncovered in the thick walls just as they burned back, back, back to days before New York had been born. The yellow cedar rafters have deepened in tint to dark brown; but round and above the fireplaces have been drawn mural paintings of every era in the Spanish history of the Trail. The Art Gallery really marks, as the late Sir Edwin Abbey predicted, a new distinctly American type of painting. This has recruited to its ranks such men as the late Mr. Lotave and Mr. Nausbaum and newcomers each year. The Archaeological Museum of which Dr. Hewett is the father, has specimens of every sort which the spade could dig. In the purely historic museum are those old treasure trunks with secret springs, which Spanish families used to bury in war and Indian raid with family plate, old coin, bars of silver and gold, scarfs, shawls from China, rugs the size of a table, valued to-day as cheap at one thousand five hundred dollars, when they can be bought at all.

One cannot do better than quote the description by Governor Prince of the Old Palace: "Without disparaging the importance of any of the cherished historical localities in the East," says Dr. Prince, "it may be truthfully said that this ancient place surpasses in historic interest and value any other place or object in the United States. It antedates the settlement of Jamestown, New Amsterdam, and Plymouth, and has stood during the three centuries since its erection, not as a cold rock or monument, with no claim upon the interest of humanity, except the bare fact of its continued existence, but as the living center of everything of historic importance in the Southwest. Through all that long period, whether under Spanish, Pueblo, Mexican, or American control, it has been the seat of power and authority. Whether the ruler was called viceroy, captain-general, political chief, department commander, or governor, and whether he presided over a kingdom, a province, a department, or a territory, this has been his official residence.

"Here, within the walls fortified as for a siege, the bravest Spaniards were massed in the revolution of 1680; here, on the 19th of August of that year, was given the order to execute forty-seven Pueblo prisoners in the Plaza which faces the building; here, but a few days later, was the sad war council held which determined on the evacuation of the city; here was the scene of triumph of the Pueblo chieftains as they ordered the destruction of the Spanish archives and the church ornaments in one grand conflagration; here De Vargas gave thanks to the Virgin Mary, to whose aid he attributed his triumphant capture of the city; here, more than a century later, on March 3d, 1807, Lieutenant Pike was brought before Governor Alencaster as an invader of Spanish soil; here, in

1822, the Mexican standard, with the eagle and the cactus, was raised in token that New Mexico was no longer a dependency of Spain; from here, on the 6th day of August, 1837, Governor Perez started to subdue the insurrection in the north, only to return two days later and to meet his death on the ninth, near Agua Fria; here, on the succeeding day, Jose Gonzales, a Pueblo Indian of Taos, was installed as Governor of New Mexico, soon after to be executed by order of Armijo; here, in the principal reception room, in 1844, Governor Martinez killed the chief of the Utes by one blow with his chair; here, on August 12, 1846, Captain Cooke, the American envoy, was received by Governor Armijo and sent back with a message of defiance; and it was here, six days later, General Kearny formally took possession of the city, and slept, after his long and weary march, on the carpeted earthen floor of the Palace. From every point of view, it is the most important historical building in the country, and its ultimate use should be as the home of the wonderfully varied collections of historical antiquaries which New Mexico will furnish."

Who says that American history lacks the romance, the adventure, the historic background of old lands? Only ignorance abysmal as it is stupid repeats the excuse of not knowing our own land.

PART VI

THE AMERICAN ARMY ON THE SANTA FE TRAIL

CHAPTER XII

THE AMERICAN ARMY ON THE SANTA FE TRAIL

IT is one of the deplorable facts in American history of the West that the heroism of the army from 1827 to 1843 is almost an official blank. You can obtain a yearly record of who was where, but of the splendid heroism quite as heart stirring as Coronado's march, there is no official account. This you can pick out from such casual visitors' narratives as Catlin's or Gregg's, or from the recollections of descendants given to the Kansas State Historical Society, or to such modern writers as Ralph E. Twitchell and Governor Prince. Except on two grounds, it is hard to explain this official silence. Either the army heads in Washington did not realize on what kind of patrols they were sending their little bands of troopers, or they did not dare reveal the ghastly ineptitude of their own orders and the rottenly wretched equipment with which they sent men to certain death in crossing desert lands.

One can hardly realize the abysmal ignorance of army heads in sending infantry soldiers on foot across a blazingly hot desert, or in using at first only the small-footed mule, which sank in soft sands or the softer sucking river beds of quicksands. The bells of the leader mule simply summoned Indian raiders. When mules were stampeded off by the fierce plains Indians, troopers and the caravans which joined the patrol simply had to cache provisions and gold on the banks of the Arkansas and foot it back by night to Leavenworth, from one thousand to seven hundred miles according to the trail followed.

From Leavenworth, soldiers were sent out as escort to protect traders bringing in the contents of the caches. Sometimes of four hundred and fifty men sent out on patrols fewer than two hundred came back. The rest died from heat or bad water, where buffalo had wallowed the pools into stink holes or frogs had died in the swale and lay putrefying to increase the illness. Such mistakes could not be put in official records. They were self-condemnatory—the common soldier called them a plainer name. You read in Catlin of a fine young lieutenant doing his best against such odds. You read a few pages farther on of the same brave young fellow lying down to die on the trail with the brave words, "Tell my dear wife"—back in Leavenworth—this, that, or the other tender message. Then with a sigh, "Give her my love but don't tell her how I died." Then life flickered out.

The body was buried where it lay without coffin; for there was no wood. Eight times in twenty-four hours, Catlin heard the muffled drums beat their sad requiem to such lonely burials and heard the ill in adjoining tents groaning with pain. Yet Catlin did not dare tell the whole story. Why? Red tape again. He was always the guest of the official commander; and if the official commander did escape death, he did not wish to block his own promotion to a more promising field, or to be formally "scalped" and demoted for giving out facts that must go only to army heads in Washington. This folly persisted to the Civil War. Then news correspondents accompanying troops began to give out facts; and even down to the 1870's there were fine officers sacrificed to red tape, of whom George Armstrong Custer and Carrington stand out as notable examples. When such cases came before men like General Grant, red tape was cut at one stroke. Custer once for a few days offended Grant. Custer could ride like a Comanche, the wildest horse almost standing on his head. He could throw himself out of the saddle, cling to the mane with one arm, stick one foot in a rope looped from the pommel and so rush raiders unseen by the foe. Once when riding a very spirited horse past a grand stand in Washington, where Grant sat, his mount took fright at the burst of music from the band. It took all Custer's strength to curb the brute from a wild stampede. He had to use both hands on the bit and could not salute. Grant was seen to frown. The army men on gentler mounts, who did not like Custer's rough and ready frontier ways, perhaps jealous that he had never lost a gun or flag in the Civil War, laughed and did not explain the seeming disregard for regulations. It was just one of Custer's crazy hair-brained tricks. Later when Custer was suspended at Leavenworth from service for a year, the true explanation came to Grant of the episode in Washington and the seeming irregularity in the West; Grant annulled suspension and at once restored Custer to service and gave him a promotion. The Carrington case is related in a former volume on *The Overland Trail* north. There Carrington was the scapegoat. Neither man was faultless but both were more or less scapegoats for the faults of men higher up.

Let us go back to the beginning of the army patrols at Leavenworth. Because of the scarcity of official records, this story must be told in episodes. They stand out like torchlights in a gloom of blackness. They almost reconsecrate the Trail of the Holy Faith, to a something finer than human effort.

Leavenworth, an officer, who had seen service in the War of 1812, came down, soon after Brown's survey, to Santa Fe, to look over the site for a fort.

He chose the location, as told in *The Overland Trail,* at Leavenworth on the west bank of the Missouri. He had the fort up by 1827 and fifteen officers and their families were there housed. He took a careful survey of the tribes on the Santa Fe Trail. He numbered the raiding Indians pretty close to what Catlin did. Perhaps he and Catlin numbered them together; for Catlin was one of his first celebrated guests early in the 1830's. There were twelve thousand warrior Pawnees including allied tribes absorbed by them; only fifteen hundred Omahas were left from Lewis and Clark's day; and the Kaws or Kansas people had some fifteen hundred and sixty warriors. Then he and Catlin went off southwest along the trail of the caravans to try and arrange more peaceful terms among these hereditary foes—Comanches, Navajos, Apaches. If intertribal peace proved impossible, then Leavenworth's duty was to impress all with the power of the white man's army. It was to be waving an olive wand to separate fighting bulldogs. Cheyennes from the north were making dashes south to raid the bands of wild horses and to plunder the caravans and caches of traders east- and westbound on the trail. These Sioux of the north had three thousand fighting warriors. Catlin describes them as winged-horse men. Their tepees left few signs amid the drift of sands by which a trail could be picked up to pursue. A

Major Daugherty was Indian agent at the mouth of the Platte—another name lost in army annals.

Catlin's pen goes quite wild over the beauty of the scenes about him. They had gone south in spring before the heat of midsummer scorched all vegetation to cinder. In one herd of buffalo passing north for summer pasture, Catlin and Leavenworth counted ten thousand animals. The roaring of the bulls, the click of horns and hoofs sounded like thunder. Leavenworth had left a garrison behind him only half manned and his men were chiefly infantry on foot. In a few hours' shooting one hunter could bag seventy-five grouse. The grass was tall as saddle pommels. In fact, in some low lying areas a man could stand up on his stirrups and hardly see over the grassy seas tossing in emerald billows from horizon to horizon. Different was the scene a few months later, when fires in this dry area created "a hell of flames."

They had traveled fifty miles southwest of the Missouri before they came on the Osages. Catlin notices a characteristic dress among the Osages, which can be seen to this day. While the main hair might hang in long braids, the topknot was *à la Pompadour,* dyed red or decorated with red feathers. All wore a profusion of silver ornaments bartered from the tribes of Old Mexico— anklets, bracelets, and bells down trouser seams. Pawnees were met one hundred miles up the South

Courtesy of the Chicago Historical Society

FORT DEARBORN IN 1803

Courtesy of the Chicago Historical Society
FORT DEARBORN, AS REBUILT IN 1816

Courtesy of Kansas City Chamber of Commerce
REMAINS OF WALL OF OLD FORT LEAVENWORTH

Platte; but liquor and smallpox were working their havoc. Liquor bought in St. Louis at three dollars a gallon, was traded to the Pawnees at twenty dollars a gallon, often doped at that price.

Fort Gibson seven hundred miles up the Arkansas was built by an officer, Arbuckle, and left in charge of a Lieutenant Seaton, again names lost in army annals. Leavenworth had set out with eight hundred men; but what with a detachment of three hundred to three hundred and fifty left at each strategic point as he went ahead, he had about five hundred to patrol and pacify a trail of fifteen hundred miles; and it was about as futile to follow these raiding tribes as to pursue a prairie wind. Leavenworth's instructions were to go as far as Red River on the False Washita two hundred and fifty miles from Fort Gibson. There he encountered the first fiendish work of raiding Comanches. A Judge Martin out on business had been caught. He and his Negro servants had been butchered, scalped, mutilated, and a little son aged nine stolen. By this time, there was much sickness from heat and bad water among all the marchers. Of all the patrol only two hundred could walk; but the soldiers had captured some of the plains horses by "creasing" the neck, or roping them on the gallop. The ponies were small bronchos and not hard to gentle for a saddle. Saddles were bartered from the Indians for a blanket or a knife.

Here we encounter another name famous in army annals, of whom more is known, a Col. Kearny, presumably Stephen, serving then as a colonel. Leavenworth now had wagons coming on from the forts behind him and in them were placed men too ill to walk or ride. Besides malaria, many of the men had a racking cough—not hard for us to explain but difficult for doctors to diagnose in that day. The high dry uplands in summer were a blaze of overpowering heat by day but chill from mountain winds at night. With underwear saturated by day sweats, bed too often under the stars, and sleep from exhaustion deep as death, the men rose stiff with rheumatism or with the seeds that bred an aftermath of lung trouble.

Stephen Kearny was not a favorite with the troopers. He was a stickler for military coats buttoned to necks, heat or cold. The soldiers grumbled but obeyed orders. Perhaps Kearny feared those night chills for his men. Perhaps he was yet too wedded to the martinet regulations of Washington.

Before taking up the gruesome phases of the trail, let us quote Catlin's first enthusiasm. His keynote changes as he, himself, fell ill and began to witness the horrors of Indian raid and murder of which no record remains. "Soul-melting scenery about me! Places where the mind could think volumes . . . but the hands palsied that would write. A place where a Divine would confess that he never had fancied Paradise, where the painter's palette would lose its beautiful tints . . . and even the soft tones of music would scarcely preserve a spark to light the soul again in that sweet delirium. I mean the prairies at sunset; when the green hilltops are turned to gold and their long shadows of melancholy are thrown over the valleys, when all the breathings of the day are hushed, and naught but the soft notes of the mourning dove can be heard . . . this prairie where Heaven sheds its purest light and lands its richest tints."

One night when the dry winds had scorched the high grass to paper, he awakened to a different scene. The roar of a cataract seemed to be advancing toward the camp. The wind became a tempest. Heath hens on wild wings flew in confusion through the darkening sky. Antelope and rabbits bounded blindly past the tents. A sea of fire was coming down the wind. It was a storm of fire above and below. In such peril, the only course was to kindle another fire beyond camp, then move to the scorched plain and camp with blankets overhead till the fire swept round. Grass fires do not drop brands and sparks. Nor do they overheat the earth at night for long. Quick movements can avert tragedy.

The scene at Fort Gibson, where Leavenworth

was to take Arbuckle's place, was one of the most imposing Catlin had ever witnessed. Horses were now in training. Each army line had different colored mounts—bays, blacks, whites, sorrels, grays, creams. The roaming Indians assembled numbered more than one thousand. The Indians then mounted their horses and showed what they could do. It was like the racing of the Cossacks in Russia.

The Comanches, Catlin says, had eight hundred skin lodges; the number seems to have been under rather than over the real census of the encampment; for Indian warriors like Arabs really travel and camp in pairs. On the Red, he found what Radisson had related by hearsay in the 1600's: though raiders, the Comanches in their own land were really a sedentary tribe with fields of corn, pumpkins, melons, beans and squashes. Here a Colonel Dodge demanded that, before any treaty could be made, the little stolen Martin boy be delivered. The Comanches denied they had him. A Negro there a prisoner told the troopers the boy was then hidden among the rascals. They swore by the pagan gods it was the Osages had taken him. The army men demanded that the little fellow be delivered. Some courage—yes! The Comanches could have wiped that patrol out. Brought in, the boy was quite naked and almost as dark from sunburn as his captors. Asked his name, he stood up and answered, "Matthew Martin." The officers with tears took him in their arms.

From that time on, Catlin did not like the Comanches. He knew they were what Indians seldom are—liars and under their own tent roof treacherous to guests in powwows or peace. The chief of the Comanches affected to weep over his raiders' bad conduct, in fact would have laid his painted cheek against the officers' faces as readily as he would have scalped them ruthlessly had he found them alone. It was on his way back from this jornada that Leavenworth, as told in *The Overland Trail,* came to his tragic death. They were near the mouth of the False Washita. The general had become very emaciated from constant sickness when every jog of the saddle must have been agony to a malarial sufferer. Indeed, in very recent wars, many a man delirious from pain and malaria has had to be strapped to hold him in the saddle and in spasms of pain has begged comrades to shoot him; but Leavenworth mounted on a fine buffalo runner was just remarking that officers too old should not attempt to hunt buffalo herds in such heat, when right into the center of a buffalo herd rode the troops. Away went Leavenworth in a wild chase. The pursued calf dodged. Leavenworth's horse tripped in a gopher hole. Heels over head went the general to faint with the words on his lips, "No, I am not hurt but I might have been." There was not a drop of water to revive the unconscious man; but Catlin got him mounted, coughing violently, and the march proceeded. Bugle call at day dawn. Ill or well, on went the troops. Rough stuff, some of them scum, none of them angels in human form these troopers were, but they did their job, tools in the hands of a Great Destiny of which they did not dream. Their job was the day's duties and they did those duties well and that is the best any of us can do. It is easy for study-chair critics to say if such and such were known of such and such man, his great reputation would be blasted. Doubtless, quite true; but how about the critic? As an old Scotch preacher used to say tapping his white-shirted front, "Mon, if ye would ken y'r ain sins, enquire within"; or as the Jesuits used to say, "Life on the frontier is seldom marked by a crop of divine grace and sanctity."

On the men rode to the head of Canadian River —the old Jornada—beautiful as a siren, cruel as death. Rotting frogs, buffalo wallows, heat and bad water added to the daily toll of the ill and dying. Catlin could hardly mount his own horse. He now hurried ahead of the little company of fifteen hanging back with Leavenworth, who came on sixty miles, when he died literally in his boots. Two weeks more and the troops were back to that same Fort Gibson on the Arkansas. Here Catlin had to be placed in a baggage wagon. He was delirious and lay on the planks of the rough wagon floor. One-third of Leavenworth's troopers had perished. Catlin awarded Col. Kearny great praise for getting any men back alive.

Catlin was astounded at the sea shells found in all this area—piles a foot deep, the margin of a vast prehistoric sea. Sometimes petrified fish were found inside the shells, again proving a tremendous inundation of sands and pressure, "thousands of feet above the level of the ocean, eight hundred miles from any sea coast."

A Captain Wharton was now sent from Fort Gibson to protect Santa Fe caravans. He was very ill; but he took the same deadly trail.

From the other old records of the trail, just as tragic episodes of the day's work can be picked out. In 1826, five hundred caravan horses had been stampeded by Arapahos and two leaders, Monroe and McNee were shot in their sleep. Some trader in fury shot a Comanche in 1828. The whole band then pursued the wagons of his caravan and their load of gold bars had to be cached on the Arkansas. Of John Means' caravan of five wagons and some score of men, Means was scalped and only two men got away alive. The bones of the rest lay bleaching on the sands. When raided and beaten, it became the custom for the men to abandon wagons and race for home by night. Walnut Creek was the head of rescue parties from the army. Major Riley comes on the scene in 1829 to protect traders to the boundary of Mexican possessions. He began to use oxen as transport animals. His jumping-off place was Chouteau's Island far up the Arkansas east of Bent's Fort. American and Mexican patrols did not quarrel in the border land of appalling danger. Sometimes a fool of a bugler at dawn would sound the call. Every raiding band heard it and scurried ahead to shoot from bluff or sandhill. The Kansas tribes now became as vicious raiders as the Comanches. St. George Cooke of whom you will hear presently was a junior under Riley and he testifies that many of the traders were so furious at the raiders that their rough drivers would scalp an Indian or skin him and leave the hide stretched on a wagon wheel as a warning. Unfortunately the warning worked the very reverse. The Indians took up the challenge.

Mexican troops so far as officers were concerned traveled "in magnificence, with wine, silver cups, much silver plate, the best of Spanish diet." The Americans were frequently in rags. That young Wharton sent to command at Fort Gibson did his best to pacify the Indians and advised the army to follow peaceful methods with them. By 1843, Cooke was in command; and a new era came on the trail.

PART VII

Army Annals of the Santa Fe

CHAPTER XIII

WAR WITH MEXICO BRINGS THE ARMY ON THE OLD TRAIL

IT would be easy to pause here and take up the old controversy on the War with Mexico. "The most unrighteous war ever waged," says one side. "Nevertheless, it was first declared by Mexico," says the other side. "It was a huge colossus grabbing territory from a weaker nation," affirms the first voice. "All right for you to say that," retorts the other side. "You are safely ensconced in a snug armchair; but how about it, if you had had daughters outraged by ruffian raids from Mexico, fathers shot and scalped, servants in your coaches butchered in cold blood, and young mothers kidnaped to be abused to death?" That argument about the colossus of the north had been used threadbare. It is used yet as a rallying cry to unify Mexican factions. "Suppose you had taken a caravan of goods to Santa Fe for sale and over and above import taxes had had to hand out graft of five hundred dollars a wagon, or have your mule skinners clapped in prison, as many were right down to the declaration of war by Mexico in 1846? Would you be so complaisant?"

This ancient controversy divides American public opinion to this day, but except for the War of 1846-48, the United States has left Mexico to work out her own peculiar way of salvation.

There was much of the heady wine of a new national feeling to intoxicate Mexico from 1820 to 1821. Revolution had heaved off the long misrule of Spain. Revolution after revolution by factional leaders had torn Mexico for twenty years. The populace were densely ignorant, eighty per cent Indian, as they are yet. Firearms were traded for goods from the caravans, and when not so traded could be smuggled across the border from the United States, or bought from European ships. England was becoming exasperated and was ready to trade bad Mexican debts for California. France was being invoked to send out a European dictator supported by the conservative element in Mexico to settle the internecine factions, which were ruining the new republic.

Let us as nearly as we can stick to facts. They have a way of discounting theories.

Mexico declared war on April 24, 1846. President Polk accepted the challenge and declared a state of war existed in May. The United States did not declare the war. The big republic to the north accepted the challenge.

It will be recalled that the most of the caravans set out from Missouri and Kansas. No sooner was war declared than the feeling in these states sent volunteers by the hundreds flocking to Fort Leavenworth to enlist. The army command of regulars was assigned to Colonel Stephen W. Kearny, first of a family for over twenty years famous in army annals of western heroism. Stephen was a student from Columbia College, a descendant of the founders of Kearny, New Jersey, who got a commission as lieutenant at the age of eighteen in the War of 1812; and who had been present at the storming of Queenstown Heights near Niagara. He was a colonel by 1846 and was promoted general the same year.

The Missouri Cavalry rallied to Fort Leavenworth under Colonel Doniphan, who like Kearny began life as a student and ended in a blaze of military fame. Doniphan came from Kentucky and had located in Missouri. He stood six feet, had hazel eyes and was the typical highest type of Irish American; but he was a Protestant, which explains his first prejudice against Mormon volunteers and later against Mexican Catholics. Both prejudices rapidly evaporated as he learned the real character of both religious denominations; for Doniphan's first, last, and middle name was fairness. It is a very good gage of the pulse in Missouri then that Doniphan could have had twice as many volunteers as the army could equip.

Kearny's first instructions from Washington were to go first to Santa Fe and then march direct overland to the Pacific and cooperate with Fremont there and the naval forces under Stockton. It is well to remember this. It was really conflicting orders which brought about the friction between Kearny and Fremont. This led to the arrest of Fremont after the war and his court martial. There may have been, too, a personal clash of temperament between the two. Kearny was a very strict disciplinarian and angered the volunteers more than once. He had good reason, too, for his policy. He knew soldiers of the army are not always angels on a march. Volunteers may be rough and ready and ragged; but they are inspired by higher motives than men who often enlist for an easy life, sure pay and a pension. I have heard Mounted Police officers in Canada say it took eight years "to turn mud into a man"; then the man was ready for promotion to be a dependable officer.

After only twenty days' drill with saber and rifle —just enough, as Kitchener said in the late war, to distinguish their left foot from their right and shoot straight—the cavalry set out from Leavenworth. War, like crops, takes no heed of seasons. This threw the march across half a continent in the very midst of the hot dry weather. Doniphan had about seven hundred volunteers till he was later overtaken and joined by the Mormon Regiment, whose part has already been told. Kearny had thirty-two light and heavy cannon, over fifteen hundred men including scouts ahead to pick camps with water, four hundred wagons to fore and rear with supplies, white topped as snow at first but soon to be gray with desert dust and torn by wild hot winds. This was to be no hit or miss expedition. It was as Doniphan says—victory or death.

The old Pilgrim Trail of the Holy Faith was to be followed; but the pilgrim trail was a very wandering path raging with flood and drought; and by June, the streams' beds were a medley of sticky sand and high banks and flood waters from the western mountains. Kearny's wagon men to the fore had to dig roads down banks and when the Kansas River was reached from Leavenworth on the 30th of June, it was in flood tide three hundred and fifty yards wide, not deep but treacherous with quicksands and the usual fords. The wagon brigade built bridges of rough corduroy, logs on beams supported by rough piles. "These plains with grass higher than saddle pommels, will be dotted with cities," said Doniphan prophetically. The Santa Fe trail was struck fifteen miles out from Independence, Kansas City, which was as yet only an outfitting port. The next rallying place of army and volunteers was to be Fort Bent on the Arkansas.

The beef cattle bellowing to the rear of the marchers, the bugles, the rattle of guns and frying pans, resulted in many a ridiculous scene amid the skittish horses broken only to saddle and bridle by six weeks' drill. Damage was greater to the rider's dignity than to his bones. In many an upset head over heels, he landed in grass soft as a pillow and had mastered in the brief drill the trick of letting himself go to the side of his mount, not in front, and of having a loose stirrup hold so he would not be dragged by his foot. The skittish horses soon settled down to a regular pace of twenty miles a day. Every class was represented in the volunteers under Doniphan—lawyers, doctors, clerks, carpenters, farm boys. In the breeze, sabers glittering in the sun, Mexican saddles giving an easy rocking-chair motion, the volunteers were happy as schoolboys on a lark. As higher desert zones were approached, mirages of heat waves at first misled the "boys." One good omen gave them great cheer on the 4th of July. Some eagle far away was reflected in great shadow against the sun. Eagle, the emblem of the American flag! The boys greeted it with a whoop. Alas, the eagle was also a symbol of the new Mexican republics; and many a cheering boy was to lay him down and die on the desert sands before victory was attained. At Council Grove one hundred and fifty miles west of the Missouri, there was a pause to mend wagons, pasture horses and cattle, and refresh the troops; but the heat was described as "awful." War is ever cruel to its votaries, be they in the right or in the wrong.

Pawnee Rock was to be the next general halting place. It was on the Arkansas, that the former Jornada across to the Cimarron began. Here fell deceptive drenching rain that gave little hint of the work across a waterless area a few miles ahead. Doniphan tells the two legends of the famous rock —where either a Pawnee had perished, or the Pawnees had lain in hiding to pounce on foes to the south. Walnut Creek, July 12, more troops behind with more mirages, more sand hills so hot in the sun they almost blinded the riders, buffalo wandering north for pasture as the south dried under the scorching winds. Kearny caught up with the Doniphan volunteers at Pawnee Rock. There were over one hundred ill men now in the baggage wagons and those baggage wagons had never a spring to save jolts on invalids, whose stomachs were an agony from cramps. Too often they had to be laid on the bare wagon floor.

Here scouts and spies and caravans coming east brought word of the Mexican army preparing to fight the American advances. There were twenty-three hundred armed Mexicans between the

Americans and Taos; but Kearny was an army man and took no chances. The caravan men who had Mexican wives, were sent back to Santa Fe to spy out the truth of how the Mexicans themselves felt. They did not go unequipped with gold. To this day, the army records refuse to divulge how much was spent on that old grafter General Armijo, who was snorting out threatenings of death to all invaders and calling in vain for a great rally. Perhaps if those records are ever given out, we shall learn why the valiant boasting Armijo vanished like the mirages as the Americans approached.

Doniphan's volunteers made twenty-seven miles a day up the Arkansas. The earth was "dry as embers." Here, Doniphan met Fitzpatrick of fur trade fame coming from Fort Bent. Fitzpatrick's warning was, "Beware of the Comanches"; so the night camps were laid out with great care. Animals turned loose to pasture were guarded by herders. Sometimes the horses took fright at the wolves, or a bark, which was not wolves, but an Indian spy. An answering bark brought any sentry to arms ready to sound his bugle.

Fort Bent has already been described. Doniphan gives it as, by his route, six hundred and fifty miles west of Leavenworth. It had practically been taken over by the army. There was a great assemblage of delayed caravans here. Again spies were sent back to Taos and Santa Fe. The Arapahos of modern Colorado did not like the look of those American "big guns." The march was resumed on August 2d. St. George Cooke, of Colonel Riley's old patrols, with twelve men hurried ahead to study out real conditions in New Mexico. Under a flag of truce, he was received by Armijo and Twitchell says about fifty thousand dollars in gold went with him. One of the Magoffin traders went with him, and both had direct instructions from the Secretary of War—Marcy. The climate seemed to belie its reputation by a gale of hail and rain, which sunk wagons to the hub, and some of "the boys" who knew the reputation of the road ahead had the forethought not only to fill the skin canteens but to hang their sabers by the handle to their saddle pommels and fill the sheaths with drinking water. This seems like a wild west yarn to the study chair man. How could bare swords hang against bare horse shoulders? Because the Mexican saddle blanket projected far before the seat. So did the tooled leather trappings and many of the riders to avoid cramped legs were sitting with feet free of stirrup or curled back over the saddle in a pace now down to a walk. The desert section was "dreary, solitary, desolate."

Turning south into Mexican territory, the troops ascended Raton Pass, that vast amphitheater, which one can see by motor or rail to-day—a panorama very inspiring but to troopers very appalling work. Owing to wagons being spread far apart, rations were down to half a pound a day. Where were the valiant Armijo's defenders which were to meet the invaders here and hurl them back? Vanished like mist.

Somewhere near the crest of the Pass, Doniphan addressed his volunteers. They could see ahead the serene fields of Mexican ranches with cattle, sheep, goats, fruit. The temptation to loot would be irresistible. Doniphan besought his men to keep their honor unsullied; and they did. Nor did the Mexicans evince the hostility which Armijo's threats seemed to invoke. They sold to his rough ragged "boys" for what pocket change the men chanced to have, vegetables, milk, eggs, chickens. A rainbow above the beautiful Pass was greeted as another good omen. Do not forget that up to this time, not a dime of wages had come up to pay the volunteers. No wonder Doniphan's chest swelled with pride over his men. He asked them if attacked not to waste a cartridge in chance shots; for till supply wagons caught up, there were barely "fifteen rounds of cartridges in camp."

Kearny and Doniphan joined forces south of the Pass. Here all received more cartridges and Kearny led the way. Doniphan followed to the rear, men all mounted and spirits sky-high. Cannon had been swabbed and rigged ready for action.

CART MEN WAITING FOR WORK

MEXICAN PEONS OF TODAY SELLING SERAPES

ROCK TRAIL, FRIJOLE CANYON

Advance sounded by trumpet and horn. Banners flew to the wind and "the boys" cheered. At the Pecos Village, then in ruins, the Indians could not be induced to oppose the Americanos. Their memories of the Spaniards were too bitter. Also they recalled an old prophecy that a fair-haired man of the white skins would some day come riding from the north and release them from their bondage to Spanish masters.

Again, where was Don Manuel Armijo, who could have defended any of these narrow bottleneck passes with a score of troops? Again vanished like morning mist! He was in fact racing for the Rio Grande as fast as he could retreat. "He was," says Doniphan, "subsequently heard of in Durango," to which may be added that descendants of the Don came back to New Mexico and lived in peace under the American flag. Was he coward or compromiser? Both perhaps; for he was a wise old serpent in reading the signs of the times. He knew from twenty years of experience that not a single revolutionary leader of Mexico had succeeded in pacifying the country.

"On the 18th day of August, 1846," at three in the afternoon, "after a tiresome march of near nine hundred miles in less than fifty days, Gen. Kearny with his whole command entered Santa Fe . . . and took peaceable and undisputed possession of the country . . . without shedding one drop of blood—and planted the American flag in the public square. . . . When the American flag was raised, a national salute of twenty-eight guns was fired from the hill east of the town . . . the streets were filled with American cavalry . . . moving rapidly through the city, displaying their colors in the gayest and most gorgeous manner. This day we completed a march of twenty-nine miles . . . over a slippery road . . . rain had fallen. . . . After incredible exertions, and late at night, the baggage trains and the merchant wagons came into camp, a few of them having failed on the way, or fallen behind; so rapid was the march of our army during the whole day. General Kearny selected his camping ground on the hill commanding the town from the east, a bare gravelly spot of earth, where neither wood nor grass was to be obtained. So constant was the army kept in motion, that the men took no refreshment during the day, nor were the horses permitted to graze a moment. At night the men lay down to rest without eating or drinking—they were almost overcome by fatigue—General Kearny had taken up his headquarters in the Governor's Palace and caused the American colors to be raised above it. The city of Santa Fe was bloodlessly possessed by the American forces. . . ." Doniphan's account does not read like an unwilling little republic being gobbled up by the Colossus of the North.

On the morning of the 19th General Kearny through an interpreter assembled the citizens in the plaza and addressed them. His address was a model of courtesy and diplomacy. He told the Mexicans frankly he had come to take possession, —"as friends to better conditions and make you a part of the Republic of the United States." All classes were to be free from molestation—not a pound of anything would be taken without full pay at market price. There would be no interference with religion. The people were no longer Mexicans. They were American citizens. He would establish a civil government at once and name as its officers Mexicans whom he found trustworthy. The oath of allegiance was then administered to a temporary governor, a secretary of state and lesser officials. At this point, the Mexicans shouted approval and an old Mexican embraced Kearny and wept.

After a famished march, it may be believed the troopers feasted. Good will and friendship so far marked all intercourse between Mexicans and and Americanos. Years later, talking to an Englishman, Armijo, described as "a mountain of fat," explained his retreat in these words: "Adios, they don't know I had but seventy-five men to fight three thousand. What could I do?"

Had plotting scoundrels out for the usual perpetual shift of revolutions not interfered with such good relations between Mexicans and Americans there need not have occurred the slight rebellion that followed the first bloodless conquest.

Horses were sent out to pasture on better ground. Discipline was relaxed a little to permit the soldiers to rest. One riotous drunk resisted arrest. "He was drummed out of the service" and had the distinction of being the only man so disgraced. Doniphan tells of one ludicrous episode. The volunteer was an Irishman with a brogue broad as his hat. "Sure, Sor, you won't object iv I take a little mice free of pay?" Of course not. Doniphan took the remark as a joke. Later Doniphan heard the man had taken some corn free of pay, and had the fellow up for examination. "Sure, Sor, you said it was all right to take *mice* and I took it." Doniphan almost exploded. The brogue meant by *mice,* maize, corn.

The next thing was to build a fort for army quarters on that sandy hill, where the men tented. It was named Marcy after the Secretary of War. The work was done by the volunteers and the adobe walls mounted fourteen great guns. You can see the old site yet but naught of a fort.

The population of New Mexico was given as a hundred and sixty thousand, one-third pure Indians and a few mixed bloods. Santa Fe was credited with six thousand people of all races. Doniphan did not like the dirty streets but he, too, felt the charm of the old place, and his soldiers were soon dancing in the wildest fandangos. The regulars did not observe the code of honor so rigidly as the volunteers and this no doubt explains much of Kearny's seeming harshness. One lieutenant had to be dismissed from the service. Six soldiers and two volunteers deserted. As their personal belongings were later found in El Paso, it is supposed they crossed the border for more free adventure than their life in the army permitted.

Despatches were sent back to Leavenworth and return order from Washington did not reach Santa Fe till after Christmas when the army had moved westward. The Mormon battalion under Cooke having reached Santa Fe, Kearny had marched by the end of September to Albuquerque —named after "the apricot." His first instructions in setting out had been to join Admiral Stockton and Colonel Fremont in California. Henceforth, Kearny's strict discipline became severer. His instructions entailed crossing that terrible Desert of Death. Here occurred the only clash between Doniphan and Kearny. Inspecting the volunteers one day on the lower Rio Grande, Kearny noticed that many men had thrown off their coats with shirt fronts open. Kearny told every man "to put on his coat or he would be dismissed from the service." It was very hot. One of the captains answered bluntly that as the volunteers had not been equipped with proper coats, and had not received a dime of pay en route, they would dress as they blank pleased, but fight to death or victory. Kearny bit his lip and passed on. He knew very well that regulars and volunteers were of different fiber.

We may ignore here a little side expedition of Doniphan's to protect some pueblos from raids by Apaches and Navajos. He saw those same old Seven Mesa cities which misled the Spanish for a half century. Many of the old mission churches were in ruins. Laguna's was, though the pueblo numbered two thousand people. At another mesa they found the people engaged in a war-dance over "the scalp" of a few raiding Navajos captured. Doniphan's young officer compared these people to Arabs or Tartars. The Spanish had noticed the same resemblance when they called their guide "The Turk." The visit was not an easy one. The horses were either wading through deep drifts of snow in the uplands or equally deep drifts of sand in the lowlands. The Navajos were friendly enough to the Americans but malignant in enmity to the mesa Indians. A sort of treaty was rigged up between the mesa people and the Navajos. Said an old chief, "You wage war for plunder. You kill, you drive off our flocks and herds. To resent this, we have plundered your villages, taken your women and children captives and made slaves of them. We have but stolen yours. You are mad. But you cannot accuse us of killing women and children. When our women and children went in the mountains to gather piñones, you killed forty of them."

Said an old Zuñi, "We have not the slightest fear of any enemy. We trust ourselves to a more honorable people,"—the Americans.

There was not much hope from a treaty between Indians in this mood. Both seemed to love war for its own sake.

This diversion for peace added seven hundred and fifty miles to the Doniphan volunteers' long march. It has, says Doniphan, no parallel in history.

Albuquerque, Doniphan says, numbered about eight hundred people. He asked one old Indian where Armijo had gone. "Armijo," said the Indian, "he—d—— rascal, gone to the d——l."

Doniphan records another joke on his gay volunteers. For sheer protection, many ranches and private houses had gardens surrounded by high walls. You can see some of these in Albuquerque to-day. By tossing a rope to the peaked rock of the wall, a volunteer had scrabbled up at night and jumped down inside to steal some fruit. Inside, he found he could not get out. The family were asleep. The fellow had to yell to his comrades to toss the rope over the wall and haul him out. If the Spanish family witnessed the escapade, they probably laughed; for in the autumn, any passer-by can have nearly all the fruit he cares to pick.

The march on to Mexico City is no part of the Santa Fe Trail and may be ignored; but the march across the Desert of Death was a section and is yet on the Old Trail of the Holy Faith. Colonel Price, enfeebled by disease, with one thousand two hundred Mormons and more volunteers, remained in Santa Fe and the army of regulars and volunteers resumed their march toward California. A despatch having come to Kearny from California borne by Kit Carson, Kit became pilot to California for Kearny. This became one of the most famous marches ever made by any army ancient or modern; and we have almost forgotten it. You can follow it to-day by steel rail or motor; and if your heart does not thrill, you have no appreciation of army heroism in the great West. It was no longer to be a bloodless march.

Let us pick out only a few of the high lights. It was pretty much the same road followed by early Spanish searchers for treasures, in their backward beat toward the western sea. On December 28, Doniphan had captured El Paso. He mentions many a ranch occupied by descendants of the same old Spanish families to this day, the

Oteros', Lunas', Chavez'. Kearney had left Santa Fe at the end of September. He had provisions for two months. The course was down the Rio Grande; where "we could see over the distant hills the camp fires of shepherds, who led their flocks afar from habitations." Isleta, Las Lunas, Socorro were passed and then, westward tramped the army and volunteers. Mesquite, cactus, the bayonet bush, sagebrush now dry and aromatic as you see all to-day. The Apaches were met on the ridge dividing the waters of the Rio Grande from those of the Colorado. "You fight for the soul," said an old Apache chief, "we fight for plunder, so we perfectly agree." Cooke's men for the most part were the advance guard to hack a road open. The Jornada over the Arizona Desert had not a cupful of water for over sixty miles. Then the mountains with streams dashing in foam through gorges. The Spanish bayonet or cactus, Doniphan described as thirty feet high. Afar were seen no longer the camp fires of herders but Apaches watching the passing army strung out in long straggling lines down the Gila River, which was crossed twelve times in fourteen miles, to that ancient Hall of the Montezumas, the famous Casa Grande, where the white soldiers wandered through the ancient ruins of a watch tower for prehistoric races. They saw irrigation ditches abandoned for centuries. Then the land of the

Pimas with their round-topped wigwams; and they met a California caravan with news of the Americans in possession at the Pueblo de Los Angeles and San Diego. Kearny received despatches about the fights at these points. An armed band of California Mexicans was encamped between Kearny's men and San Diego. They were entrenched in the valley of San Pascual. The men were called to arms at two in the morning and in battle array advanced. The valley was entered at daylight. The California Mexicans were waiting in their saddles. The Californians seemed to retreat. After them plunged the Americans scattering in the pursuit. The Californians charged with their lances "and it became a hand to hand fight." The California Mexicans were defeated; but seventeen Americans had perished and Kearny was wounded. "The dead were lashed to mules. . . . It was a sad and melancholy picture. The wounded were unable to travel and the packs were released from the mules and the dead buried that night, and ambulances made for the wounded." This was thirty-eight miles from San Diego and "at sunset we were again attacked." It was an even race for each side to get possession of a hill. A blast of bullets came from behind some rocks. For four days before help came through from San Diego, the Americans were down to rations of horse and mule meat. On December 11, two hundred men joined Kearny from San Diego. The Californians had fled to the hills and San Diego was entered on December 12th. The march from Santa Fe had traversed one thousand ninety miles. Kearny's account does not differ much from Doniphan's. He says the Mexicans at San Pascual had one hundred and sixty men. Kearny was bleeding badly from three different wounds. When the surgeon dashed up to help him, Kearny said, "No, go dress the wounds of my soldiers first." Then Kearny fainted.

It was here the friction ensued between Kearny and Fremont; and as the cause of that friction has never been fully revealed, and as Doniphan refused to give any verdict on the historic quarrel between two great commanders, perhaps we had better leave it aside. Kearny had proceeded on his march to Los Angeles. Fremont was at this time in San Francisco. He raised the standard of his country. Perhaps this was resented as exceeding his instructions from Washington. Kearny drove the Mexicans from the hills round Point Angeles. Fremont with four hundred Californian volunteers met Kearny on his way to Los Angeles. "I fear," said Stockton's report on January 11, 1847, to the Secretary of the Navy, "all absence of Colonel Fremont's battalion of riflemen will enable most of the Mexican officers, who have taken their parole, to escape to Sonora." It did and the regular army men and naval officers resented Fremont's on his own responsibility freeing other Mexican officers. For this, Fremont was afterward arrested at Leavenworth by Kearny.

Strict disciplinarian as he was, Kearny limped one hundred and forty-five miles on a return trip to San Diego in order to permit soldiers with blistered feet to ride his horse.

As Brigham Young had predicted, the Mormons did not need to slay a man, nor did they lose one. Kearny assumed the reins of civil government.

The march back across the Desert of Death was a very terrible one. It was cold in December and the dry palms fired for warmth "would blaze up like a flash of powder and die down almost at once." On Christmas Day, the volunteers were on the east bank of the Rio Grande and yelled to keep their hearts up with "Yankee Doodle" and "Hail Columbia." At El Paso Doniphan's volunteers were dispersed to go back up the Mississippi to Missouri, via New Orleans. If you add to their march to and from California the march down into Old Mexico they had covered six thousand miles, "a feat with not a parallel in the annals of the world."

Then let the curtain drop on one of the most

famous patrols of the army. Not one such march can be recorded of Greek conquerors or Roman in the Old World annals. It surpassed that of Alexander the Great, when he wept because he had no other worlds to conquer.

CHAPTER XIV

OTHER ARMY PATROLS ON THE SANTA FE

BIG movements backed by the army heads of Washington go down to history duly chronicled; but there were smaller patrols on the Trail of the Holy Faith of even greater heroism seldom known. They are rapidly fading in oblivion. They would have tried the patience of a Job or the faith of a St. Paul. Yet which of all the early army heroes wavered on the line of duty? Not one. Which of all the commanders was guilty of those awful breaches of good faith with the Indians? Only one and he had under him local volunteers, not carefully chosen like Doniphan's men, and provoked by outrages on settlers; and this one terrible deed has been quoted many times to prove the superiority of regulars, or to sustain the charge that the Indians were not the first offenders. It would be impossible to relate all these little patrols in twenty volumes, no, not in a whole Parkman series. All that can be described are a few that like torches shine as they seem to recede in the past.

There were a lot of motives tempting adventure

to the Southwest both before and immediately after the Civil War. Primarily were the hard times following all war. Men hard up, prodded by necessity, do not look before they leap. They shift uneasily and keep moving till they find a niche in which they fit or from which they cannot very well escape. Mrs. George Custer tells of the early days in Kansas. Custer's troopers came on an abandoned homestead with this sign stuck up: "Toughed it out here two years. Stock on hand, five tow-heads, seven yaller dogs—two hundred and fifty feet down to water—fifty miles to wood and grass—Hell all round—God bless our home." Not a name, just a sign-board of failure and an epitaph to blighted hopes. Where the five young tow-heads and their dad went and what had become of the mother, the dreary sign did not record.

Besides hard times were other temptations to adventure. Gold had been discovered in California, in Colorado, in Montana, in Idaho. While few drew the lucky cards in the lottery of mining—the majority of those stampeding to new gold finds lost and would have fared better by plodding slowly at home—the few who did draw the lucky cards emerged with riches beyond dreams. Before Kearny's and Doniphan's victories had added New Mexico, Arizona, California, to the Southwest, revolt against what government there was—bad and fraught with tumult and spoils—had been set up. Such spoliation as Manuel Armijo's stopped; and for contests over land grants, there was always resort to the courts. Very few land areas in these Indian territories were carefully surveyed till long after the Civil War; but squatters knew that if they sat them down and put up their rough wire fence lines, the courts would ultimately honor the claim of one hundred and sixty acres to each member of the family, fathers, brothers, wives, or sisters. This gave vast ranches for cattle, sheep, horses; and all were in great demand during the Civil War and almost as great during the rail-building era, following the war. Stages and mails demanded protection; so the famous patrols of small battalions began southwest from Leavenworth.

Philip St. George Cooke was a severe but great commander. Do not confuse him with another George Crook equally famous both in Custer's last tragic campaign to the north and in later campaigns against the Apaches. The Crook of the Apache wars really paved the way for General Miles' triumphs; but because Crook was not the final victor, little is known of his brilliant fearless penetration through mountain passes, as narrow as a man's shoulders literally, to beard "fighting tigers" in human shape. Price was in feeble health when left in command after the Mexican War and that perhaps explains why he advocated pacifist motives with tribes who never once observed nor kept a treaty till General Miles' victories forced such action. Yet no man in all the army was ever a truer friend to Indian rights. General Hancock's switching to pacifist policy is harder to explain. Perhaps he was influenced by the outcry in the East against the enormous expenditures on the Indian Territories. The policy of both men was furiously opposed by such army authorities as Sherman, Sheridan, and Grenville Dodge. You can read that in their despatches to Washington, in which one signed by Sherman dated 1868 draws attention to the ugly facts.

"Where the settlers received them (the Cheyennes) kindly, they were given food and coffee, but pretending to be offended . . . by the use of tin cups, they threw it back in the faces of the women, began to break up the furniture and set fire to the houses. They seized the women (the rest is not tellable) killed the men . . . I at once hurried to Fort Harker, troops were sent in pursuit—rescuing the women and children."

Under another date, he reports worse outrages. When more than eight hundred settlers had been slain in the Indian Territories in a few years, public fury forced action in Washington; so the little patrols which began after the Mexican War, ran on to the coming of the steel highway after the Civil War.

Let us take a look at the army as given in General George Forsyth's book. The army had increased from nine thousand men before the war to thirty-four thousand men after. Yet the population had grown only from twenty-three millions to thirty-eight millions. The howl for economy went up to high heavens. Forsyth explains how the ugly term "soldiering on the job" came in as a description of the sluggard worker. Army pay was in early days only six dollars a month with keep, enlistments for three to five years. Hard-ups, idlers, flocked to the ranks. Untrained soldiers among volunteers inspired by patriotism were splendid in action but apt to be unruly in intervals of peace. West Point and Annapolis graduates as officers began to enforce higher grade standards for rank and file. Their Spartan training of fourteen hours a day with certain pay of five hundred and forty dollars began to result in infantry, cavalry, artillery, bridge engineers who would tackle and master any job and never flinch. Those destined for western service were sent to Leavenworth for postgraduate training in cavalry duties. Forsyth describes Kearny as "peculiar" but awards praise to any officer who tackled a job on the Santa Fe Trail eight hundred miles from his base of supplies with fewer than one thousand seven hundred men. Of St. George Cooke he tells how for three days on one march, neither men nor animals had any water, and the feet of both troopers and horses were often wrapped in canvas, wool, or cotton to afford relief. He tells how when the clash with the Mormons came in 1857, even St. George Cooke, who had such an admiration for the Mormons in the Mexican War, almost suffered a peaceful defeat. The cause of that clash has been given in *The Overland Trail*. The Mormons blamed the traders in Jim Bridger's old fort at the entrance to the mountains for trading firearms to the Utes to raid the Mormon settlements. They doubtless did; but it almost caused a Mormon War. When Cooke reached Fort Bridger to take it over for the army, it was winter. Over five hundred horses and oxen had been frozen to death. Fort Bridger was found "a blackened ruin." Men hauled wagons through the snow for fire-wood and set up tents where they had expected to find warm quarters. There was not one complaint. Through the drifts they waded two miles a day. Pay at this period ran at thirteen dollars to thirty dollars monthly and keep. The allowance for food and clothing was very liberal—one overcoat, two uniform coats, three wool blouses, three light blouses, seven pairs trousers, seven pairs undersuits, three extra trousers, three overalls, seven dark blue shirts, nine undershirts, nine drawers, thirty linen collars, twelve cotton, twelve wool socks, nine pairs of shoes, two pairs wool blankets. The cavalry had besides leather gauntlets. Food was one and a quarter pounds of fresh meat, bread with vegetables in proportion, per day. Coffee and chocolate were liberally supplied. Even to men toiling like trojans, this was an ample ration. Each man had his dinner and soup plate, his bowl, saucer, drinking cup, and spoons.

All this worked well when supply wagons could keep up with the troops; but a new situation confronted the army working its way through the mountains to Salt Lake City. Brigham Young was too wise a man to fight a government army. That would have been rebellion and brought on the Mormons all the persecutions of early days, and now the Mormons had a colony rich from peace and plenty; but wherever the troops advanced the Mormons had fled to the hills and not a pound of supplies had been left, which could be bought. The army did not leave blackened ruins behind them. They left dwellings intact and there was probably never a stranger entrance to a city by any army than the march through Salt Lake City. Through a ghost city with never a soul in it filed the army hour after hour. Young was determined to leave the reproach of loot and destruction on the invading forces. The army was equally determined that such reproach should not rest on the troops and took up quarters outside Salt Lake City. When the Mormons returned, they found not an article had been purloined from their houses. What Forsyth calls the awful Mountain Meadow Massacre fell on California Overlanders. It was a repetition of the Jim Bridger's Fort experiences. The Mormons had said Jim's traders had given aid to the Ute Indians raiding them. The California Overlanders now said the Mormons had inspired and led the attacking forces against one hundred and thirty-five passing emigrants, every soul of whom but seventeen young children was shot down under flag of truce in cold blood. "Twenty years later," says Forsyth, "a bishop in the Mormon Church was legally executed on the very spot in which his victims perished."

This very bitter dispute may be left aside. It is only a part in the history of one of the most amazing Trails in the world. A will-o'-the-wisp, call it illusion or delusion, may have lured the vast movements of humans westward. The fact remains, though the motive may have been illusion or delusion, that motive led the way for tens of thousands trekking to a new Empire.

One of the shocks to fresh army men coming to forts on the frontier was the character of the army posts. Walls, houses, storage buildings, hospitals, very few at first, were all built of adobe-clay bricks baked in the sun. The appearance was very somber and dingy. Till whitewashed, the fort resembled a squatty huddle of mud houses. The flag fluttering to the breeze was the only sign of color. Fort Leavenworth, Kearny on the Platte and Grande Island three hundred miles northwest, Laramie, Wyoming, Fort Bridger, Bent's Fort, Wallace, not far from modern Wallace, were all beads on the rosary of the Trail of the Holy Faith. In the cemeteries were many stones and wooden crosses with only the name of the dead and the sad words, "Killed by Indians." Many a burial had been held at sunup or sundown with every attendant soldier standing at arms with rifle ready to shoot any raider peering like a black snake over the sand drifts.

The life was not all drab. Dances, dinners, cards, theatricals, band concerts kept up the cheer. The forts were always near a good water supply. Officers and men were encouraged to hunt either buffalo or the other game, bird or deer. Riding was a passion with officers and ladies. Looking back, we may criticize the presence of women at all in these posts of danger; but their presence contributed to the contentment of officers and men. "Soap Suds Row" where laundresses, wives of troopers, added to the family pay envelopes, became a regular feature of the forts.

In the cavalry regiments, near each stable door saddled and bridled and with a loaded carbine in the socket of each saddle, "could be seen three

Courtesy of the Union Pacific Historical Museum

A BUFFALO HERD IN THE '70s

A MEXICAN CATTLE RANCH

extra horses ready for instant call." That is the truest index I know to the danger in these frontier forts. Men who had expected an easy life were disappointed. The bugle or trumpet blew at sunup during summer and a little later in the dark dawn of winter. Breakfast was served at six-fifteen. Woe betide the man, who appeared in slovenly attire. Drill began at eight and duties did not cease till supper at six-thirty. Then lights had to be out at "taps." Between drills, the men could box, play ball, tug on ropes of war, go hunting, or study for promotion to commissioned ranks. In this era there was very little jealousy between the officers who had come up by the route of the military schools and those who advanced by the rougher route of shirt sleeves and necessity. The army was too keen for officers fit for promotion to care by what route they arrived. The jealousy, which did later exist between such sets of officers, really resulted from the demobilization of rank and file after the Civil War. From army surgeons to young lieutenants, there were more good men available than the army could use; and under the howl for economy, many a professional man loving army life enlisted in the ranks. A wicked feature of fort life was the clutter of "hog ranches" outside the fort, drinking dens with the worst of whisky and gamblers' devices. The army fought them but not very successfully, no more successfully than they are fought to-day under strict prohibition laws.

Let us take now just one minor little patrol of which Forsyth himself was the unconscious hero. One could give many such. The duty of this patrol was to guard the Santa Fe Trail. The Indians were on the rampage. Cheyenne Sioux now raided south as far as the Comanche lands; and they were equipped with firearms and telescopes obtained in trade. They still used the smoke signal as a sign to rally raiders; but they also used white men's flags and tin mirrors to semaphore. Treaties had been signed by tribes to permit unmolested passage of immigrants and caravans across their lands; but it was one thing for a good chief to set down his mark to such treaties and quite another thing to control chiefs who would not sign.

It was in 1868. Forsyth had accompanied Sheridan in a tour of inspection from Fort Leavenworth. He had waived his rank and was going out as scout with fifty men to Fort Wallace. His equipment consisted of a blanket each for his men, saddle and bridle, rope and picket pin, a canteen, a haversack, butcher knife, tin plate, tin cup, a Spencer repeater—six shots besides one in the chamber—a Colt revolver and one hundred and forty-five rounds for rifle and thirty for the revolver; all this carried in the haversack of each man. Forsyth says distinctly that though the new Henry repeaters were coming in use, the most of the men used Spencer carbines and old Springfield loaders. These were very unreliable in action. Many were mere junk left over by the Civil War. One of his best lieutenants was Fred Beecher, a nephew of Henry Ward Beecher. Forsyth had ridden for Saline River, where the signs of Indian camps indicated raiders all round.

It was September. At Fort Wallace he learned of terrible raids on settlers. He camped on the trail of the settlers' wagons and of the Indian tepee poles which had dragged along the horse tracks, when on the morning of the sixth all trail disappeared. Circling what must have been the trail on the fifth day out from Fort Wallace, Forsyth came to the north bank of the Republican River. There he found an old "wick-i-up"—a branch wigwam. The sign was "hot" of very recent occupation—ashes less than twenty-four hours old, not yet dispersed by the winds. Hotter and hotter became the signs of a very large Indian camp. Forsyth's men were almost out of rations. On September 16th, he was going in camp on the south side of the Republican River. In midriver was an island in the deep swale of slack water. It was about seventy yards wide and twenty long covered with willows and brambles. The water rippled over gravel at shallow depths of a foot or less. Grazing their horses, the scouts camped just opposite the little island. The horses were picketed and hobbled. Each man slept with tether rope over his arm and uncased rifle beside him. The men knew they were going to see presently what they had come out to report—where the raiding band was.

"At the first flash of dawn . . . we heard the thud of unshod horses' feet . . . and between us and the skyline we caught sight of waving feathers on the war bonnet of a mounted warrior just moving over the crest of ground a little way above us . . . as we raised our guns, we saw him joined by others. The sharp crack of our rifles caused the men to spring to their feet" and grab horses before the shout of "Indians—turn out!" could reach the warriors' ears. Running back to camp, Forsyth saw the aim of the raiders was to stampede horses; for "they were yelling at the top of their lungs." "Saddle and stand to horses," shouted Forsyth. Bridles and saddles were on in a trice. "Oh, heavens, General, look," said one scout. "Indians appeared to spring full-armed from the very earth." They were all round Forsyth's little band in a circle. There were women, too, on the crest of the hills screeching their warriors on to what seemed easy and instant victory. All warriors had rifles. Forsyth ordered his men to wade for the island, where they could conceal their movements in the weeds and brushwood; to tie horses, and dig rifle pits from which they could fire. The ford was crossed and the men dropped to the ground and began digging pits with knives and tin plates. Down in these they lay flat with rifles pointed and orders not to shoot till each raider was near enough so that not a bullet would be wasted. This rush for the island seemed to baffle the Indians but they came down the hills with a shout. The tethered horses fell first. One of Forsyth's men lost his head and yelled, "Don't let us stay here and be shot like dogs." Forsyth stood up—"I will shoot the first man who attempts to run," he said. Beecher yelled, "You addleheaded fools, have you no sense?" Discipline told, and the panic fool dropped back to his wet pit. Every shot hit as a raider attempted to cross the shallow ford. Forsyth walked from man to man, bidding them lie low and aim at every Indian trying to cross the ford. A bullet struck his right thigh and bedded close to the bone. Another bullet crashed in his left ankle and as he fell in a pit, yet another whisked his hat away and splintered off a shallow piece of skull. He describes the pain as the most intense he ever felt in his life.

The mounted bands were in hundreds about the little group of scouts. They could see Roman Nose, a famous Cheyenne raider of the Sioux, who usually went out with a thousand warriors. Some of the white boys began counting them but Forsyth interrupted. He feared it would render his men hopeless. Dr. Moor had rushed to Forsyth but was hit by a rifle bullet in his forehead. Though he lived for three days, he was never again conscious. Evidently puzzled as to how many whites lay hiding behind the brushwood across a ford which the Indians could have jumped, the Indians now plugged Forsyth's last horse down and deployed back to tempt the scouts to rush out. The scouts never budged. They reloaded rifles and revolvers and drew across the firearms of the dead and reloaded them, then did the hardest thing on earth—waited for what seemed certain death. Then came at the little island again the rush of the foes perfectly naked but for cartridge belt and moccasins. Roman Nose was heard addressing them in passionate harangue. Even the squaws and families now descended the hills to celebrate what seemed an easy massacre.

Roman Nose led the charge. The crimson silk sash round his waist whipped to the wind against his magnificent chestnut horse. The squaws and children broke in a wild exultant cry. Roman Nose rose in his stirrups and uttered a whoop. Beecher, McCall, and Forsyth's men uttered as wild a cry back from the island pits. Just as the raiders were about to jump the ford on all sides, the rifle pits spat fire and each shot tumbled a foe to the ground. "Roman Nose and his horse went down in death together." The fighters were not a hundred feet apart. The scouts were so exultant they sprang up—"Down men," shouted Forsyth; and they threw themselves flat just in time to duck a rain of answering bullets. "We are good for them," yelled Forsyth, bleeding from all his wounds.

Beecher in the pit next to Forsyth had turned his face on his arm. "I have my death wound, General. I am shot in the side and dying," he whispered quietly. "My poor Mother," he murmured, and life went out. In the lull the Indians had retreated with the dead Roman Nose; but to avenge their chief's death they essayed another rush at six in the evening; but their confidence had been broken and they retreated to their camp. Of fifty-one men Forsyth had lost five by death, and had twenty terribly wounded. He knew another day's fighting would exterminate his little band. He had his men draw saddles from the dead horses and heap them to the fore as additional screen. He then picked two men, one an old trapper, another a beardless boy, and giving them his only map, bade them try to break through the foe's encircling line under cover of darkness back to Fort Wallace, a hundred and ten miles.

They took off their boots and strung them about their necks. They walked out backward to mislead the Indians as to the direction taken and stole away to arrive at Fort Wallace in four nights. All the troops on the island had to eat was raw horse flesh. The next day was horribly hot but the Indians still held back, so the second night Forsyth sent out two more men. They could not get past the Indian lines; but these two saw that the Indian women and children were preparing to decamp. That was a good sign. Forsyth's note to the commander at Wallace was very urgent. He asked for seventy five men and ambulance. "I can hold out for six days but please lose no time." Again two more men set out, and these two fell in with another little patrol who rushed to the rescue.

Afraid his wounds might putrify in the heat, Forsyth asked his men to see if they could not dig out with his razor the bullets in his legs. They could not bear to try; so Forsyth himself pried them out and felt an immediate relief from pain except his splitting headache. Horse meat had become bad in the heat but they had shot "a little gray coyote wolf and that helped." On the sixth day, Forsyth called his men together and told them they had better try to break through to Fort Wallace and leave him to die. "Never!" they exclaimed. "We'll stand by you to the end. We've fought together and by heaven, we'll die together."

The men were now straining their eyes to the crests of the sand hills for help. It came on the morning of the ninth day. "By the God above us," gasped a man leaping to his feet, "It's an ambulance." That other little patrol band had come jingling over the sandy wastes to the rescue. There is a curious human story told of the first two scouts' experience. It seems in hiding one day, the only screen they could find was a bleaching buffalo skeleton; but in lying down and crawling up to it, they found the old buffalo premises already occupied by a good-sized rattlesnake. One of the scouts spat tobacco on its head and the rattler vacated the premises.

Such was the life of the army patrols on the plains.

Can one add or take from such simple heroism in the day's job by one more word?

CHAPTER XV

SCIENTISTS' REPORT PARALLEL TO ARMY RECORDS

FOR those who love accuracy there is no authority superior to the report of Lieut. Col. Emory, sent out in 1846-47. He was to lead an advance guard for the army with a band of scientific scouts. They were to pick camping places for the main body of the troops, under Kearny, where pasture and pure water could be obtained. Only about ten thousand copies of this old volume were ever printed and they are very scarce. Mine was given me by descendants of the Chavez-Otero-Luna families. Good as the report is, even the best of all, it is not always accurate to a mile. Mules tumbling over precipices broke instruments. At times when the instruments were true, cloudy dust blizzards obscured sun and stars; but from the ground described, the plants, and the trees, the most of the points named can be identified by travelers in motors and parlor cars.

I give them simply as a roughly correct guide—

Leavenworth—rain—June 23
Kansas River—clear—June 29

Oregon Trail—clear—June 31
Santa Fe Road—cloudy—July 1
Cottonwood—clear—July 7
Little Arkansas—drizzling—July 9
Santa Fe Road—misty—July 12
Pawnee Fork—clear—July 13
Jackson Grove—clear—July 19
On Arkansas—all sorts of weather to July 29
Bent's Fort—overcast sky—July 29 to August 2
Hole in Prairie—clear—August 4
Purgatory River—clear—August 5
On Purgatory—clear—August 6
Below Raton Pass—clear—August 7
Top of Raton Pass—fair—August 7
Canadian River—fair—August 8 to August 10
South of Pecos—rain—August 17
At Pecos Village—clouds—August 18
Sante Fe—clear generally—August 19 to September 1
The Rio Grande near Albuquerque—fair—September 6
Chavez Ranch—fair—to September 7

There follows a backward and forward movement to and from Santa Fe—

Clear Weather to September 24

Strike the Rio Grande—cooler—September 27
Pass Albuquerque—clear—September 30
Isleta—clear—October 1
Socorro—clear—October 5
East of Rio Grande—fair—October 9
Leave Rio Grande for West—clear—October 15
Gila River—clear—October 20 to October 31
River San Francisco—clear—November 1
Mountains to arid bends in rivers—clear—to November 3
San Pedro River—clear—November 6 to November 7
Carson's Plain—murky skies—to November 11
Pima Villages—clear—November 11 to November 24
On Colorado River—clear—November 25
On the Jornada—clear—November 25 to November 30

(This was not the desert Jornada east of the Rockies. It was the modern Mohave Desert, where the old travelers used to say that the Devil having forgotten a few points of torture put them in the Mohave.)

San Pascual Battle Ground—all sorts of weather—December 6 to December 13
San Diego—all sorts of weather—December 13 to December 29

The temperature of each camp is given; also the altitudes of climbs for mounted troopers and supply wagons. For instance, I quote very roughly to explain the slow or swift movement of troops—

Purgatory is given as 5,560 feet above sea level.
Raton Pass, 7,169 feet to 7,500 feet
Village Vagas—6,418 feet—here Kearny got word of his promotion to a generalship.

The population, the prices for food, the old ruins, are described in great detail. The old ruins are drawn so accurately in the pictures as to be recognized to-day. The houses are described inside and outside. Once the Mexicans knew that the army was not to raid, prices for food dropped like a stone to figures that leave us lamenting the good old days—a few cents a pound for beef, less for all the fruit and vegetables and poultry hungry men could devour. A lady's most elaborate hat cost one dollar and fifty cents because the most of the ladies wore beautiful silk scarfs that "revealed all they concealed," while the "Judy O'Gradys" didn't wear any hats or scarfs.

Many episodes I would have quoted but they would fill a six hundred page volume. For instance, among the Navajo and Comanche and Apache raiders, whom the caravan scared into good behavior, were seen squaws of pure white skin, also boys, who could not speak a word of English; and no offer could persuade them to leave the Indian life. The inference is self-evident. Though the Indians said that they were half-bloods from white men and abused squaws, these whiteskins were captives from childhood, who did not know their own origin. They rode for the most part almost as naked as the Indians in a hot zone. One boy remembered his native tongue well enough to answer "No—me too long Indian to become white now." One does not know whether to wish we had the record of his parents' death, or to thank God we have not. Any oriental would say that the incense of their prayers went up to God's throne as the sacrifice of martyrs on a Holy Trail. A cynic would say, serves them right for taking chances on a dangerous trail. You can take your pick of either argument. As arguments, both have holes. The incense prayers did not assuage the awful suffering. Also people do not challenge dangerous trails unless necessity of one kind or another prods like a bayonet. I simply set down the facts as nearly as I can gather them.

There are slips in the *Army Report* of Spanish names, like Chavez, Isleta. These may be due to the Washington Bureau of Printing; for in the report six to ten pages are repeated in bad binding. Carson and Fitzpatrick, both familiar with the mountains were the guides on the trail. As to the Apaches, vowing friendship after seeing the long range guns, Kit Carson said, "I would not trust one of them." The giant cactus, the pulque cactus, the little groundling cactus called jocularly, "The Devil's nail keg," or "Devil's cushion" are all described and pictured.

The Pimas are portrayed as the best of all the Indians. The habits of the clean Indians in never eating the beef of old males or fish except from deep cold water; their medicine purges, medicine plasters from berries and plants; all have points which whites have not yet adopted as helps to perfect health. The pictographs drawn on rocks, which the early priests thought devices of Devil worship, are ascribed to picture-history, which scientists now recognize as true. The Saviour of mankind is depicted as a fair-haired montezuma born of sinless flesh, a Virgin Birth. The picturesque fantastic dress of early settlers is described. Some wore the remaining uniform from British Naval Squadrons. Some wore the clothes of gentlemen who had once had velvet and satin trousers but now added buckskin leggings as protection from Devil Cactus and regarded life as a passing show, taking things pretty much as they came and went.

Near San Pascual the bugle sounded "call to horse" at 2 A.M.

The San Pascual Fight is given very fully. It was there Kearny showed his real heart for troopers, neglecting his own wounds for the suffering of the soldiers. In fact, any one who desires a full account should read Colonel Emory's report. Several of the army officers traveled with a copy of Horace, a Greek Testament, and sometimes a small Shakespeare. None took up much space. All could be reread many times and are an index to the culture of the officers.

Acequias or irrigation ditches were noted all along the Trail. Sumach berries made red dyes. Green came from copper ore. Pitch was fused on sore hoofs. There was a rattlesnake weed which cured snake bites. All the Indians had a legend of coming from the north, "long-long time ago," ninety seemed the limit of numbers counted. Beyond that, the Indians computed so many "nineties" where we computed so many hundreds. Very few could even remotely grasp a general idea. It had to be a pictured specific idea. In other words, the Indian's was a childhood race.

Their sign language was the same as a white child's: plenty to eat,—a sign "full up to the mouth." A "chorus of wolf packs" played the nightly band from end to end of the march; it is called, "a serenade of inimitable music." The dust was a horror, the bad water worse. The scenery was so gorgeously spectacular it set the troopers "whooping," though it strained muscles to a toothache. The salt lakes encountered, where thirsty men and horses plunged, played havoc but purged of poison; then the fresh stream from the mountains restored health and strength. From all of which it is self-evident that Kearny's mathematical slow but sure procession was wise as the tortoise of fable that out-raced the hare. The shouts of the mountain streams was "a joyful cry" in which soldiers joined. The pulque was not so strong and intoxicating as that used to-day and the soldiers drank it in gulps without bad results. The rattlesnakes made even "mules jump." Down some of the precipice roads, the mules had to be blindfolded before they would venture a step. Troopers were kept away from corn fields for fear they would pillage after dark. Until assured there would be no pilfering, the Mexicans would not look an Americano in the face. The red-winged blackbirds chanted a chatter of joy above irrigation ditches as they do to-day. The wild raging music of the Mexican funerals shocked the staid

Eastern reverential officers. They forgot that many of those mestizo Mexicans still believed in scaring away the Devil; and the Americanos had to admit the music was a wild vent for overwrought emotions. The most of the gold mining was pure placer out of holes or quartz which the Mexicans crushed with rocks, then washed. Don Jose Chavez was one of the foremost miners. Goat milking was a comical scene. If nanny's horns were not held, she was likely to charge at the man on the milking stool and he went over backward, a fine target for the rams. Sheep were the great and profitable crop. Some ranchers had forty thousand head of sheep. Navajo blankets sold to the officers at fifty dollars to one hundred dollars. No good don would accept a cent of pay from officers for lodging and board. A beautiful description is given of the churches with the clash of hammer-hit bells, of the hooded friars in blue and gray, of the crimson lights through mosaic windows, even of the plaza with its gambling dens, and of the beautiful homemade bread at (praise of thanks from the Americanos) two dollars and fifty cents for one hundred and forty-four pounds of loaves, of the portales which the records spell "portails," of the fine paintings which money could not buy. In a word the charm of Santa Fe and Taos captured the conquerors. They were like Roman conquerors captured by Grecian beauty.

The report gives an interesting explanation of "Cibola" which the early treasure-hunters thought meant the Seven Golden Cities. Cibola meant to the old Indians the country whence came "the buffalo"; so they sent the treasure-hunters on to the land of the buffalo—Kansas. Alas for the poor "Turk" strangled by the treasure-seekers, and the poor Negro Estevan hurled to death over a precipice! They did not intend to mislead but mistook a phrase in Indian translation. I set the explanation down for what it may be worth. It is the best explanation I have ever read. To question from the officers then among the Mexicans, both Indians and Mexicans when they did not know definitely answered—"Quién sabe?"—who knows? "Quizas," perhaps. It would—says the report—have made Cervantes weep in despair. It would. Poor Don Quixote would have charged with his steed and lance at a windmill, as we too often do.

Now let us skip to the Jornada in the far western Desert of Death . . . the Mohave. The Indians were not wilful liars. They saw "through a glass darkly." Mexicans were so polite, they staggered the best of the officers, "God grant, sir, that you may live to see the last years of thousands," with the sweep of a sombero and a deep bow. Cold, abominable cold at night, heat beyond endurance by day. Fiendish cruelty by Apache raiders.

The last part of the report has an official record by Colonel St. George Cooke of the march to San Diego. He gives the distance from Kansas City to San Diego as one thousand eight hundred miles. All the reports shy off the quarrel between Fremont and Kearny.

It was one thing for the scientists to pass westward in summer protected by big guns with the army. It was another thing to get through the mountain passes in snow and across the plains amid treacherous raiders. Some of their staff were crippled for life by frozen limbs. The Indian raiders —Pawnees, Cheyennes, Kaws—were bold and brazen. Mules were run off by night and the scientists were glad to reach Independence (Kansas City) alive. They had no illusions about Indian raiders and called them "treacherous liars." I set their reports down for exactly what they are worth —which to me is a great deal.

CHAPTER XVI

GENERAL GEORGE ARMSTRONG CUSTER'S PATROLS IN THE SOUTHWEST

SEVERAL causes contributed to embolden the Indians in raids along the Santa Fe Trail. Up to 1869, they had been uniformly triumphant in the north. Then, if they completed their raids by September or October, they had a fixed idea that no white troops could pursue them through the mountain fastnesses where they camped for the winter. Also the leaders knew perfectly well that the cry for economy in the East, the howl about Indian rights, the wobbly policy of politicians, were embarrassing army action.

As the raids went on against settlers, General Sheridan grew furious. He was in charge of this section and daily received reports of the settlers' suffering in fiendish tortures. The ironical feature was that the raiding Indians from the north had not the excuse that the settlers squatting on land were encroaching on the red man's hunting ground. It is in the year's report of 1868-69, that General Sheridan, to silence well-meaning humanitarians, gives details of the suffering among women and children. Do not think for a moment that such suffering was from frost-bitten hands and feet. Few humanitarians could bring themselves to read General Sheridan's pages. White blackguards in rare cases might scalp and skin a bad Indian, but they did not brain babies nor tear to pieces the bodies of living victims.

Ignoring the hue and cry for economy, General Sheridan determined to strike the raiders an unexpected blow—a smashing blow—in midwinter, a campaign during the very wildest and coldest of blizzards. To army heads in the East, this seemed "an unheard-of" proceeding, "an impossibility." To this campaign, Sheridan called a young Colonel who had the records of never having lost a battle nor a flag in the Civil War—George Armstrong Custer. A word as to this picturesque figure, whose life went out in such dark tragedy in the north. Custer was born in Ohio in 1839. He plowed. He taught a country school and had worked up to West Point, where he made brilliant records. In the Civil War, he had the same undimmed record.

Kearny always regarded him as "peculiar." Naturally, a Kearny buttoned to his chin in strict regimental dress, could not see things just the same as a young cavalryman who led wild charges with shirt front open. One won battles by sheer careful mathematical precision, the other trusted to dash, courage, nerve. But Sherman and Sheridan had boundless faith in Custer. Custer could have had any of a dozen diplomatic appointments after the Civil War, but he chose the Western field as better suited to his temperament. Rough he was, in a way. When cavalrymen grew sluggish in movement, his orders were more likely to be, "Plug up your old chugs" than some precise phrase. He had been detailed to Fort Riley on the Arkansas. He came up with Mrs. Custer by way of Louisiana and grew to have a distinct distrust of colored troops as dependable. He also acquired a habit in the hot zone of marching from 2 A.M. to avoid heat. He was at the head of four thousand men and acquired another habit of riding not according to army regulations. It was the use of the Mexican rather than the army saddle. The Mexican saddle gave an easy rocking-chair motion on long patrols and did not jolt bones to pieces as the stiff rise and fall of cavalry motion, too often did. Though rough and ready, he kept up the amenities of civilized life when on the patrol. He had buckets of water, camp stools, camp table and never let himself nor his men become careless.

Mrs. Custer gives a very full account of life at Fort Riley but we are more interested in the army patrols. Custer kept his men eternally busy. When not hunting nor drilling, target shooting nor boxing, he had them "sharpen swords on the grindstones." Every man in the cavalry had to have a hundred rounds of cartridges. That old Pond Creek of Brown's Report in 1825 had become Fort Wallace, the jumping-off place to the Southwest.

Sheridan's plan was to keep scouting the whole area and wherever he heard of raids, send his troops summer or winter. The Indians in camp would not expect punishment in winter and by spring they would scamper and again raid. A hundred miles south of Fort Wallace, Sheridan opened a Camp Supply. It was to be support as a basis of supplies for the patrols, and Sheridan took up his field headquarters right there. Custer, then only a lieutenant-colonel, in command of the famous 7th Cavalry, was instructed to take the field on Nov. 22 and track down a raider band of Cheyennes under Black Kettle, the most notorious of the cruel chiefs. At four in the morning of the 23rd, the bugle sounded. It was too dark to see beyond the tent flap except that the snow was a foot deep and a blizzard raging with the scream of a wolf pack. Breakfast was eaten standing knee deep in snow. Tents were down by daylight and the regiment of men moved out in a long procession of two abreast amid snow so thick the Indian guides could not see twenty yards ahead. Custer took out his map and guided his course by compass to Wolf Creek fifteen miles away. Wagon trains with supplies followed after the horses breaking a way through the drifts.

The morning of the 24th, the blizzard calmed to be followed by bitter hard frost. Game big and little was noticed everywhere sheltered under bluffs from the blizzard. The 25th of November was Thanksgiving Day and many a boy in rank must have recalled happy old home scenes of turkey dinners and warm blazing hearth fires. The next night Custer was very close to Canadian River. While he moved across Canadian River, he sent Major Elliott with a small detail of troops fifteen miles up stream in search of the Indian camp, which he knew was lying ensconced here. Just as Custer got across the Canadian at eleven next morning, a scout came back from Elliott with word that the trail of an Indian war band had been found.

"Leaving," says Forsyth, "his train under guard of eighty men to follow as fast as possible, Custer set out to overtake Elliott." Each rider carried one hundred rounds of cartridges, coffee and hard bread. Tents and blankets were to follow in wagons. At 9 P.M. Custer caught up with Elliott. The horses were saddled and took the trail by moonlight—another surprise, for the Indians hitherto had encountered whites only in daylight. "Not a word was spoken. Strict orders prohibited the lighting of a match or smoking of a pipe."

Some scout thought he smelled camp smoke. The cavalry halted. Over the crest of a hill, a large winter camp could be seen in the ravine below. Custer ordered his men to avoid the clanking of any sabers. Then dividing eight hundred men in four bands, one on each side of the Indian camp, one circled behind the ravine tepees, and a central fourth band of cavalry under his own leadership, Custer waited for the groups to take up their stations. The waiting troops drew capes of overcoats over their heads and snatched sleep lying in the snow or leaning against horses. Dawn had barely stolen over the gray white landscape, when overcoats were off, strapped to saddles, rifles loaded, pistols loosened from holsters. Then the command ran along the lines. Men sprang to saddles and grasped reins; then there was a blast of bugles and trumpets.

A quarter of a mile below lay the raiders' camp. The troopers charged down hill in Custer's whirlwind fashion. The Indian camp sprang from sleep in awful confusion. "It was," says Forsyth, "awful retribution on Black Kettle's band." Let it be said in fair defense of the Cheyenne Sioux that they never would assume guilt for Black Kettle's doings. They said he was no coward but a bad Indian and would abide by no agreement with white or red. Black Kettle was one of the very first to fall. To Custer's surprise he found

Comanches and Apaches with Black Kettle's Sioux.

Custer burned the village with all its supplies and captured more horses than his men could herd back; so except for mounts for the captured women and children, he ordered the Indian horses shot. He then sent men to hunt for Elliott and his band of scouts again out to report movements of foes. They were not found till the 10th of December. They had been surrounded, shot and mutilated. It was while searching for Elliott's scouts that the bodies of fourteen little white children dropped by the raiding Sioux were found frozen to death. It was here, too, Custer rescued two white women, Mrs. Morgan and Miss White, from a cruel captivity. The prisoners were sent back to Camp Supply. This was one of the worst blows the raiding Indians had yet suffered. It justified Sheridan's policy and he determined to go on before the clack of protests could arrest the army's action.

Whether Custer split his own forces or his forces were split by the strategy of the Indians, it will be evident from this one battle, that the very tactics which won victory on the Santa Fe Trail brought defeat in the north. These victories brought Custer a great deal of public recognition as a new type of army man. They also brought on him a deal of criticism for rough and ready methods. It was for infraction of one regulation that he was tried and suspended from duty at this period. He had absented himself from duty without leave to go to his wife for three days; but General Grant, as told elsewhere, promptly reinstated him.

Fort Wallace in these years could house only five hundred men. The troops were expected to be kept in constant motion on patrols. When more troops came in than could be housed, if it were winter, the family men went in sod shacks. In Hancock's régime, while patrols were out over the plains, Fort Wallace was left with fewer than fifty men to defend it of whom twelve were unreliable Negroes. The Indians were now fighting the progress of the Union Pacific Westward. One of Custer's patrols took him one hundred and fifty-four miles in four days. Another led him to the bounds of northern Colorado. Poor young Beecher was one of the boys who drove off many a raid. His fate has already been given in the account of Forsyth's patrol.

Seventy-five miles from Wallace, Custer once waited for supply wagons to come up. There was not a night his camp had not been attacked. He was waiting at Fort Sedgewick for a Lieut. Kidder to come along with despatches. Kidder did not turn up. Kidder's body and ten of his scouts were found bleaching on the prairie. The bodies had been mutilated and partly burned. The bones were buried in one grave by lantern light. This was a year before the defeat of Black Kettle's band. Frontier posts from 1867 to 1870 were in bad shape.

Terrible tales could be told of the suffering among white families; but they are much too harrowing. The story of the Germine or German girls is one that can be told. It is given very fully in all Kansas State annals. The massacre occurred east of Wallace. The parents and seven children had come from Georgia. They had camped twenty miles east of Fort Wallace. The girls were gathering fire-wood for supper. The father and son had milked the cow and the others were preparing supper. It was September, 1874. They rose before breakfast and were loading to move toward Wallace. The father paced on foot ahead. Mother and girls were in the wagon. A boy and a sister had gone out to drive in the milk cow when yells were heard. All but four girls were slain in meanest fashion by seventeen raiders and two squaws in less than five minutes. There was no provocation of any sort. Yet the girl with the longest and loveliest hair was compelled to hold her hair to be scalped because such locks would make a showy decoration. An Indian would have shot Adelaide who was about five years old but a little squaw jumped between and claimed the white as her slave. The wagon was ransacked and burned, the stock driven off. Then the Indians, Cheyennes, went back to camp to dance a wild scalp celebration of victory. The children were drenched to the skin by autumn rains. The eldest captive was seventeen, the next twelve, the others mere babies. They were given Mexican saddles and not treated too badly. Catherine, the eldest, probably escaped abuse by fighting like a wildcat and nearly tearing the eyes out of a young buck, who would have seized her. On horseback, this band under Kicking Horse of South Dakota, raided two hundred and thirty miles south from Fort Wallace. The two youngest children were dumped on the prairie because they became troublesome. How they ever escaped prowling wolves cannot be guessed. They were picked up by another band of Cheyennes. It was General Miles' men who rescued them almost naked and they were forwarded to Leavenworth. A year later, Miles compelled the surrender of Catherine and Sophia. Funds were raised by raffle and collection to clothe the girls till an appropriation could be made by Congress and Miles was appointed their guardian.

Very much sadder is the story of the two women whom Custer rescued on his patrol. They were Mrs. Morgan the bride of a few months and a Miss White. They had been captured in Kansas and held for eight months, but Custer had captured

GENERAL CUSTER'S PATROLS

three chiefs and held them till the two white women were delivered. Miss White was only eighteen, Mrs. Morgan nineteen. They had never seen each other till they met as captives. Miss White's father had been at work in the field when she saw four Indians enter her father's house. When she rushed to the house, the Indians spoke broken English and seemed very friendly. They asked for something to eat. The White family fed them and off went the mask of friendship. Miss White found herself grasped and being carried to a horse on which she was tied. Mrs. Morgan's capture was almost similar. Her husband was out in a field. She was stunned by a blow and came to consciousness to find herself tied on the back of a Cheyenne raider's horse. Custer heard of the girl's captivity through the eagerness of a boy to join his patrol. The lad was a brother of Mrs. Morgan. Custer forced the delivery of both women by threatening to shoot two Cheyenne chiefs on the spot. Let Custer tell the story: "The sun was perhaps an hour high when the dim outlines of about twenty mounted figures were discerned against the horizon . . . two or three miles to the west of us. . . . Securing my field glass . . . I could only determine at first that the group was composed of Indians . . . two figures mounted on the same pony. . . . Several of my companions exclaimed, 'Can they be the girls?' One seemed to have a short heavy figure . . . the other was slender. Young Brewster (Mrs. Morgan's brother) . . . responded, 'the last must be my sister . . . she is tall. . . . Let us go and meet them. This is more than I can endure.' But this I declined fearing it might provoke young Brewster beyond control. The two figures approached near enough to enable one clearly to determine they were really white. . . . Three senior officers went beyond our lines to conduct the two girls to camp. Young Brewster bounded away and was running at full speed to greet his long-lost sister. He clasped in his arms the taller of the two girls. In a moment officers and men were struggling to take them by the hand. Eyes filled with tears. They were clothed in dresses made from flour sacks. Both wore leggings and moccasins and their hair in two long braids. I had a white woman in camp who enabled them to improve their wardrobe. . . ."

The two had been sold from camp to camp and abused by both squaws and men. They were used as transport beasts of burden and seldom had more than a little raw meat to eat. They were beaten unmercifully by the squaws.

Making a brief halt at Camp Supply, Custer passed Fort Hayes and came to Fort Dodge (Wallace). Here awaited Mrs. Morgan's husband. Neither could express their gratitude to the troops. A collection was taken up by the troops to enable them to go back East where Mrs. Morgan inherited a considerable property. She lived for a few years after her restoration but died insane from her memories.

Such were the heroic duties of the little patrols.

PART VIII

NEW MIGRATIONS FOCUS ON THE HOLY TRAIL

CHAPTER XVII

FIVE MIGRATIONS FOCUS ON THE HOLY TRAIL

FIVE migrations began to focus on the Holy Trail and to create what we now regard as a Pacific Empire.

Fifty years before the California War brought in new territories under the Stars and Stripes; in fact, from the days of Gray's discovery of Columbia River, whalers and other sea hunters had paused going north and paused again going south to buy provisions from the Spaniards in California. Lemons, fresh fruits, vegetables, prevented scurvy among the ship crews. On the Pacific was a peculiar form of barnacle, a worm, which left a shell beautiful as flowers embossed in lime: but "the sea worm" as the sailors called it riddled to a honey comb stem and stern, and stuck fast to all ship timbers below water line as it sticks fast yet to a whale's sides. I have watched whales come in at night to scrape their skin of these parasites by floundering and splashing against sharp rocks; but rocks sharp as knives in a high tide were dangerous to ships; so for scraping they came in to Spanish ports along California. The favorite ports were Los Angeles, Monterey, San Francisco, where the ranches and missions had provisions, tallow, oakum, timber, for sale or barter. The Spaniards of Old Mexico did not like these Washington ships, which the Indians called "Bostonnais," intruding on their closed sea, but so far from base of action in Mexico City, both missions and ranches largely ignored the orders to give no help to Americans' ships. They wanted the oriental spices, condiments, silks, corn, which the traders proffered. They might officially "shoo" them out; but privately they welcomed them in and treated them with regal hospitality.

Then, when Spanish power was ousted by revolution after revolution, the new republics of Mexicans reversed the policy of old Spain and opened their embraces to the intruders. The reason was plain. The revolutionists, and there were fourteen revolutions in ten years, had to have firearms and bullets and pistols and swords and what not. It sounds as if California could not have been a very peaceful habitat in such days of disorder. The very reverse was the truth. Outside the presidios, the general population did not take these revolutions very seriously. The period from 1821 to 1846 was really a Utopian era in California life. The missions with adobe walls, the ranches with the same type of wall round dwellings and stables, were

FREIGHTING WITH AN OXCART

FREIGHTING WITH DONKEYS

A MEXICAN ADOBE HUT

DWELLING OF A NATIVE RANCHER

really little independent republics, where the good will of the Indian was protection and each little settlement had become self-sufficient for its own needs. The climate made living conditions easy. The vines introduced by the friars gave raisins, grapes, and wines; the cattle and sheep grazing on ten thousand hills required no winter housing and afforded hides and wool, which again the friars had taught the Indians how to weave in blankets and clothing. It was an easy delightful leisurely life in an easy delightful sunny clime. People did not just exist to fight a harsh climate or to fight what was still more difficult—intervals of hard times. They lived independent of vicissitudes which created a hard life.

From the time when Lewis and Clark's expedition had opened the Northwest to a procession of fur traders up the Missouri and across the plains by boat and horse brigades, many a fur trader's platoon or brigade had drifted south of the Columbia to California. Many a fur hunter had stumbled down to California bounds. The fur traders' life was a perilous one to scalps and health. Men wore out with terrible speed. Those whose health or courage was broken remembered California. A few dollars to the revolutionist who chanced to be on top would purchase ranch areas in thousands of acres. This drift of migration began in a dribble at first but after the discovery of gold became a stampede.

But prior to this migration, was another which had prepared for it. The holy friars, who had come back to their missions after the terrible massacres of the 1680's, had come overland through desert and mountain defile northward from Mexico City and Sonora and Sinaloa to the Trail of the Holy Faith, which long ago had led Coronado as far north as Kansas.

Then came the discovery of gold on the heels of the Mexican War. If the discovery had come before the war, Mexicans might have said it was an attempt by a colossus of the north to gobble up a little independent republic; but the discovery came a year after the war; and the rush of people from every section of the East and Middle West became such an insane stampede as the world had never witnessed nor has witnessed to this day. As many as sixteen thousand people a year passed along the old Overland Trail and the Oregon Highway and the Mormon trek by pushcart and wagon; but instead of following these old paths northward this movement now struck southwestward for California, some by Fort Hall across the narrow section of the Inland Desert, some across Utah, the broad belt of greatest peril from lack of water, yet others from Santa Fe southwestward across that Mohave Desert of Death, the most dangerous jornada of all.

Though the winners of the prize in the gold-mining lottery drew millions in a few years and men began to think in millions where they had formerly thought only in hundreds of thousands, the majority of the stampeders found themselves poorer than if they had stuck and plugged on a slower, surer path to security as lawyers, doctors, carpenters, or farmers, but having exhausted their all in rushing to the new Eldorado of blasted hopes, they had not the means to go back. Costs of food were enormous—almost starvation prices. Of housing at many mining centers, there was none. Tent roof had to be used. The rifle and fishing line gave food. It is almost comical to read in many a poor boy's letters back East that "California afforded no agricultural possibilities." The hills browned by the summer sun, the gold areas of sand, the nugget pockets in rocks did not look like agricultural lands; but the hordes of men and women stuck fast by necessity began to revise that bad depressing first verdict. When the rains came, the browned land changed to deep emerald green —the pasture for cattle and sheep. The waters tumbling tumultuous from the snowy peaks shouting a jubilate of triumph gave good water for man and beast. What is more, it gave water for irrigation ditches and flumes. Families began to stay and plant fruit farms and buy the black cattle of Mexico and the woolly herds of sheep, which meant permanent settlement, a new Pacific Empire. When the gold rush subsided, prices for food, for cattle, for sheep, dropped like a stone. Cattle could be bought for five dollars a head, sheep and lambs for one dollar and a half to seventy-five cents; and ruined argonauts sticking each to his own job as doctor, lawyer, printer, carpenter, could earn enough to buy a supply of stock and begin life anew. The doctors taking fees in nuggets at one dollar and a half or "six bits"; the boys handy as carpenters earning five dollars a day as builders, the printer at five dollars a day either paid in nuggets or notes or shares in the little plant, where he slept over a counter and cooked his own meals; these presently became governors, rich merchants, influential editors, rail builders. Huntington of the Central Pacific had begun as a merchant and ended a rail millionaire. Families beginning as squatters round Los Angeles and then buying lots at a few dollars, or camping on the arid hills round San Francisco and San Diego, buying lots for permanent homes, found themselves at middle life by no virtue but that of necessity owners of real estate priceless in value.

There was riffraff. There was scum. There was crime rampant. It was like the backwash of an evil smelling tide, which the outwash carried away; but it all led to the migration of settlement. This came slowly from the East at first, then as reports brightened, the slower movement became a permanent upbuilding of the new Pacific Empire.

There were a lot of curious coincidences in these migratory movements, which people ascribe to manifest Destiny, to Providence, to God. I shall set down a few. Then you can apply any explanation that seems adequate.

The discovery of gold came almost simultaneously with the terrible Whitman Massacres, which stemmed the tide to Oregon.

The revolutions from Spanish control were all contemporaneous with the migrations of Americans to California.

The revolutions, which continued under republican Mexico, had disgusted the best Mexicans in California with any control from Mexico City. They began to despair of any stable government under revolutionist leaders and were therefore ready to welcome any stable government, British or American.

The unutterable stupidity of the British government in rejecting the proposal of Sir George Simpson to swap the bad debts of Mexico for California left the field open for a stable government under Americans.

Governor McLoughlin of the Hudson's Bay Company—of whose plans more presently—made the mistake of sending as envoy to San Francisco his own son-in-law, Glen Rae. The latter again made the double mistake of backing the weakest revolutionist there and of falling in love with a Spanish señorita, which alienated him from Governor McLoughlin. He blew his brains out leaving as a legacy for the Hudson's Bay Company forty thousand dollars of worthless debts contracted for supplies to the defeated Mexican leader.

Fremont the army man, Stockton the navy leader, chanced to be in California ports just when the Mexican War broke out and really paved the way for Kearny's victories.

The friars, too, on the discontinuance of financial help from the King's Treasure Box of Old Spain and the dismantling of their missions, had no motive for loyalty to Mexico City authorities and were eager for a stable government.

So one could go on and enumerate many motives that prepared the way for American occupation. You can call these lines which gradually came to a focus in an American California any name you like. There is hardly any historian of California who does not offer "a Manifest Destiny" as the only explanation of such divergent motives coming to a focus in a Pacific Empire.

Drake's Nova Albion of the sixteenth century might have preceded the settlements of the Atlantic colonies if England had followed that discovery up; but she did not. Nova Albion was forgotten in European wars except as the magnificent exploit of a great English sea rover. English sea traders following Cook's explorations wanted furs, not settlement. Spanish ports in California became to them points of repairing ships and buying supplies. The poor little official presidios with a few ragged soldiers and fewer dismantled guns became to them havens of refuge. The Spanish commandant might be a lion of courage but he was powerless as a protector. Indeed, the story is told of one, who, enraged beyond the bounds of patience by the impudence of a bold Indian chief seized the fellow and swung him round through the air by the hair. It was not courage the Spanish commandants lacked. It was adequate support from Mexico City for such local authority. Apaches, Comanches, Yaquis—all Indian raiders—were tireless foes. From San Diego to Monterey in 1770 were fewer than forty-three soldiers. The Yumas would behave if they received gifts; but with fewer than eleven soldiers, four religious assistants and perhaps thirty to forty civilians on surrounding ranches, what could presidios or missions do but hold what they had inside their fort walls and strive to become independent of supplies from the outside world? In 1790, two years before Gray discovered the Columbia, there were only twelve hundred whites in all California. Whether they were Americans or English, Mexicans or Spaniards, the common peril of Indian raid and of such massacres as had devastated New Mexico and Arizona in the 1680's, held all the whites in a unit for self-defense. Let it be said right here, though the missions became holders of magnificent economically independent plants, not a friar received a centavo of salary. Monterey, San Diego, Los Angeles, San Francisco, were the radiating centers for the missions. The Bostonnais' ships seem to have begun their coming and going from 1788 on, the English from Vancouver's day in the 1790's; and one of Vancouver's officers wrote of Monterey, "to live much and without care, come to Monterey; this is a great country . . . healthful . . . good bread, meat, fish . . . plenty to eat . . . one lives better here than in the most cultured court of Europe."

There is an alluring idyl of a romance, which has been told once in a novel and once in a poem. Rezanof had been sent south from the Russian settlement of Sitka in 1806 to open a commercial treaty for supplies from California. It was really, as Professor Chapman says, "a race with death" against starvation. When he came to San Francisco Bay, the Spanish commanders ordered him to keep out.

"Yes, Sir! Yes, Sir!" answered the Russian

through his sea trumpet; but he steered his ship right inside the ample harbor, beyond range of the poor presidio guns. The friars were eager to barter food. The commandant became friendly and the friendship became a family affair when the commandant's daughter, age sixteen, in all the beauty of blooming womanhood, fell in love with Rezanof, who was some thirty years her senior. He, too, fell deeply in love with the Spanish señorita, especially as love and need for supplies to Sitka coincided in a common aim; but Rezanof was a royalist officer from the Czar and like St. Denis of Louisiana in an earlier day, he had to have the court's permission for a marriage. He returned to Sitka and set out for the Czar's court. In crossing Siberia he was very ill and either died of disease or was drowned fording a river. He never returned to California. Despairing but never doubting his loyalty to her, the little señorita took the veil and became a charity nun. She lived for twenty-two years in Santa Barbara. When Sir George Simpson, Governor for the Hudson's Bay Company came to California in 1842, quite by chance, in the hearing of the nun, he told of Rezanof's death. Her dark eyes were seen to gleam and her pallor to whiten. She left the room like one stricken to death. She lived on to 1857 and died, Chapman says, "the most cherished figure in the romance of California." Bret Harte relates the romance in imperishable verse.

The romance has almost a parallel in Glen Rae's when he came to California to negotiate Simpson's plans for the purchase of California by a swapping of bad debts. Rae's romance was a forbidden one. He already had a wife, a devout Roman Catholic from whom no divorce would be recognized by McLoughlin, who was also a devout Catholic. Whether Glen Rae committed suicide because he had advanced forty thousand dollars in supplies to the revolutionary leader who failed, or because he could not marry the Spanish girl of his choice—we do not know. He was found in his rooms with a bullet hole in his temple.

Secrecy was a necessity to ships between India and California. This was the result of the difficulty in getting papers to leave ports. It was equally necessary among competing fur trade ships from Boston. As Professor Cleland says, "a Yankee captain would take a leaky, worm-eaten craft, man it with a crew made up of broken down sailors and deserters from other vessels, sail out half way round the world in spite of storm and mutiny and make his fortune on the cargo." Sea otter was the great prize. In those days both fine seal and sea otter were found as far south as Los Angeles and San Francisco. A sea otter could be obtained in barter for a handful of nail spikes and resold in

China for from forty to two hundred dollars according to the market. One trader bought such furs for a rusty chisel and resold them for eight thousand dollars. Inasmuch as such vessels could not obtain official recognition from Californian commandants, they often made harbor in the Catalinas and took their frolic in the presidios. This was safe and satisfactory to both parties. It really put the vessels in the class of smugglers but it relieved the commandants of responsibility for receiving what the Mexican City officials called "piratical adventurers."

Sometimes a commandant of ugly temper would seize the furs of the traders, when the Yankees were apt to take law in their own hands. This happened to Shaler and Cleveland in 1803 at San Diego. The Spanish commandant seized their furs. Then he seized the sailors. Did he want to force a bribe? If so, he did not get it. Cleveland got a brace of pistols and rescued the sailors ashore from three Spanish soldiers on guard. Down came "horse and foot" to punish the Yankee free booters; but the dismantled ship was by this time up on her sea legs. She ducked the poor cannon shots from ashore and got away. Similar adventures beset Captain Eayes' vessel in 1808. His ship and crew were hustled to Santa Barbara. He was not successful in getting away and his protests bombarded the Spanish commandant at San Diego for six years. He received no redress.

Meanwhile Rezanof's ill-starred mission had obtained a settlement for the Russians eighteen miles from Bodega Bay in 1812. There a hundred Russians raised their own supplies. The fort, with good strong cannon, was called Ross. It was one hundred yards square, amid ranches for cattle. The cannon by 1821 had increased to one hundred and twenty. It was at this period the American government set up and pronounced the famous Monroe Doctrine—not over Spanish America but against Russia—that the American government would no longer recognize "the American continent as subject for future colonization by any European power."

The Russians wisely held off from any embroilment with Americans or Spanish. Furs were decreasing yearly and all they wanted was supplies. The whalers succeeded the fur hunters; and the cattle on ranches at the terminus of what used to be the western end of the old Santa Fe Trail now numbered sometimes forty thousand, sometimes ten thousand on one ranch. Ranches covered from four thousand to forty thousand acres. Hides and tallow brought in an enormous yearly revenue, from twenty-five thousand dollars to one hundred thousand dollars a year. Is it any marvel that this period became in California life the Utopian Era?

Now let us take the overland migration on the old Trail. It was to terminate in less than thirty years in what seemed to ditch Santa Fe in a back-water on seas of sand; but it did not, as we shall see. Jedediah Smith had led the procession of fur traders going first up the Missouri, then down across the Inland Desert over the Jornada, then across the Desert of Death among the Mohaves through the Cajon Pass of the Santa Fe Trail past San Bernadino. He is credited as the first American "to make the transcontinental journey to California." Either contemporaneous with him or soon after, Peter Skene Ogden from Fort Vancouver on the Columbia crossed east on the broad belt of Salt Lake and Utah. Whereas Jedediah Smith prayed and carried his Bible, poor roly-poly Peter, suffering from heat and alkali water and no water for beast or man, too often cursed both the country and his rabble of hunters; swore never again would he lead a brigade to such an arid waste of sand seas; but the very next year he would be out toiling eastward to Jackson's Hole and Pierre's Hole under the Tetons in the Rockies. Ogden was really following the later pathway of the Central Pacific and Union Pacific where Smith had been following the future right of way for the Santa Fe Railroad. We know how Smith met his death on the Cimarron and Peter lived to a good old age to rescue the victims of the Whitman Massacres.

One could give many examples of the wines, the fine food, the hospitality of all the Spanish Missions to these wayfarers of the Santa Fe Trail. While they tried to avoid the heat of torrid summers by traveling in winter when snows would avert death from thirst, they too often found themselves trapped by depths of snow in the mountain passes where horses starved to death.

People who regard these fur traders as rough irreligious toughs should read the pathetic prayer penned by one Rogers, "O God, may it please Thee in Thy divine providence to still guide us through this wilderness of doubt and fear, as Thou hast done heretofore and be with us in the hour of danger and difficulty . . . do not forsake us, Lord, but be with us and direct us through." Among the victims of Indian raiders were hundreds of fur traders just as fine as Smith. Rogers perished like Smith somewhere between the Columbia and California. Who can say the travelers on the Santa Fe Trail were not still inspired by a Holy Faith that took its toll of martyrs?

Pattie came in 1824 from the Missouri with one hundred and sixteen men and finally reached Santa Fe by November. They set out westward for California, passed Socorro, reached the Gila and with a fine cargo of furs set back for Santa Fe.

They were robbed of all their horses by Indians and cached their furs to come back for them from the Spanish settlement of Santa Fe. They found every cache robbed and golden hopes of fortune blasted. Yet Pattie like Ogden set right out again on the most dangerous trail in the West. Pattie in his fur trips pretty nearly followed the whole course of the Colorado River but he had no eyes for its majestic beauties, not he! He was too desperate for means to cross its dark tumultuous treacherous waters. To the Canyon now frequented by tourists in thousands, the Indians did not follow. They were too fearful of its "demons." A younger Pattie went as far south as that ancient Casa Grande and El Paso to try his luck at mining. He had very bad luck. Once jumping from a large bear that met him on a narrow ledge, he knocked himself senseless. His companion rushed down with a "hatful of water" and was just preparing to bleed the fallen leader, when Pattie regained consciousness and assured his "pardner" he had bled quite enough from his gashed chin. The Apaches had shot him in the hip and the arrow head stuck, so he carved it out from the bone.

Again, amazing to credit, the two Patties left Santa Fe in the fall of 1827 for the Gila westward. Here their men threatened to desert and the Patties had to stop mutiny by threatening to shoot the first malingerer. The Colorado was swelling from snow fall in the mountains and again both had to cross the Mohave without horses, only a rifle, blankets on backs, and a remnant of food. Eyes were almost blind with dust. Throats and lips swelled from lack of water. Only the discovery of a mountain stream saved the lives of the marching men. The Mission of Santa Catalina seemed a gateway to an earthly paradise. The Americans were ordered to report to San Diego and were there clapped in jail. The food was rancid tallow, dry bread, and a pint of bad water a man. Young Pattie was so furious, he threw it all down. His ignorant jailer then flung all the water and bread in Pattie's face. The younger Pattie later died of disease contracted in this prison and the father "died alone in his prison cell." Smallpox sweeping California, young Pattie offered to vaccinate the Mexicans against the epidemic. The Americans were given their freedom. Revolutions were rocking California and Mexico; so young Pattie went to Mexico City to get some redress. He got sympathy but no redress and came back to the United States by way of Vera Cruz and New Orleans. He went to Kentucky broken financially and ruined in health.

Why did these migrations of adventurous traders go on unconsciously winning an empire? For material gain just ahead like the pot of gold at the end of the rainbow? Perhaps; but also with an undying faith that the rainbow was an emblem of hope justifying faith in works. Manifest Destiny says the other side to the argument. You can take your choice right down to the Mexican War when a new coincidence comes—the gold rush.

Let us go back now to the old Spanish trail up from Mexico parallel with the sea.

It was a jornada through Apache land, through the Mohave Desert of Death; and it was tramped by the friars with seldom more than fourteen soldiers to protect them. Yet they carried church ornaments, farm tools, and seeds for the orchards soon to become so famous and to lay the foundations of California in a great fruit industry. I shall quote only the brief description of one commander dated about 1773. "We reached Monterey after struggling thirty-eight days . . . through an ungracious country . . . of rocks, brushwood, rugged mountains where we were without food and did not know where we were. . . . We seemed all under hallucinations." Any desert traveler knows that sensation from mirages, from exhaustion, from hunger, from dreaming in half sleep, half drowsy delirium, of the waters that could not be found and the food so scarce.

"At the end of each day's march, I ordered that one weak old mule should be killed . . . for food. We shut our eyes and fell on that scaly old mule like hungry lions. When we entered San Diego, we smelt frightfully of mules. . . . We remained nine months at San Diego waiting for ships . . . and refreshing ourselves on geese and fish. . . . We had scarcely clothing to cover our backs . . . the ship brought corn, flour and rice. . . . We then went on to reconnoiter the port of San Francisco, a labyrinth of bays . . . where the natives were very friendly and gentle."

Such was the Via Dolorosa by way of the south to the north. It could be paralleled by many such records officially sent back by commandants and friars to heads in Mexico City. Full of superstition these records may be, full of miracles easily explained, by men taking desperate chances with death but all animated by a quenchless faith and undying ardor. California was peopled by this trail as far north as the Sacramento, as far east as Santa Fe. Every blessed place was given a name prefaced by a saint. Do you wonder? The first comers had need of faith in saints or they would not have had courage to go ahead.

It is almost pathetic to set down that the gold which the Spaniards ever sought was under their feet. The oil which far exceeded the yields of gold had not yet been discovered, and the fruit industry which was to exceed all had barely begun outside mission fort walls.

Such were the first great migrations. The next came in the mad gold rush.

CHAPTER XVIII

HUMAN GHOULS AND VULTURES ON THE HOLY TRAIL

SOME description has been given in *The Overland Trail* of the pirate criminal type infesting every No-Man's-Land: the border ruffians, who set out with skull and cross-bones on their flag, traded liquor and firearms to the raiding Indians, invaded lonely settler cabins to terrify women and children, ran off stock and usually came to their merited fate, from cross-bars erected between wagons with a noose dangling below for the neck.

But there was a more insidious crafty type of criminal on the Santa Fe Trail. It is axiomatic in all Indian lands that a lone settler or two partners cannot go in the wilderness and not be reported as "going in," or "coming out." Like sails at sea amid far distant ports of call, the departures or returns are duly noted; and if there is no return, in the chronicle of the sea is set down the taking toll of so many lives. Likewise of the lonely wilderness prairie then attracting so many settlers. Some settlement, some army patrol, a chance traveler, was sure to report a couple going in. Where were they going? Where were they last seen? Had they money or other valuables on their person? Where had they settled? Had they come out? To this day in the Far North, a sort of moccasin telegram keeps tab on the movements of hunters and settlers, and when two partners go in and only one comes out, the Mounted Police patrol have a way of examining the abandoned homestead shack. If the slimmest trace of crime has been noticed, a new-made grave, a filled-in well, a stained axe, that clue must be taken up and pursued to earth's ends. Cases could be cited where the clue led to China, from China back to Texas, from Texas to the scene of the crime, and within a few weeks to trial and conviction and execution.

In the migratory throngs then traversing the plains, similar types of criminals began to come in. It was a No-Man's-Land. Roads crossed thither and yon to Santa Fe, to California, to Oregon, to new settlements in Kansas. There a family might set itself down, knock up a cheap road house and by serving meals to passers-by make quicker, easier, surer money than by the slow plugging on a homestead or wild lottery in a mine. In the passing throngs were soldiers, settlers, adventurers, Germans, Swiss, Swedes, Norwegians, Russians, and Americans from every part of the

United States. Amid such colonists came in a family called the Benders. This story has been told by Edith Connelley Ross in the Kansas Historical Collection of 1926-28. It is told in a classic recital that out-herods fiction.

In 1871, "the Bender family simply appeared." They pushed on with wagon and team and family across the southeastern corner of Kansas. They squatted where four cross-roads east, west, south, and north seemed to promise good returns to an eating-house: but there were unusual features about this family. People in the new West did not usually question much about the past. Bygones were bygones. Start anew. But they had a rough good-natured curiosity about present plans. Colonists from the same sections usually settled together —Germans with Germans, Swiss with Swiss, Missouri folk with old neighbors. No one seemed to know whence these Benders had come. A roadhouse went up where a well had been dug. Partitions for sleeping apartments consisted of cheap colored cotton hung from bars at right angles. The big room outside combined kitchen and dining purposes. There was nothing unusual in all that. You can see to-day similar road-houses in all settlements far from rail centers. There was a cook stove. There were candles for light. There was a rough table. There were crude beds like the berths in a ship. The modern location of the mystery family is twelve miles from Thayer, five miles from Cherryvale.

Nothing extraordinary in the location so far: but it was over the family itself that mystery seemed to hang in an impenetrable curtain. The curtain somehow seemed to resemble a shroud. The family gave many an army officer a guess. It was an inexplicable enigma. The father and mother were German peasants of the roughest type, between fifty and sixty years of age. They were sickly, stooped, stolid, a sullen silent pair, almost like human ghouls. Neighbors compared the big whiskered father to a hairy gorilla. The very opposite were the two children. The son about twenty-four was fair-haired, erect, tall, handsome. It did not take much figuring to guess that these Germans had dated the births of these children about the time of the great German migration in the 1840's; but it was in the daughter that the contrast became startling. Kate Bender was perhaps a year younger than her brother. She held herself erect with the haughty pose of a queen. Her hazel eyes were of great depth and brightness, her lips very red and full but delicate in outline, and her hair a glory of Titian red. She moved with light airy grace, talked vivaciously and was intensely interested in the spirit rapping and other spiritualistic phenomena then a vogue. She liked company, went to church, sang well and sent many a young farmer back to his lonely bachelor homestead with visions of red hair and hazel eyes.

Whence had come such a daughter to such parents? Was she a throwback to some worthier ancestor, or a lawless waif adopted from some noble family in Germany? Older thoughtful heads could not help asking themselves these questions. She was as alien to her surroundings as a song-bird amid vultures, and as vultures the Benders seemed soon to be classed for no valid reason but their own extraordinary establishment. The road-house had the sign "meals, lodgings, groceries." There was a trap-door in the floor leading to a cellar which had another outlet to the yard. Dirt, disorder, flies were everywhere.

What set rumor going at first in whispers was the fact that many a wayfarer, who paused at the Benders' for a night's lodging, was never seen to go on or come back. There seemed to be hay in a stone barn for the traveler's ox or horse. Kate bloomed out as a faith-curer and first gained business by working in a hotel at Cherry Vale where her claims became known as a spiritualist. Was Kate the beautiful bait for a deeper criminal game? It was an ugly rumor but it gained currency as more and more lodgers failed to go on or come back. The family had a trick of speaking only in German, not unusual; but their glances were evil sinister signals.

There came to army patrols and little frontier post-offices letters asking for missing relatives. These missing travelers could be traced to the Benders' but no farther. Two stalwart old women, who often wandered over the prairie pot-shooting rabbit or prairie chicken, began to relate odd experiences at the Bender shack. There were times when Kate's eyes went quite wild and she would sidle up to the old women with a mad gleam and the whisper, "the spirits command me to kill you." People did not know whether this was one of Kate's practical jokes to rid herself of garrulous long-staying neighbors, or what we would perhaps call to-day emanations of a double-personality— one sane, one insane; but the poor old Dianas of the chase took to their heels with a firmer grip on shot-gun and with tales to make their neighbors' eyes pop. However, their gossipy evidence became later terribly vital. One of the elderly wandering pot-shooters told how when a traveler leaned his chair against the bar partition waiting for his meal he chanced to glance at the ceiling. The shadow on the ceiling played odd tricks. It looked as if an ax or hammer behind the flimsy partition were raised to come down on the traveler's head. He raised the curtain. Either the candle behind was extinguished by the draft, or was it all a trick of shadows? That traveler did not stay over night and he came out. A well known priest of the Jesuits had a similar experience. He felt the atmosphere of a criminal haunt and made his horse, tied out in the gathering storm, an excuse to decamp.

The crisis came in the disappearance of a Dr. York in 1873. He had a brother—Colonel York—in the army. Dr. York was traced to the Bender house. Colonel York took up the clues from Fort Scott to the Benders', where all clues stopped. He then came back with a posse of men. The Benders said Dr. York had stopped for the night and gone on. Kate asked Colonel York to stay for the night. "I'll find your brother for you, even if he is in hell," Kate boasted of her spiritualistic powers. Colonel York gave her a chance to explore those shady realms.

Here the story of the Benders splits—one story, that given out for the public, one what really happened. When Colonel York came back with picks and spades, the Benders had vanished. Only the little yipping terrier barked lonely about the place; but the cellar was found full of blood-spattered clothing and in a garden patch well hidden was found a deep grave crammed with bones of the dead. By this time, neighbors were gathering in hundreds. There was evidence of hurried flight, rags, dirty dishes, beds disordered.

Dr. York's body was found amid the bones in the garden patch. An iron hammer in the house fitted the broken skull. So much for facts given to the public.

Colonel York did indeed come back for the promised séance and with him came a posse. Each man took an oath of silence at "the mouth of a smoking pistol." The Benders did disappear and they disappeared there and then to eternity. Before neighbors came back at sunrise, the Benders had been cleaned out like "a den of copperheads." Only the little dog seems to have escaped. Victims had been identified by clothing found in the pit and sent home to relatives.

Of quite another character was the one great stain against the army record, or rather against Colonel Chivington's Volunteers of Colorado. Public sentiment had been terribly incensed by an Indian raid and massacre in Minnesota. I prefer to quote General Miles: "The Sand Creek massacre is . . . the foulest and most unjustifiable crime in the annals of America. It was planned and executed under the personal direction of J. M. Chivington, Colonel of the First Colorado Cavalry, on the 27th of November, 1864, at a point in Colorado about forty miles from Fort Lyon. . . . But for this horrible butchery it is a fair presumption that all the subsequent wars with the Cheyennes and Arapahos and their kindred tribes might have . . . been averted. In the Indian Peace Commission of 1868, the statement is made.

... 'It scarcely has its parallel in the records of Indian barbarity. Fleeing women and children holding up their hands and praying for mercy were shot down; infants were killed and scalped: men were tortured and mutilated. No one will be astonished that a war ensued, which cost the government thirty millions and carried conflagration and death to the border settlements.' " It only illustrates with what strict discipline it was necessary to hold the troops for the army and how important it was to hand-pick volunteers.

Of a much similar character was the border ruffianism at Lawrence. Missouri was largely peopled by southerners, Kansas by northerners. Kansas borders became the cock-pit of fights over slave and free. It was easy for border ruffians under the flag to raid little towns famous in their stand for the free. Quantrill was the leader of these Missouri guerrillas. To illustrate how chaotic frontier justice was at the time, the story is told of a rough fellow in 1868 coming on another charge before a judge. He boasted of his raids under Quantrill's Band in Lawrence. The judge was a sympathizer with Missouri. "You're a d— fool for tellin' it. I discharge ye for want of ividence."

Perhaps it is well to let these sleeping dogs lie. There were many of what General Sears called Paul Revere Rides to save the doomed city of

Lawrence. The ghastly part is that each side in the fight considered itself in the right; and so each was in a measure; but in the shift and drift of contending sides, lawlessness slipped between and wrought its usual evil.

William Connelley tells of one of the Paul Revere Rides to save Lawrence from Quantrill's band of ruffians.

"When the guerrillas had gone from her house, Mrs. Jennings determined to send tidings to Lawrence . . . with her servant and children she went to the home of William Guest, who lived half a mile north. Guest would not believe her story and she could not prevail on him to go to Lawrence. Henry Thompson, a Negro, who was working for Guest offered to go if Guest would furnish a horse for him to ride. Guest refused. Thompson then set forth afoot to do the best he could for the doomed city. A justice of the peace came upon Thompson on his way . . . Thompson soon told his story. . . . The peace officer hurried back sounding the alarm. . . ." Citizens gathered and heard the account of the passing of Quantrill. Volunteers to go to Lawrence were called for and three responded. . . . "Of these, one was thrown from his horse. He never recovered from the fall." The other two rode at a wild gallop in the direction of Lawrence. They had reached an intersection of roads at dawn. One was mounted on a fine black Kentucky mare called "Crow." She stumbled and fell. The rider was crushed to death. By the time aid was called for the crushed man, Quantrill was entering Lawrence.

A Shawnee Indian was another of the heroic riders to save Lawrence from Quantrill's raiders. The Shawnee was given an army horse, a sorrel mare, a Kentucky racer. It was one in the morning when garbed as an Indian, the Shawnee "mounted to race against fate." He knew the timber clumps and kept to no beaten highway. He was going at terrific speed, the mare in long regular strides, neck straightened, nose thrown well forward. Her breath coming hard, the Shawnee pulled her down for rest, rubbed her limbs, her quivering flanks, her head. He cleaned her mouth of foam and allowed her to drink a little water, then he remounted and again rode away. The mare had found her second wind. . . . Miles melted under the steady hoof beats. . . . Round a long sweep of the winding trail, the Shawnee saw far to the southwest the black line that marked Lawrence and he knew if his faithful mare could hold her pace another hour he could save the city. . . . "At the top of a hill she faltered. The Shawnee was a man of resource. He was racing with death . . . so he resolved to urge her with a death stab. She bounded forward for a few miles, plunged in death and with a cry of protest almost human, pitched forward dead." The Shawnee sprang from the falling mare and raced on afoot. He saw far down the forest aisles the cabins of Delaware (Indians). He sounded his "quavering war cry. He took an Indian pony and recklessly rode for the Lawrence ferry." He reached the goal only to hear the roar of battle and the city doomed.

"On the fateful morning of Friday, August 23, 1863, outlying villages could see the city in flame. In Lawrence perished by sheer murder one hundred and fifty-three unarmed men."

Why on all holy trails the ghouls stalk and the vultures flock is one of the enigmas of life. Why do not these creatures of prey, beast and bird, keep to their own kind? Perhaps it is as Eastern legends aver that to keep the faith holy, the Sifter, the Adversary is always tirelessly at work.

CHAPTER XIX

BEFORE AND DURING THE GOLD RUSH

JUST before the Mexican War, a drift of emigration to California overland had begun. The great Twin Panic of 1837-38 had passed and hard times were picking up. The minor panic in 1857 had not begun. The great colonization movement of Germans in 1848 did not yet afford Americans in the Middle West the golden chance to sell good homestead lands at from twenty dollars to thirty dollars an acre and move to a genial clime where ranches of four thousand to forty thousand acres could be bought for a song from contending revolutionists; but climatic conditions in the Middle West were not easy to people over forty years of age. The work was a race to get crops in before the dry summers, to harvest before early rains; and of connections with an outside market, there were none. Not a rail extended till later beyond modern Chicago. Perhaps that is one explanation. What profit to race yourself to death to get crops in when there was no market for them?

Yet, when you look deeply, there were economic

reasons. Three concrete examples, which came to me as I wrote these pages, explain. A hundred years ago, it was customary among neighboring farmers, who knew one another's families well, for the man with a less numerous family than his neighbor, or with better soil, to take as apprentice on his farm a boy from a near farm. The lad was apprenticed by drawn contract from early age to twenty-one to work. All wages were to be paid only to his father—from two dollars or three dollars a month with keep to perhaps ten dollars or fifteen dollars at twenty-one. It may have been because a boy was careless of his pantaloons. It may have been because the family taking him in as a member of their own circle had little to spare; but in some contracts it was stipulated that the boy had to supply his own "patches for pantaloons." Imagine the sense of freedom that such a lad would feel on reaching twenty-one. He longed to kick free of thraldom. He heard of a land far away, which he could reach by acting as "mule skinner"—that is driver—at five dollars to ten dollars and keep, as "boss of five or ten wagons" at ten dollars to twenty dollars; as captain of a caravan at forty dollars a month; and he could have glorious adventure all the way west for six months and reach his destination with from sixty dollars to two hundred and forty dollars, more cash than he had ever seen in all his previous life. He could reach California and buy a ranch of four thousand acres for twenty-six dollars, lambs for two dollars and fifty cents, cattle for five dollars a head, horses for from ten dollars to twenty dollars. As for each ranch being a little independent, self-sufficient kingdom, had not his ancestors peopled the country from New England to Pennsylvania in that very way? Was not every household seated round its hearthfires full of such tales and adventures with Indians? Indians and scalp raids? Pah! Give him a gun and he could take care of himself.

Take another case hardly a hundred years old. I was driving past an old Indian burial ground with an old gentleman. I was asking about the old cemetery now with stones flat amid weeds and pasture lots. "That is not my most intense memory of this valley when I was a boy. The mansion house has been burned down; but I recall I was nervous about passing it—it was supposed to be haunted because the father was such a brutal tyrant he used to beat his wife and she died from the effects of such a beating. I suppose in those days, he regarded his wife as a chattel, whom he could treat less mercifully than he did a cow; and he was rich, too, so well off people were afraid of him; but his wife is supposed to have interfered with his treatment of his children—"

"And what became of his children?"

"Oh, of course, they ran away west as soon as they were big enough to run away."

The last example is of a different character. There is in one of the most beautiful valleys of lower New York, what is now known as the Locust Valley School for children who live an almost ideal life outdoors summer and winter with work and play. Over seven hundred acres had been cleared in the lap of the hills amid hard wood forests. The pass through the hills was so narrow, that Indian raiders would hardly penetrate it. It was a little self-sufficient kingdom in itself. The old mansion-house stands yet intact as a dormitory; but the heads of the school have built for themselves beautiful little bungalow cabins above a stream. What was my amazement to find to the rear of one cabin an old tombstone erect as the day it was raised, with the inscription "Vanderburgh —died 1688." Who in the West needs to be told that this was the ancestor of the Van der burghs famous as fur company leaders from Lewis and Clark's day? As the family grew more numerous, the younger sons pushed west to do what the ancestors had done soon after Manhattan was transferred from Dutch to English and transformed from English Colony to American Republic.

All this gave the west a fine brave stock of humans to lay foundations for a new Pacific Empire.

Other explanation apart from economic really

lies in the character of California itself. There was a genial clime all the year round. There the black cattle could range in the hills and the sheep run unhoused. There each ranch itself could become a little self-sufficient republic. It was an easy life. There not sections of six hundred and forty acres could be preempted free, but vast ranches of four thousand to forty thousand acres could be bought for few dollars. Often as many as one hundred vessels lay rocking in the harbors of Monterey, San Diego, Los Angeles, San Francisco Bay, eager to carry cargoes of dried cattle hides back round the Horn to Boston. There the leather really laid the foundations of the shoe factories in Massachusetts. Equally eager were these vessels for cargoes of wool, which laid the foundations of another industry in the East. Industrially East and West were becoming one before the advent of the steel rail bound all in unity. Tallow, fruit, mutton, dried beef, wheat, could always be sold for supplies to the whalers and fur traders farther north.

Fremont's explorations by land to the Columbia and from the Columbia south to California had made California fairly well known—so well known that President Polk would willingly have paid up to forty millions of dollars for California. Wilkes's expeditions by sea had added to the general knowledge of the Pacific Coast. Both proclaimed California an empire capable of expanding in population to forty million people. Revolution after revolution was rocking California. It was like ripe fruit waiting to drop in any mouth open under the tree. Perhaps Kit Carson's explanation is the simplest of all. "Well," he drawled, "I began in Kentucky. I reached the Missouri and the Mississippi. Then I crossed the plains. Then from the mountains, I came to Santa Fe and here I am on the Pacific Coast." So there you are! Debate any explanation you like! Through a chaos of hardships, of deaths, of sufferings untellable in the mountains to the point of cannibalism among white people—the urge lured and pushed settlers to California before the gold stampede. The drift had begun from Oregon before the California War.

There were Western Emigration Societies from Missouri to Massachusetts. One was led by John Bidwell of Ohio from the Missouri in the spring of 1841. "We knew," says Bidwell, "that California lay west and that was the extent of our knowledge." Hard to credit, there were fifteen women and children in this party. Each member supplied his own food, arms, horses, mules, oxen. Of money, says Cleland—"there was less than one hundred dollars cash" in the entire party. Fitzpatrick, a Rocky Mountain fur trader, acted as guide part of the way.

KANSAS CITY, 1872, LOOKING EAST ON 10TH ST. FROM ROOF OF COATES HOUSE

Courtesy G. C. Hebard Collection
FORT HALL, NEAR POCATELLO

From "The Life of Frémont." From collection Dr. G. C. Hebard, Wyoming Univ.
FRÉMONT ADDRESSING THE INDIANS AT FORT LARAMIE

From Westport (Kansas City) the emigrants followed up the Platte. Laramie and Independence Rock were passed. They then came to the famous South Pass. On the fur trader's advice, they went on north to Pocatello, Idaho, where they hoped to cross the narrow section of the desert. There the trouble began. The fur traders went on north to Fort Hall. There thirty-two of the emigrants also decided to go north to the Columbia. One woman, Mrs. Kelsey, and her daughter went on to California. The quest was not unlike the old Negress' response to an evangelist. "Where I'm gwine, I don't know where; and how I'm gwine, I don't care"; and she danced on. Utah and Nevada were bewildering. Thirst drove the travelers nearly mad and mirages led them astray. They abandoned wagons and pressed ahead on foot and on horseback.

At Humboldt River—Ogden's old trail, which he cursed—eight men on horseback hurried forward for help from California. Twenty-five pressed on for the Sierras. They were terribly alarmed at the slender prospect of getting through alive. They turned south and killed the last ox for food. The eight scouts on horseback now came back baffled. They could find no direct path west, so all struck south in frantic haste to get through the Sierras before snow fall. They came on the head waters of the Stanislaus. This was a dangerously rough gorge and all animals had to be killed. When they struck the river they were down to a diet of coyotes; but from the stream on their hearts almost burst with joy. There were antelope so tame they were easily killed. There were ripe grapes. There were green well watered valleys. They reached the ranches in November. It was from such ancestors that California like Oregon was first peopled.

The Russian settlement of Bodega Bay had passed into the hands of John Sutter, a Swiss, who had bought out the Russian fort. There he had set out a little kingdom of his own, a fort, cannon, wheat fields, flour and lumber mills, herds of cattle, weaving plants for wool, a launch down to San Francisco. There, to make himself strong enough to defy Indian attack, he welcomed all settlers. People from Oregon were helped by Sutter. By 1845, Cleland says there were 250 new colonists overland in California. Clyman, whose journal is so often quoted on the Oregon Trail, was one of the Bidwell party. The cost for a concession of land fifty-three square miles was twenty-six dollars. The rewards were richer than the pot of gold at the end of the rainbow trail; and word of these went back east in letters that often cost two dollars and fifty cents in postage and required six months in transit.

Advertisements began to appear in New York

papers of emigration societies, with the significant phrase tacked on to the tail, "every person is expected to be well armed with rifle, heavy shotgun and ample shot and lead." Cattle could be bought in California for five dollars, mares for six dollars, sheep at two dollars. No need to clutter and hamper swift movement by taking these along.

The Donner party was one of the saddest in all the overland migrations. It was led by George and Jacob Donner in 1846. It numbered two hundred people and fared well to old Fort Bridger. There the majority elected to go north by way of Fort Hall across the narrow belt of desert. Eighty-seven decided to go across by Salt Lake. The two bands planned to meet on the Humboldt River. The big band got across safely to California. The small group lost time rounding south of Salt Lake. Stock was fagged, food scarce, panic frayed nerves to jumpy judgment. Disputes waxed to quarrels, quarrels to delays, delays to death among horses and mules. Wagons had to be left and women and children floundered forward on foot.

Near Reno, Nevada, a relief party sent back by Sutter gave food enough; but it became the usual race against death to get through the Sierras. The snow caught the marchers near Truckee City. Those with strength got through the Sierras. Each storm deepened the snow for weary laggards, incapable of quick pace. It was necessary to winter in the snow; but the deep snow robbed animals of fodder and they disappeared in the storms. Of course, game had "holed up" or receded to lower levels; snow walls during winter are thirty feet deep. Camps of wood and canvas were knocked up.

Then seventy-nine people faced starvation. Fourteen were women, thirty-eight were children. Five women and two men reached a ranch in the Sacramento. The main camp behind has been known as the Camp of Death. Those who survived in delirium ate the flesh of the dead.

Relief parties came from Sutter by February and April. In one camp was found only one poor living skeleton of bones and skin. How he survived was self-evident. The bones told plainly how. He lived an outcast for the rest of his life. Only forty-five survived the winter.

The Donner party was the most tragic; and fair minded people prefer to drop the curtain on the guilty. The guilty were insane from hardship. In the far north, similar tragedies occurred on scientific expeditions, such as that of searchers for Franklin, almost contemporaneous in date.

Then came the Mexican War and a year later— the gold stampede.

Every new era has its birth pangs. The darkest hour at midnight precedes the dawn. Let us try to picture what would happen now if a new gold area were found, in which pure nuggets could be washed out, or dug out with a jack-knife, exceeding a billion dollars in a couple of years. You cannot picture it. The kaleidoscope reels off too fast for eye or fancy to follow. At first, people said, "Impossible!" The nuggets of six pounds went back east to prove the truth. People did not go mad from starvation then. They went mad, delirious, insane with a subtler poison—greed. Wise the man, steady the head, that stuck to "his last" and "plugged on his job" and took his pay in gold. Wise the dame who opened an eating-house, washed for the miners and took her pay in gold dust and nuggets; and many a woman of good birth and better sense did that. She came out financially better than the woman who had put her all in a mine hole. Some drew a prize. The majority drew a blank; but shopkeeper and general worker amassed wealth, which reinvested in city lots and rail systems left the owners like Stanford and Huntington multimillionaires.

In one of Sutter's mills, a man named Marshall noticed some glittering sands. He picked them out. They were gold pebbles and gold sand to the value of five dollars. Other little gold bits had been found elsewhere but not to the value of five dollars each. Why the Spaniards never found gold in California, I have told. They did not dare go inland or away from presidios with fewer than a dozen ragged lawless soldiers. If they had discovered gold it is a guess with fate if the United States would ever have possessed California. It might have been a northern province of Mexico. For a few weeks Sutter and Marshall kept the secret and obtained mining rights; but teamsters and workmen let the secret out and by May, all California was talking. When a messenger came down to Monterey, he met a sea of "upturned faces" and as he dismounted his horse and drew lumps of pure gold from his pocket, people simply rushed home to dash for the mines. Husband and wife, says Cleland, packed all night. The blacksmith dropped his hammer, the carpenter his plane, the mason his trowel, the farmer his sickle, the baker his loaf, the tapster his bottle. All were off for the mines, on horses, on crutches, on litters. One woman departed before her lodgers had time to pay bills. The only human beings left were prisoners and their keepers. San Francisco went wilder. Crews left ships. Newspapers quit be-because they had no printers. Not a magistrate was left in town.

Two men in a week took out one thousand seven hundred dollars in pure gold. Some averages ran one hundred dollars a day to each digger. Within six months six hundred thousand dollars had been taken. Steadiest heads went dizzy. Oregon was almost deserted. The East was no longer skeptical. The odd thing was that for once facts surpassed exaggerated fancy. The Eastern press was filled with advertisements telling how to go to California and what to carry along from lamp glasses to canned soups. Travel clubs had to put up two hundred and fifty dollars each to take passage to California by sea or overland, which was entirely inadequate as the sequence records. Fifty vessels departed from the East by the spring of 1849, two hundred and thirty later, and seventeen thousand persons took passage. At least eighteen thousand people crossed the Missouri; and over eleven hundred wagons went streaming in dust across the plains with three or four people in each. Nearly thirty-five thousand people went in a year overland. Then things became a frenzy. Ship expenses mounted to one thousand dollars for steerage by way of Panama. Here, pedlers swapped the contents of their packs at an increase of one to four dollars for provisions and mining tools. Cholera, fever, malaria, took their toll in death. Huntington was one of the pedlers, who reached Panama with one thousand five hundred dollars increased to almost five thousand dollars for his supply store on the Sacramento. Salt Lake City made a fortune selling goods. So did Santa Fe. Every trail that had ever been traversed was now followed by people who knew less of the way than a child chasing a rainbow. Wheelbarrows, "prairie schooners," horses, mules, oxen—all were used. The marvel is not that so many gold-seekers perished. The marvel is that so few did. The Fort Hall route became a favorite; and the stench of dead horses and oxen became a guide. In fifteen miles one man counted three hundred and fifty dead horses, two hundred and eighty oxen, one hundred and twenty mules. Goods had to be abandoned to permit faster pace and wagons costing one hundred and twenty dollars lay warping in the heat—three hundred and sixty-two wagons to ten miles.

Criminals were thick along the road as vultures over battle fields. The rifle and pistol in quick shot became the only umpire. Californians in a frenzy sent relief to all unfortunates on the trails. But in many cases help did not come soon enough. Meat went up in price to seventy-five cents a pound, milk to fifty cents a gallon. Butter and sugar were luxuries. Our friends Fremont, Kearny and Riley, of the war remained successively in command of troops. There were all sorts of scraps between military and civilian authorities. It took mighty quick work to organize a state local government and Burnett of Oregon became first governor. Statehood came because it must to preserve some semblance of order amid crime. Then the wild boom did what all booms do—it collapsed. There were more losers in the lottery of mining than gainers. Rents of one hundred dollars a month fell to a few dollars. Ghost cities abandoned with signs of Gomorrah, Hell Hole, Ground Hog, Hang Town were left: suburbs without a soul, of towns with not a living man or woman. It is another irony of fate that below many of these deserted mining centers, where men starved, oil later spouted, surpassing in value all the gold ever washed or dug. Explain it who can. Men called it luck and a trick of that jade— Fate.

Let us now follow some of the vessels going round the boisterous Cape Horn for the gold mines in California. Though they did not know it, they too were following a famous waterway of the Englishman Drake and the Spanish sea captains and Vancouver and such other ships as Grey's and the whalers of Boston and New Bedford. Even good old stable Philadelphia with its cautious Quaker ancestry was not exempt from the frenzy of the gold stampede. Printers had read the reports of the gold finds. Carpenters had scanned the Emigration Society advertisements for wages paid. Masons exchanged hammer and trowel for pick and spade. Young medicos guessed rightly that there would be much disease amid raw new mining camps where fees in nuggets would yield greater return than any diggings.

There was not a class of people in the Quaker City untouched by the frenzy. The fact that the vessels round the Horn escaped much of the disease taking toll on other routes may be ascribed to the length of the voyage, requiring at least seven months and setting out less crowded. Each passenger, first-class or steerage, had his own berth, bed, or hammock. Cleanliness had to be observed and the heat was never great by sea. There was no herding of passengers thick as ants on deck and a clutter of baggage that could not be stowed below hatches. If delayed by the boisterous roar of wind and wave round the Horn, there was of course the constant danger of provisions running short and scurvy setting in; but antidotes to scurvy were well known by 1848; the sea charts pretty well laid the course, showing which passages to attempt, what reefs to avoid, and above all, cautioning to keep off rocks by chancing the winds of deep seas rather than reefs hidden by the crest of billows but fearfully dangerous when the vessel dipped in the trough. Steam was by 1846 used in vessels but the supply of fuel was so uncertain between far distant ports of call that the majority of the craft going round the Horn went under sail, a great cloud of sail subject to calms but very swift with a good wind to rear. These old "windjammers" could show heels to the most of the

A WINDJAMMER

AN EXCURSION TRAIN AT 1,000 MILE TREE

BEFORE AND DURING THE GOLD RUSH

steamers. Let us follow a vessel prepared to use either sail or steam.

The crews were a pretty unruly lot. The captain had frequently to use fists, a belaying pin, the lash plied on a mutineer tied to a wheel. His job was to get his passengers safely to land and he used the weapon nearest at hand.

Enos Christman's letters written in 1849 and rescued from an attic trunk in 1930 give a most vivid picture of how the gold frenzy swept the Quaker State of Pennsylvania. He had been a printer in West Chester and the news came to him in his twentieth year. He hoped to make a quick fortune in the gold mines and return with wealth to marry the girl of his choice. For her, he kept a daily journal. He describes the bread, hard as a brickbat. The cabin passage cost two hundred dollars, the second—which was really steerage—one hundred and sixty dollars. Some of the men and a few women on board were members of emigration societies, Christman's group consisted of friends, lads like himself, and each was amply fortified with personal provisions in addition to the allowance by the ship's company. They had bread, pork, beans, dried beef. They had tents, axes, hatchets, spades, shovels, picks, nails, pots, kettles, and clothing for both warm and cold zones. To their outfitters they were to hand over fifty per cent of returns for two years. Christman had fifty dollars of his own money, two rifles, pistols, plenty of lead, powder, balls. On board were fifty-one passengers, six women of the best and worst types.

At first, so merry were the gold-seekers that they celebrated the 4th of July all night. By July 21, the ship was one thousand two hundred miles from Philadelphia. The winds so favorable at first fell to dead calm. The porpoise gamboling round the ship were a sign of bad sea weather. Christman read a chapter of the Bible each night. Nearly every ship signaled semaphored back, "Bound for California." The flying fish were, of course, only the fish with fins taking a joyous leap in air to splash back in the sea. Passengers began to bet on the time to reach California—six or eight months. As the tedium of the slow pace began to weary the travelers, midnight "busts" as Christman describes them became more frequent. Civilization began to shed to a thin veneer. There were wife beatings and quarrels over the gamblers' winnings.

The Equator was crossed August 31. Sailors and passengers celebrated the event in the usual fashion—a dip in the sea, or clown dances in fancy rags over the decks. South of the Equator began the storms. The ship rode like a gull but the wash of billows tossed furniture and passengers about in junk. When a drench came down open hatches, it set the furniture swimming. The dampening of the sea-biscuits resulted in green mould and grubs. Whales were counted in schools of sixty. As the Horn was neared, "snow fell in squalls," and from the masts hung sleet and icicles. Just one hundred days from Philadelphia, the Horn was passed. One mutinous sailor had to be flogged. The supply of fresh water fell to one quart a day per passenger. Though this resulted in loud grumbling, looking back now on the ship service of the day, the Philadelphia vessel did well. But the captain's job was no easy one. He had to pacify grumbling passengers and force unruly men, many of whom had enlisted only to reach the gold diggings, to do their duty, whether he used the lash, the belaying pin, or his own pistol. The Pacific belied its name as far north as Chile. It was tempestuous. In Valparaiso lay eighty vessels, the most bound for California. Fruit was purchased to supply the most of the passengers as far as San Francisco. It cost from twelve cents (rials) a hundred oranges to less for raisins. Postage for letters to go back home cost thirty-seven and a half cents each. A week before Christmas, the vessel left Valparaiso and sped on north for San Francisco.

February 7, 1850, the yell "Land ho!" announced the first glimpse of rugged rocks near San Francisco Bay. It was foggy and the captain "lay off" until the 11th, when the bay was entered. Alas for high hopes. The town looked like a mud hole. Few of the boys had more than a pocketful of small change left. They camped outside "the mud hole" and began to try their hand at cooking. Four days later, one of the group died from that frail health which ought not to have risked the rough and tumble of frontier hardships. "Thousands will curse the day that brought them to this golden land," wrote Christman. He began to understand that roseate hopes are one thing, realization another and plugging through prosaic work is a surer pace. "Money here go's like dirt. Everything costs a dollar. . . . I purchased a single potato for forty-five cents." Tin pans cost two dollars and fifty cents each. The boys went on up the San Joaquin and paid thirty dollars for passage on a launch for fifty miles. At Stockton breakfast cost one dollar and fifty cents and bread twenty cents a pound loaf. The Mariposa Diggings were yielding scarcely returns of board for work. Honking of mules passing nightly with miners' packs, coyote howls and dangers day and night from criminals on the trail began to darken prospects. Christman was making seventy-five cents a day from gold sands, one of his chums twenty-five cents, the others nothing; but they pooled their earnings.

Then they struck camp and tried another location. Atkins' health began to fail under the combined hardships of climbing hills and packing possessions in blankets on backs. Only two of the boys were by April in condition to put over a day's hard work digging; and their backs nightly felt as if the spine had been broken. Yet their hope for a change of luck persisted; for they met a man, who had taken out in nuggets over five million dollars in two years; but it was becoming more and more evident that the richest surface diggings had been exhausted. The boys tried on Sundays to cook ahead for a week and wash up soiled clothing and patch pantaloons; but the razor for whiskers was going out of fashion and all began to resemble roadside tramps. The idea of fortune in a few years and a sort of glorified hunting trip was fading under stern reality. Money was exhausted by April and they were buying food on credit. Flour in one hundred pound sacks cost thirty-five dollars. Atkins was not mending in health. He was daily weaker. Letters to and from home cost two dollars and forty cents. This was hard on lovers. Raiding Indians and Mexican outlaws were becoming nightly dangers. Men in camps slept with rifles loaded within hand reach. Men out at their digging came back to find tents ransacked, blankets and sheets stolen. Hunger, too, was common. Often mules run off would be found chopped up for food and this left travelers stranded. Wayside merchants were very liberal in credit. They figured that the high charges on those who could pay would compensate losses on the bad credits; and many poor credits could be taken out in manual work. Christman being a horse for work did his best, but when the rains fell in torrents as they did in April, even Christman felt the effects, like toothache in his back bone, of toil in water to his hips. When a few fellows went in pursuit of stampeded mules and one came back with scars of eight arrow shots, white blood began to boil and trail travelers were not too careful whether they shot up the guilty band of Indian raiders or the innocent. The food cooked was bad medicine for the strongest—"the coffee strong enough to float a millstone" . . . "the pan-cakes heavy as lead." Their best days yielded about three dollars; so Christman hired out at five dollars a day to work for others.

So one could follow the Quaker boys to the Tuolumne, to the Merced, to the Stanislaus. Poor Atkins grew worse and worse but "rich or poor, I shall stick by him when health and fortune fail." Good sports but challenging a gambling game they could not beat. The poor Quaker boys tried cutting hay for a living, then Christman struck out for work as a printer and received just what he could have earned back in West Chester. He slept on a counter to avoid rats running over his face if he lay on the floor. He had his first permanent job "to stick type" on the *Sonora Herald*. Hundreds, yes thousands, of parallel cases could be cited about the experiences of stranded miners.

Castles in the air were crashing down. "Individual mining is over," Christman pens in his daily journal. "It must be carried on by large companies with . . . machinery." Wise lad! This has been the record of every new gold, silver, copper camp in the world. Big money must come in to get bigger money out. Half a dozen claims must be tied up in one company so that if this, that, or the other claim peters out, those still held will compensate outlay, risk loss.

Just about the time when one paper on which Christman worked owed him four hundred and sixty-seven dollars, it went bankrupt. This finished Christman's hopes of easy quick fortune in mining. He now aimed only to get out of debt and earn enough money to go home—penniless.

There remains only to tell the humble heroism of these Quaker lads to their dying comrade, Atkins. Atkins had refused to go home with Christman. He contracted black smallpox in Sonora and lay in a wet cold cabin. He was almost blind from the disease and had a little fire and sat shivering beside a small tin stove with his blanket round him. Three of his Quaker friends stayed with him, cut wood, made a good fire, carried his medicine in through the drifts of snow and slush, nursed him and during the downpour of a rain in January of 1853, with no sound but the patter of slush and howl of wolves, saw him breathe his last at dim day dawn. They buried him that afternoon in a gulch. "I'll say no more," wrote Haines, as unconscious of his heroism as a soldier in the ranks.

Vigilantes had to organize in every town. These were not, as pictured in fiction, lawless bands of "necktie parties." They were good citizens who tried at once by extemporized jury, and on proof hanged or shot at once, those convicted of crime. It is a misrepresentation of early California life to play up the Vigilantes as a sort of Ku Klux Klan. The Vigilantes never at any time numbered more than nine thousand in all California. It is worse than false to play up the leaders of the robber bands as daring young gangster heroes. It is as one professor of history says, "sheer rot." To be sure one such leader was barely twenty-four; but he was a murderous little beast of prey running round in human frame with not a streak of honor in him or loyalty to his own friends.

PART IX

WHEN RAILS CAME ON THE PILGRIM WAY OF THE HOLY FAITH

CHAPTER XX

WHEN RAILS CAME TO THE OLD SANTA FE TRAIL

WHEN rails finally came to the old Santa Fe Trail, the Mexican War and the gold rush had already prepared the way sanctioned by Congress. War and gold stampede had proved that East and West must be bound together by more than sentiment. The factories of the East needed the wool from the West. The country as a whole needed silver and gold to pull out of the panic of 1857. Both metals were now pouring from mines in the West.

Asa Whitney had talked himself into bankruptcy and senators and congressmen deaf, blind, and dumb, on the subject of rails to the Pacific. Politicians had told him to run away and play, that is, they had down to the Civil War. Then the need of rails to bind West and East in a unity became self-evident. The Civil War delayed action but did no harm to the West. It enabled rancher, farmer, bankrupt miner, to sell both labor and supplies to the army at figures exceeding any prices ever paid. It did more. It established manufacturing plants west of the Mississippi when supplies to the East were cut off by the War and goods back from the East could not be obtained.

Flour mills were built from Minneapolis to Kansas City. Leather industries such as shoes and saddlery centered in St. Louis. Lumber men erected plants on the Pacific Coast. All this was gain to the good through the Civil War. It gave the farmer a near market for his supplies and a near market for what he must buy. Farm machinery plants began to dot little towns on the Mississippi and transform them to cities in a few years. For at first the making of plows, harrows, wagons, scythes, sickles, shovels, they expanded later to manufacture selfbinders, mowers, and in our day tractors, motors—every device to lessen hand labor and increase output. All were necessary to beat short seasons for crops. Not one of these industries has ever been dislodged and displaced by movement back to the East. As to wages, they ascended to a scale not known in even the gold rush. Many an immigrant struggling knee deep in debt and hardship to put his farm on a pay basis could earn during the Civil War twelve dollars a day hauling timbers for bridges, or food for army supplies; and the army needed these teamsters more than it did soldiers. Many an army engineer like Grenville Dodge graduating from the Civil War became later an equally necessary adjunct for the rails.

Fortunately, before the Civil War, Lincoln, a raw young lawyer, had been as far west as Omaha and Council Bluffs. He was quick to grasp the fact that one of the first things Congress must do after the war, no matter what the cost in cash or land subsidy, was to run a railway right across the broadest midmost belt of the new territory from the Mississippi to the Pacific. Hence were born in the thought of the country lawyer who became president, the Union Pacific, the Central Pacific, and later what became known as the Santa Fe railroads. Grenville Dodge tells how when he met Lincoln by chance at one of these old taverns, the future president, with his long legs braced against piazza railing and his chair tipped back at rickety angle, "had shelled his brains" of all information on the best routes westward before Dodge realized that such facts should have gone first to his employers then using him as a young surveyor. What was the character of the lands, Lincoln has asked. Would they support a large farm population? How about the mountain passes? Could lower levels than South Pass be discovered? What would be the cost per mile for prairie, for barren uplands, for mountain guides? How could settlers be attracted fast enough to support traffic? Would he advocate granting blocks of land continuous along the rail right of way, or only alternate sections?

We know how Dodge answered these questions. Rights to bridge the Mississippi and the Missouri must be obtained in spite of steamboat opposition. It was in one of these lawsuits that Lincoln won his first big fee of five thousand dollars. He had to pause in the midst of his argument to whittle a match and anchor his braces, for a button had jumped off his trousers. Carnegie was one of the bridge engineers at this period. Prairie land would yield crops on the turning of a furrow. Colonists would come wherever they could make a sure independent living. From the barren uplands, there was not much to count on but pasture for sheep. Lower levels might be found than the caravan wagon had traversed across the mountain passes. The granting of land in alternate sections would be wisest. It would give the homesteader a chance to take up land close to rails and the rail a prospect of immediate traffic to pay its way, to pay interest on bonds for construction. As to costs, Dodge told Lincoln frankly he was convinced that both cash subsidies and land grants would be necessary to attract capital from the East.

Why? Plain enough. The lands could be assigned to rails only as surveyed and they could not be surveyed within a year, no, not within twenty years; and they must be lands that could be sold at from two dollars and fifty cents to five dollars and twelve dollars an acre, or settlers would not buy them, when they could have free homesteads between blocks, or go back behind the preempted blocks and haul to the rail stations. Later, when the Civil War had passed and Dodge went back to rail work, he was electrified to receive a call to Washington. He responded with quaking. Had he failed in his army work? No, the president wanted to know if on a grant of cash and land, would Dodge undertake to push a Union Pacific as far west at least as Utah? The land would be assigned only as earned by construction and it would be a race between the Union Pacific and Central Pacific which would earn the more lands and cash subsidy. The Union would go west from Council Bluffs and Omaha, the Central from the Pacific east to Utah. The river could never be safely bridged from Fort Leavenworth. Except for army needs, Fort Leavenworth must be left out of the picture. The river was too wide there for bridge spans. Also the bottoms were too insecure for bridge supports. They were shifty quicksands. To the disappointment of many a speculator, the eastern terminus must be Omaha, west of the river. Events have demonstrated the correctness of that judgment. Many an early bridge both at Kansas City and Omaha has had to be abandoned, sheer loss because of the tricky river bottom below its piers. We know how Dodge beat his rival by almost four hundred miles; but to go back to the Santa Fe.

Cyrus Halliday, a young capitalist from the East, who knew what rails had done for the East, had been thinking along these very lines. He came to Kansas. He figured that where land would grow almost anything, especially southwestward, where farmers could figure always on two crops a year, there rails would ultimately come; so he picked on Topeka as a rail raiding point and made a second fortune selling real estate. When he got a dinky little train made up of cheap junk he had picked up in Chicago, rattling over shaky rail bed, his enthusiasm as to the future of the Southwest went what the crowd called "crazy." The mob, assembled to witness the feat of a train running over twelve miles of real rails, simply booed and hissed him. He might be sound on real estate but plainly he had gone off his head as to rails. Halliday lived to see his most derisive scoffer become mayor of Topeka. Halliday, swelling up with a father's pride, had predicted that the Santa Fe—then known under another name—would yet extend from Chicago to the Pacific Coast. A cowboy fell back in a feigned faint and kicked up his heels. He was the future mayor of Topeka City.

Courtesy Union Pacific Historical Museum
WAGON TRAIN MOVING DOWN ECHO CANYON, BRINGING SUPPLIES TO THE BUILDERS OF THE UNION PACIFIC

GROOVES MADE BY PIONEER WAGON WHEELS IN SOLID ROCK NEAR SPLIT ROCK, WYOMING

Courtesy of the Union Pacific Historical Museum
UNION PACIFIC AND CENTRAL PACIFIC ENGINEERS AT THE DRIVING OF THE GOLDEN SPIKE

But again who can say Halliday's faith was not another example of that sublime holy faith in a Santa Fe—a holy way? To ascribe such results to chance is an illogical argument for proponents who hold there is no chance—all is cause and effect. What was the cause? What was the beginning from Coronado to Halliday? A holy faith, perhaps faith in an illusion; but the illusion proved a reality the faith backed by works, by hardships, by toll of death, by blind human instruments good and bad, with high and low aims.

It seemed one of the great tragedies of little Santa Fe ensconced in the lap of the snowy mountains that when the rail finally did reach within a few miles of the holy city, two obstacles seemed to block the way. One was the grade and expense of circling the hills to enter the city. The other was that some of the old Spanish ranchers did not want it, or demanded an extortion figure for right of way. The old Spanish ranchers were quite comfortable, thank you, without rails. Was not labor cheap? Had not they sent herds of sheep across on the hoof to California for almost thirty years? Why chance a change? So the Santa Fe Railroad put up that beautiful little Lamy Station for travelers to jump off and run up by a twisty rail to Santa Fe. The rail proceeded on down by Albuquerque, Laguna, Acoma, and those well known stations and pausing spots of old caravan and helmeted horsemen, of mesa and pueblo and desert tribes, now seen by passing travelers by motor or rail.

Santa Fe felt literally ditched in "a backwater of sand seas" for all time. The Spanish ranchers were glad or indifferent. They saw Americano changes blocked. The Americanos eager for what they called progress were in despair. Santa Fe's days of prosperity were over forever. That was the sentiment. There was a little bitterness, a little depression, an eclipse of faith in the future, a little cloudiness of hope, that is, as much cloudiness and depression as people could feel in a sunny land, where conditions for happy living were still easy. Food was cheap. It is yet for beef, for mutton, for fruit, for vegetables. For humble folk, who had the looms, clothing, too, was cheap. Houses could be constructed of adobe, rugs woven; and wages were, compared to those paid elsewhere, ridiculously low. In fact, right down to the Great War of 1914 wages continued low. Give the peon herder five dollars to ten dollars a month, his keep, a few lambs, his guitar, mouth organ, or concertina, and what else did he want to be happy? In old age, he could retire to his own little fruit or sheep ranch. He and his good wife did not want a thing on earth which they did not possess.

But what seemed a blasting of hopes for Santa

Fe, proved as so often in its past, a blessing in disguise. Santa Fe rested in the old tranquillity of accepting things pretty much as they came and went. Can that be said of another spot in the restless modern world of turmoil to-day? Nor was it the dry rot of fatalism. It was in the words of the old prophecy—"In repose and rest are your confidence."

The city preserved her peculiar forms of old architecture, which have been the inspiration of the small bungalow and of the open-window one-story mansion. She preserved her old love of art, of music; and these are now coming back in a new school of Southwestern art and in the radio music to which millions nightly listen. She became the center of one of the world's greatest schools of archeology; and from that first Emory Report of the Mexican War, which was so timid of suggestions as to seas amid lava lands, she gave birth to a new geology. Vast seas had preceded the lava flow, the eruption of a volcano that hoisted ten thousand feet peaks above sandy seas and left marine monster bones and little sea shells and ferns in levels of high area. Perhaps most important of all, yearly growing in scope, Santa Fe became known as one of the greatest health centers in America. When I predicted more than seventeen years ago that Santa Fe had a great future, the audience was too polite to laugh but plainly thought that the high ozone air had gone to my head. "How long have you been out here," an army man asked me. I told him twice only, for six weeks each trip. "I thought so," he answered tersely. Though I was not contradicted, one adorable cartoon came out, which I regret I lost. It predicted motors tumbling out of a great tooting horn over precipices in their haste to reach a new El Dorado. I wish that army officer were alive to-day and could witness more than my wildest prophecy verified. Bad as traffic both travel and freight has been since the Great War, which traffic has slumped the least in North America? I'll not provoke contradiction by other sections in any answer; but look up the figures for yourself in freight, passenger, holiday-seekers, each season of the year. Only one type of transportation has beaten the old Santa Fe Trail—the trans-Atlantic; and that does it largely by rates on steerage quarters changed to travel suites; and it does not yet appear in returns, whether profits from that are sufficient to warrant reduced rates, or whether these are only a stopgap till incoming and outgoing traffic revive from present conditions.

Has, then, the Drop Curtain fallen on the old Santa Fe Trail? No; and it never can.

As Doniphan said of the trail in the Mexican War, it is not only one of the longest and oldest in recorded history, it is one of the epic trails in the racial migrations westward of the world. It links East and West together in the United States. It links Occident and Orient together on the Pacific.

What of the future?

As the Spaniards always say of *mañana: Quién sabe?* Who knows?

INDEX

Acoma Indians, 48, 79, 115, 116
Albuquerque, 182, 239
Alvarado, 40, 46, 49
Apache Indians, 13, 37, 90, 102, 105, 167, 180, 191, 199, 200, 211, 238, 241, 248, 268
Armijo, Manuel, 9, 42, 118-120, 181, 194-196, 203, 230-233, 235, 248
Army post life, 253-255

Beecher, Lieut., 257-261, 282
Benders, the, 313-318
Bicknell, Capt., 173
Bidwell, John, 328-330
Black Kettle, 278-281, 283
Black Mesa, the, 110, 115
Bodega Bay Settlement, the, 304, 330
Bridger, Jim, 155, 156, 177
Brown's Survey, 191-193, 210

Cabeza de Vaca, 16-25, 27, 33
Cadillac, La Mothe, 60, 61, 66, 71, 167, 168
California, 11, 150, 240, 242-244, 291-310, 327, 328, 333-335
Caravans, 167-188, 219
Carson, Kit, 173, 185, 200, 240, 269, 328
Casa Grande, the, 36, 45, 79, 81, 108, 109, 241
Catlin, 208-219
Chavez, Antonio, 199, 241
Chavez, Jose, 272
Cheyenne Indians, 5, 13, 211, 256-263, 274, 278, 283-285
Chicago, 129, 147
Chihuahua, 169, 173
Chouteau's Island, 173, 185, 192, 220

Christman, Enos, 339-346
Cimarron, the, 173, 174, 180, 184, 185, 190, 192
Cities, Seven Golden, 15, 19, 23, 24, 27, 32-35, 41, 45, 47, 49-50, 55, 77, 91, 94, 176, 238, 273
Comanche Indians, 66, 77, 90, 167, 180, 191, 192, 211, 213, 216, 217, 230, 268
Cooke, St. George, 203, 220, 231, 237, 248, 250-252, 274
Coronado, Francisco, 32, 38, 41-52
Cortes, 43, 47
Council Bluffs, 134, 147, 191
Council Grove, 184, 229
Crane, Leo, 26, 54, 73, 93
Crook, Gen., 248
Culiacan, 34, 43
Custer, George Armstrong, 5, 6, 76, 209, 210, 247, 276-287

De Soto, 27-33
Diaz, 42, 47
Dodge, Grenville, 147, 249, 350-354
Doniphan, Col., 225-244, 358

Elliott, Major, 279-281
El Paso, 107, 109, 111, 240-244
Emory, Lieut. Col., 264-274
Enchanted Mesa, the, 48, 116
Estevan, 17-24, 32-39, 46, 273

Fitzpatrick, 230, 269, 328
Forsyth, Gen., 250-263, 279, 280
Fort Bent, 177, 184-186, 192, 220, 228, 230
Fort Bridger, 141, 146, 251, 253
Fort Dodge, 184, 286
Fort Gibson, 213, 215, 218, 220

361

INDEX

Fort Hall, 294, 329, 331
Fort Riley, 277
Fort Wallace, 8, 193, 254, 256, 261, 262, 278, 282-284
Fremont, 226, 237, 243, 244, 274, 327
French, the, on the Trail, 19, 59, 60, 61, 123, 167-169
Friars, the, 28, 29, 100, 102, 106-109, 112, 293, 294, 298

Germine girls, the, 283, 284
Gold rush, the, 333-346
Grand Island, 138
Grant, Gen., 6, 209, 210
Great Salt Lake, 133, 140, 156
Gregg, 177, 186, 193, 207

Halliday, Cyrus, 354
Hancock, Gen., 5, 6, 14, 249, 282
Haw-ai-kuh, 38, 45
Hewett, Dr. Edgar, 88-91, 94, 201
Hopi Indians, 12, 23, 37, 39, 77, 183
Hotoville, 37, 78, 79

Independence, 180, 190, 199, 227, 274
Indians of the Southwest, 12, 16-18, 20, 22, 23, 28-31, 33-39, 73-94
Isleta, 54, 109, 110, 241

Kane, Col., 133
Kansas City, 170, 180, 190
Kaw, or Kansas, Indians, 211, 220, 274
Kearny, Stephen, 119, 132, 134, 203, 214, 225-245, 250, 274, 276
Kidder, Lieut., 282, 283
Kivas, the, 82, 83, 106

Leavenworth, Gen., 210-219, 225-245
Leavenworth, town or fort, 8, 134, 167, 181, 190, 199, 208-211, 226, 227, 248, 253
Lincoln, Abraham, 147, 351-353
Los Angeles, 242, 243
Louisiana, 15, 60-62, 167-169

Marcos, Fray, 33-38, 41-46
Martin, Judge, 213, 316
McLoughlin, Gov., 297, 298, 302
Means, John, 219
Mendoza, 32, 41-42
Mexico City, 4, 9, 18, 24, 32, 43, 52, 55, 66-70
Mexican War, 223-245
Migrations over the Trail, 291-310
Miles, Gen., 7, 11, 12, 73, 248, 284, 318
"Misery Bottom," 137
Mohave Desert of Death, 44, 183, 237, 240-244, 266, 273, 295, 305, 309
Morgan, Mrs., 281, 284-287
Mormons, the, 11, 123-163, 227, 237, 244, 251-253
Mountain Meadow Massacre, 253

Narvaez, 16-20, 27, 59
Nauvoo, 126, 128-131, 135, 138, 153
Navajo Indians, 77, 90, 102, 105, 183, 191, 211, 238, 268

Ogden, Peter Skene, 305
Omaha, 51, 154, 155, 353
Oraibi, 37, 47, 53, 78, 79
Osage Indians, 191, 212, 216
Otermin, Gov., 106, 108, 110, 111

Padilla, Juan de, 44-52, 54, 55, 81
Patrols, army, 207-220, 226-287
Patties, the two, 306-308
Pawnee Indians, 132, 138, 191, 211-213, 274
Pawnee Rock, 191, 229
Pensacola, 4, 9, 42
Pike, Lieut., 172, 174-176, 177
Pilgrim Path of the Santa Fe. See Santa Fe Trail
Pima Indians, 36-39, 269
Pope, 105-109
Price, Col., 240, 248

Quantrill, 319-322

Rae, Glen, 298, 302

INDEX

Rails to the Pacific, 349-356
Raton Pass, 182, 192, 231, 232
Reports of scientists, 264-274
Rezanof, 300-302, 304
Riley, Major, 220
Ross, Mrs. Edith C., 7, 313

St. Denis, Juchereau, 61-71, 103, 104, 119, 167, 168, 182, 190
Salt Lake City, 144-150, 156-158, 160, 252
San Diego, 179, 242, 309, 310
San Pascual, 240, 270
Sand Creek Massacre, 318, 319
Santa Fe, 9, 25, 54-56, 107, 111, 113-120, 130, 169, 171-175, 181, 184, 189-203, 233-237, 355-358
Santa Fe Trail, the, 3, 4, 10, 15, 27, 59, 100, 105, 175, 189-193, 227, 250, 254
Sheridan, 6, 147, 249, 275-278
Sherman, 6, 147, 249, 277
Simpson, Sir George, 297, 301, 302
Smith, Jedediah, 179, 180, 305
Smith, Joseph, 123-130, 151-153
Spaniards, the, 12, 15-25, 27-32, 42, 75, 99-102, 104-120, 291-293, 303
Stockton, Admiral, 226, 237, 243

Sutter, John, 330-334

Taos, 65, 91, 112, 171, 181, 193
Topeka, 182, 354
Tragedies on the Trail, 219, 281, 284-287, 311-322, 331, 332
"Turk," the, 48-50, 273
Twitchell, Ralph E., 26, 33, 72, 177, 207

Ute Indians, 141, 142, 167, 203, 251

Vargas, de, 42, 104, 111-119
Vera Cruz, 170
Vigilantes, the, 346

Wharton, Capt., 219, 220
White, Dr., 199
White, Miss, 281, 284-286
Whitney, Asa, 147, 349

Yaqui Indians, 13, 25, 44, 77, 90, 102, 105, 167
Young, Brigham, 130, 142, 145-163, 171, 252
Yuma Indians, 25, 44, 47

Zuñi Indians, 23, 37, 39, 77, 115, 183